ESCAPISTS
AND
PROPHETS

BLOOM'S LITERARY CRITICISM 20TH ANNIVERSARY COLLECTION

Dramatists and Dramas
The Epic
Essayists and Prophets
Novelists and Novels
Poets and Poems
Short Story Writers and Short Stories

ESSAYISTS
AND
PROPHETS

Harold Bloom
Sterling Professor of the Humanities
Yale University

CHELSEA HOUSE
P U B L I S H E R S
A Haights Cross Communications Company ®

Philadelphia

Printed and bound in the United States of America.
10 9 8 7 6 5 4 3 2 1

Library of Congress Cataloging-in-Publication Data
Bloom, Harold.
  Essayists and prophets / Harold Bloom.
     p. cm. — (Bloom's 20th anniversary collection)
  ISBN 0-7910-8523-6 HC   0-7910-8524-4 PB
  1. Philosophers. 2. Essayists. 3. Bible—Criticism, interpretation,
etc. I. Title.
  B29.B56 2005
  100—dc22
                                        2005005523

Cover designed by Takeshi Takahashi
Cover illustration by David Levine
Layout by EJB Publishing Services

Table of Contents

Preface

Harold Bloom

I BEGAN EDITING ANTHOLOGIES OF LITERARY CRITICISM FOR CHELSEA House in early 1984, but the first volume, *Edgar Allan Poe: Modern Critical Views*, was published in January, 1985, so this is the twentieth anniversary of a somewhat Quixotic venture. If asked how many separate books have been issued in this project, I no longer have a precise answer, since in so long a span many volumes go out of print, and even whole series have been discontinued. A rough guess would be more than a thousand individual anthologies, a perhaps insane panoply to have been collected and introduced by a single critic.

Some of these books have surfaced in unlikely places: hotel rooms in Bologna and Valencia, Coimbra and Oslo; used-book stalls in Frankfurt and Nice; on the shelves of writers wherever I have gone. A batch were sent by me in answer to a request from a university library in Macedonia, and I have donated some of them, also by request, to a number of prisoners serving life sentences in American jails. A thousand books across a score of years can touch many shores and many lives, and at seventy-four I am a little bewildered at the strangeness of the endeavor, particularly now that it has leaped between centuries.

It cannot be said that I have endorsed every critical essay reprinted, as my editor's notes have made clear. Yet the books have to be reasonably reflective of current critical modes and educational fashions, not all of them provoking my own enthusiasm. But then I am a dinosaur, cheerfully naming myself as "Bloom Brontosaurus Bardolator." I accept only three criteria for greatness in imaginative literature: aesthetic splendor, cognitive power, wisdom. What is now called "relevance" will be in the dustbins in less than a generation, as our society (somewhat tardily) reforms prejudices and inequities. The fashionable in literature and criticism always ebbs away into Period Pieces. Old, well-made furniture survives as valuable antiques, which is not the destiny of badly constructed imaginings and ideological exhortings.

Time, which decays and then destroys us, is even more merciless in obliterating weak novels, poems, dramas, and stories, however virtuous these may be. Wander into a library and regard the masterpieces of thirty years ago: a handful of forgotten books have value, but the iniquity of oblivion has rendered most bestsellers instances of time's revenges. The other day a friend and former student told me that the first of the Poets Laureate of twentieth-century America had been Joseph Auslander, concerning whom even my still retentive memory is vacant. These days, Mrs. Felecia Hemans is studied and taught by a number of feminist Romantic scholars. Of the poems of that courageous wisdom, who wrote to support her brood, I remember only the opening line of "Casabianca" but only because Mark Twain added one of his very own to form a couplet:

The boy stood on the burning deck
Eating peanuts by the peck.

Nevertheless, I do not seek to affirm the social inutility of literature, though I admire Oscar Wilde's grand declaration: "All art is perfectly useless." Shakespeare may well stand here for the largest benign effect of the highest literature: properly appreciated, it can heal part of the violence that is built into every society whatsoever. In my own judgment, Walt Whitman is the central writer yet brought forth by the Americas—North, Central, South, Caribbean—whether in English, Spanish, Portuguese, French, Yiddish or other tongues. And Walt Whitman is a healer, a poet-prophet who discovered his pragmatic vocation by serving as a volunteer, unpaid wound-dresser and nurse in the Civil War hospitals of Washington, D.C. To read and properly understand Whitman can be an education in self-reliance and in the cure of your own consciousness.

The function of literary criticism, as I conceive it in my gathering old age, is primarily appreciation, in Walter Pater's sense, which fuses analysis and evaluation. When Pater spoke of "art for art's sake' he included in the undersong of his declaration what D.H. Lawrence meant by "art for life's sake," Lawrence, the most provocative of post-Whitmanian vitalists, has now suffered a total eclipse in the higher education of the English-speaking nations. Feminists have outlawed him with their accusations of misogyny, and they describe him as desiring women to renounce sexual pleasure. On this supposed basis, students lose the experience of reading one of the major authors of the twentieth century, at once an unique novelist, story-teller, poet, critic, and prophet.

An enterprise as vast as Chelsea House Literary Criticism doubtless reflects both the flaws and the virtues of its editor. Comprehensiveness has been a goal throughout, and I have (for the most part) attempted to set aside many of my own literary opinions. I sorrow when the market keeps an important volume out of print, though I am solaced by the example of my idol, Dr. Samuel Johnson, in his *Lives of the Poets*. The booksellers (who were both publishers and retailers) chose the poets, and Johnson was able to say exactly what he thought of each. Who remembers such worthies as Yalden, Sprat, Roscommon, and Stepney? It would be invidious for me to name the contemporary equivalents, but their name is legion.

I have been more fully educated by this quest for comprehensivness, which taught me how to write for a larger audience. Literary criticism is both an individual and communal mode. It has its titans: Johnson, Coleridge, Lessing, Goethe, Hazlitt, Sainte-Beuve, Pater, Curtius, Valèry, Frye, Empson, Kenneth Burke are among them. But most of those I reprint cannot be of that eminence: one makes a heap of all that can be found. Over a lifetime in reading and teaching one learns so much from so many that no one can be certain of her or his intellectual debts. Hundreds of those I have reprinted I never will meet, but they have helped enlighten me, insofar as I have been capable of learning from a host of other minds.

Introduction

Harold Bloom

AFTER TWO BOOKS OF THE HEBREW BIBLE, AND ONE FROM THE GREEK New Testament, this volume contains meditations upon twenty essayists and prophets. Pascal, Rousseau, Samuel Johnson, Carlyle, Kierkegaard, Emerson, Thoreau, Ruskin, Nietzsche, Freud, Scholem, Du Bois in their very different ways took up stances as wisdom writers resembling prophets, whereas Montaigne, Dryden, Boswell, Hazlitt, Pater, Huxley, Sartre, and Camus can be regarded as diverse essayists. Many of the prophets saw themselves as essayists, and all twenty writers were moralists, though the great aesthete Walter Pater would have denied the role.

What holds the twenty together is a literary category that defies simple categorization. Montaigne, though following the ancients Plutarch and Seneca, invents the modern essay, and can be regarded as master of most who come after him here. Pascal, Christian moralist and mystic, was unhappy with Montaigne, yet all but plagiarized him. Dryden, Johnson, and Boswell belong to English neoclassicism, yet all owe subtly concealed debts to Montaigne, who is to literary prose reflection what Shakespeare was to literary fictions, whether in verse or prose: the undoubted progenitor. Rousseau, whom Boswell interviewed, was a precursor of Romantic reflection, with its very different incarnations in Hazlitt, Carlyle, Kierkegaard, Emerson, Thoreau, Ruskin, Pater, and Nietzsche. Freud, Romantic rationalist, has affinities with several of these, but his exuberant originality tends to emancipate him from much that was traditional.

The final five writers in the volume are difficult to associate with one another, though Sartre and Camus were friends, until they quarreled. Du Bois, African-American prophet, owed much to Emerson, while Aldous Huxley mingled his friend D.H. Lawrence's vitalism with a mystical Perennial Philosophy. Gershom Scholem, who invented the modern study of Kabbalah or Jewish mystical speculation, stands by himself, though many have followed after him.

Dr. Johnson, Hazlitt, Emerson, Pater, Nietzsche, and Freud are the writers here who have most influenced my own work as a literary critic, while Scholem, whom I knew, has been the strongest of personal guides. That, I surmise, is the ultimate use of prophetic essayists: to aid us in becoming ourselves, as caring singularities rather than as individualists indifferent both to ourselves and to others.

The Bible

THE BOOK OF JOB

For Job could not better prove his patience than by resolving to be entirely naked, inasmuch as the good pleasure of God was such. Surely, men resist in vain; they may grit their teeth, but they must return entirely naked to the grave. Even the pagans have said that death alone shows the littleness of men. Why? For we have a gulf of covetousness, that we would wish to gobble up all the earth; if a man has many riches, vines, meadows, and possessions, it is not enough; God would have to create new worlds, if He wished to satisfy us.
—JOHN CALVIN, *Second Sermon on Job*

And yet there is no hiding place in the wide world where troubles may not find you, and there has never lived a man who was able to say more than you can say, that you do not know when sorrow will visit your house. So be sincere with yourself, fix your eyes upon Job; even though he terrifies you, it is not this he wishes, if you yourself do not wish it.
—SØREN KIERKEGAARD, *Edifying Discourses*

THE POET OF JOB EMULATES A STRONG PRECURSOR, THAT ASTONISHING prophet, Jeremiah. Though the Book of Job is less shocking, rhetorically and dialectically, than Jeremiah's book, it remains profoundly troubling. Like *King Lear*, which is manifestly influenced by it, the Book of Job touches the limits of literature and perhaps transcends them. Lear desperately prays for patience, lest he go mad, and even declares, "No, I will be the pattern of all patience, / I will say nothing," as though he would be a second

1

Job. In the play's greatest scene (4.6), perhaps the finest in Shakespeare or in literature, Lear advises Gloucester to join him in the Jobean fortitude:

> If thou wilt weep my fortunes, take my eyes.
> I know thee well enough, thy name is Gloucester.
> Thou must be patient; we came crying hither.
> Thou know'st, the first time that we smell the air
> We wawl and cry.

Patient Job is actually about as patient as Lear is. *Ha-satan*, the adversary, is provocative enough, but Job's comforters are worse. William Blake bitterly wrote that "in the Book of Job, Milton's Messiah is call'd Satan," and clearly Job's abominable friends are what *The Marriage of Heaven and Hell* calls "Angels," or pious time-servers, fit to become minor officials of Kafka's court or Kafka's castle. Despite pious tamperings, such as the absurd epilogue, the Book of Job is not the work of a trimmer or of a self-deceived saint. Its best expositors remain two fierce Protestants, John Calvin and Søren Kierkegaard. Calvin condemns us for not being Jobean enough:

> Meanwhile God will be condemned among us. This is how men exasperate themselves. And in this what do they do? It is as if they accuse God of being a tyrant or a hairbrain who asked only to put everything in confusion.

Kierkegaard exalts Job as a hero of the spirit, a champion who has overcome the world:

> But he who sees God has overcome the world, and therefore Job in his devout word had overcome the world; was through his devout word greater and stronger and more powerful than the whole world, which here would not so much carry him into temptation but would overcome him with its power, cause him to sink down before its boundless might.

I take from Calvin his accurate sense that Job does not condemn God, does not accuse him of being "a tyrant or a hairbrain." From Kierkegaard, I take his realization that it is not the Behemoth or the Leviathan that causes Job to sink down when God comes at last to confront the sufferer and speaks out of the whirlwind to him. Martin Buber shrewdly notes that "Job cannot forego either his own truth or God." Protesting the incommensurable, suffering far in excess of sin, Job is answered by a God who speaks only in terms of the incommensurable. Like Jeremiah, the poet of Job returns to the J writer or Yahwist whose Yahweh is uncanny. We are made in Yahweh's image and are asked to be like him, but we are not to presume to be too much like him. He can be argued with, as when Abraham argues him part way down on the road to Sodom, but he also is subject to peculiar vagaries, as when he tries to murder poor Moses at the outset of the prophet's reluctant mission or when he alternately entices and warns the people on Sinai. I take it that Job recognizes the reality of Yahweh's extraordinary personality after the voice out of the whirlwind has completed its message, a recognition that is the resolution of the book.

It seems clear to me that the Book of Job is not a theodicy, a justification of the ways of God to man, as Milton defines the genre in his sublime theodicy, *Paradise Lost*. The voice out of the whirlwind does not seek to justify. Rather, with an ultimate exuberance, it bombards Job with a great series of rhetorical questions, which attain their summit in the vision of the Leviathan:

> Canst thou draw out leviathan with an hook? or his tongue with a cord *which* thou lettest down?
>
> 2 Canst thou put an hook into his nose? or bore his jaw through with a thorn?
>
> 3 Will he make many supplications unto thee? will he speak soft *words* unto thee?
>
> 4 Will he make a covenant with thee? wilt thou take him for a servant for ever?
>
> 5 Wilt thou play with him as *with* a bird? or wilt thou bind him for thy maidens?
>
> 6 Shall the companions make a banquet of him? shall they part him among the merchants?
>
> 7 Canst thou fill his skin with barbed irons? or his head with fish spears?
>
> 8 Lay thine hand upon him, remember the battle, do no more.
>
> 9 Behold, the hope of him is in vain: shall not *one* be cast down even at the sight of him?
>
> 10 None *is so* fierce that dare stir him up: who then is able to stand before me?

Ahab's answer in *Moby-Dick* was a fierce affirmative until his life ended with his outcry "*Thus*, I give up the spear!" as he rammed his harpoon vainly into the White Whale's sanctified flesh. Job is no Ahab, nor an apocalyptic seer. But it is difficult not to prefer Ahab to Job, when God taunts us with such vicious irony: "Will he make a covenant with thee?" In Kabbalistic prophecy, the companions do make a banquet of the Leviathan when the Messiah comes, but Job is no Kabbalist. The Book of Job is the strong, implicit opponent of that belated doctrine Gnosticism, and nothing could be further from Job than the Lurianic doctrine of the breaking of the primal vessels of creation.

Confronted by the Leviathan, Job declares that he had lacked knowledge:

> therefore have I uttered that I understood not; things too wonderful for me, which I knew not.

The Hebrew text does not say "things too wonderful for me" but "things beyond me." Confronting the sublimity of Yahweh, Job understands his own tradition, which is that the sage must rise to the agon, as Abraham and Jacob did, and so behave pragmatically as if he were everything in himself while knowing always that, in relation to Yahweh, he is nothing in himself. Job prefigures Martin Buber's theological vision: the "eclipse" of God. God's answer, out of the whirlwind, is read by Buber as being "not *the* divine justice, which remains hidden, but *a* divine justice, namely that manifest creation." Buber cites Rudolf Otto here on the playful riddle of God's creative power. Karl Barth in his *Church Dogmatics* makes a nice point illuminating this riddle, which is that God shrewdly allows creation to speak for him:

> He obviously counts upon it that they belong so totally to Him, that they are so subject to Him and at His disposal, that in speaking of themselves they will necessarily speak of Him.

Like Rudolf Otto and Karl Barth, Martin Buber sees Job as a "faithful rebel" and so as a servant of God. All three men of God seem to fall short of the Book of Job's bitter ironies, which is why I prefer the answering irony of John Calvin, "God would have to create new worlds, if He wishes to satisfy us," or the more complex irony of Kierkegaard, "Fix your eyes upon Job; even though he terrifies you, it is not this he wishes, if you yourself do not wish it." We cannot be satisfied, because Yahweh will create no more new worlds, and we need to be terrified by Job, even if he does not will to terrify us. The limits of desire are also the limits of literature. Kierkegaard is singularly perceptive; it is not the creation but the creator who overwhelms Job. Our desires for the good are incommensurate not with the good but with the creator of good. Shelley, in the accents of Gnosticism, declared that good and the means of good were irreconcilable. Job, in the accents of Jeremiah, accepted his election of adversity.

The Song of Songs

Rabbi Akiba, who is the dominant single figure in the entire history of normative Judaism, insisted upon bringing the Song of Songs into the canon of Scripture:

> The entire world is unworthy of the day the Song of Songs was given to Israel, for all of Scripture is holy, but the Song of Songs is the Holy of Holies.

Akiba is even reported to have said that the Song of Songs would have been sufficient to guide the world had Torah not been given. There is enough evidence of how Akiba interpreted the Song of Songs to suggest that he was the effectual originator of the immense history of allegorizing this poem or poems, though such allegorizing must have preceded him. The question of literal versus allegorical reading of the Song of Songs should be set aside forever; the work is so strong that it demands every mode that can be brought to it. My own emphasis here will be neither literal nor allegorical, but interpoetic. I cannot reread the Song of Songs without involuntarily rereading its greater poetic descendants, from the Kabbalists through Renaissance erotic lyricists on to Walt Whitman. To meditate upon the Song of Songs, for any reader conversant with Western imaginative traditions, is an activity that calls into play poems and prose by Isaac Luria and St. Teresa of Avila and St. John of the Cross, and by Fray Luis de León and Edmund Spenser, by Coventry Patmore and Walt Whitman, and many others.

The origins of the Song of Songs always may be in dispute, but my own ear for the Hebrew original tells me the work had one author, however many the redactors, and that she or he is unlike any other biblical poet. The notion, still held by some scholars, that we are reading a suite of folk songs is not worth arguing against; the sequence is as folksy and simple as Ovid or Spenser or the young Shakespeare of *Venus and Adonis*. I also cannot take seriously the rival scholarly camp, which holds that the Song is cultic in character, reflecting the survival of pre Judaic Canaanite fertility rituals. What I hear in the Song is a court poet, akin to the Spenser of the *Prothalamium* and the *Epithalamium*, a poet of enormous urbanity and cultivation, and of a highly sophisticated eroticism. I mean "court" in a very loose sense, and perhaps "aristocratic poet" would be a more useful phrase, since the likely date of composition is between the time of Ezra and Nehemiah and the Hellenistic period, with 400 B.C.E. a reasonable guess, making the Song roughly contemporary with that very different body of poetry, the Psalms.

Erotic poetry of such power and distinction must have stimulated normative misreadings almost from the start, and one sees how the interpretation of God as bridegroom and Israel as the beloved was inevitable. I do not believe that the poet of the Song had any intention of employing that prophetic trope, which had figured in Isaiah and even more strikingly in Jeremiah. The rabbis assimilated the Song to the prophets, an assimilation whose final consequence was the canonical passion of the great Akiba. Arthur Green, following Saul Lieberman, surmises that Akiba and his colleagues continued an esoteric tradition of interpreting the Song as commemorating the actual revelation of the body of God in the Sinai theophany From this developed, centuries later, the grand Kabbalistic vision of the sexual union taking place within God, between God and the *Shekhinah*, the indwelling Sophia or wisdom-principle or female aspect of the Creator.

To this day, Kabbalistic interpretation seems to me the most fruitful of approaches to the Song of Songs, since it fuses the erotic and the spiritual, as the Song itself does, and since in essence it contains every thing that is vital in an interpoetic or intrapoetic reading. Isaac Luria's Aramaic chant for the Sabbath joins itself to the Song of Songs by a great epiphany of God as bridegroom coming to embrace the Sabbath as his bride. God "enters the gates of the holy orchard of the apple trees" and "brings his Sabbath bride intense joy, in double measure, so that light and blessings pour upon her." In a related mode, St. Teresa of Avila celebrated her own union with God:

> By certain words that wound the soul who loves you, words scattered by you in the Canticles, and which you teach me to say to you! ... My Lord, I ask nothing else in this life but "to kiss me with the kiss of Your mouth," and to do this in such a manner that I should not be able to withdraw myself from this union, even if I wished it.

Closer even to the unique ethos of the Song of Songs are the *Ascent of Mount Carmel* and the *Living Flame of Love* of St. John of the Cross, each of them a commentary upon his ecstatic lyrics that recapture vital moments in the Song. It seems a strange path from the positive ecstasies of the Song to St. John's Dark Night of the Soul, but we will see the darkness that is there in the Song, and read the Song better, if we juxtapose to it:

4. This light guided me
More surely than the light of noonday
To the place where he (well I knew who!) was awaiting me—
A place where none appeared.

5. Oh, night that guided me,
Oh, night more lovely than the dawn,
Oh, night that joined Beloved with lover,
Lover transformed in the Beloved!

6. Upon my flowery breast,
Kept wholly for himself alone,
There he stayed sleeping, and I caressed him,
And the fanning of the cedars made a breeze.

7. The breeze blew from the turret
As I parted his locks;
With his gentle hand he wounded my neck
And caused all my senses to be suspended.

8. I remained, lost in oblivion;
My face I reclined on the Beloved.
All ceased and I abandoned myself,
Leaving my cares forgotten among the lilies.

Luis de León, who was descended from a New Christian family of Jews who converted in 1492 so as not to suffer the Expulsion, and who brilliantly translated the Song into both verse and prose, is closer to the Song itself and to Kabbalistic tradition in always affirming his own identity even in the negative moment of union with the Divine. Willis Barnstone defends Luis de León from Spanish critics who see him as falling short of his contemporary mystic and poet, St. John of the Cross, since Luis de León never allows himself to lose a sense of his own separate identity. I think Barnstone is right and that the Judaic element in Luis de León reminds us of the Song of Songs's own awareness that love unites only in act, not in essence. That may be why Spenser and Whitman seem to me closer to the Song of Songs than any other poets have been. Spenser's Puritanism, and Whitman's Hicksite Quaker heritage alike gave them a crucial consciousness of their own abiding individuality, and prevented them from totally losing themselves in visions of erotic union.

There is a final sense in which no poet has come close to a certain quality in the Song, to a terrible pathos that is unsurpassed in Western erotic literature:

> Set me as a seal upon thine heart, as a seal upon thine arm: for love is strong as death; jealousy is cruel as the grave: the coals thereof are coals of fire, which hath a most vehement flame.

The Hebrew is a little sharper than this, the unmatched King James version, since it calls love as fierce or intense as death or dying, and the Elizabethan "jealousy" is closer to "zealous" in its meaning. In the Hebrew, the poet chants that "passion is as strong as Sheol," or Hades, which affirms again the parallel intensities of loving and dying. The "coals of fire" are "darts of fire" in the Hebrew, and so confirm again the aggressive power of sexual love, so intimately related in the Song of Songs both to the death drive and to the transcendental possibilities of human existence.

THE GOSPELS

> "Your father Abraham rejoiced that he was to see my day; he saw it and was glad." The Jews then said to him, "You are not yet fifty years old, and have you seen Abraham?" Jesus said to them, "Truly, truly, I say to you, before Abraham was, I am." (John 8:56–58)

This exchange from the Gospel according to St. John will be my text. In the Christian triumph over the Hebrew Bible, a triumph which produced that captive work, the Old Testament, there is no more heroic stroke than the transumptive trope of John's Jesus: "Before Abraham was, I am." Too much is carried by that figuration for any range of readings to convey, but one reading I shall give is the implied substitution: "Before Moses was, I am." To my reading, the author of the Gospel of John was and is a more dangerous enemy of the Hebrew Bible than even Paul, his nearest rival. But I can hardly go on until I explain what I intend to mean by "an enemy of the Hebrew Bible."

It is now altogether too late in Western history for pious or humane self-deceptions on the matter of the Christian appropriation of the Hebrew Bible. It is certainly much too late in Jewish history to be other than totally clear about the nature and effect of that Christian act of total usurpation. The best preliminary description I have found is by Jaroslav Pelikan:

What the Christian tradition had done was to take over the Jewish Scriptures as its own, so that Justin could say to Trypho that the passages about Christ "are contained in your Scriptures, or rather not yours, but ours." As a matter of fact, some of the passages were contained only in "ours," that is, in the Christian Old Testament. So assured were Christian theologians in their possession of the Scriptures that they could accuse the Jews not merely of misunderstanding and misinterpreting them, but even of falsifying scriptural texts. When they were aware of differences between the Hebrew text of the Old Testament and the Septuagint, they capitalized on these to prove their accusation.... The growing ease with which appropriations and accusations alike could be made was in proportion to the completeness of the Christian victory over Jewish thought.

Yet that victory was achieved largely by default. Not the superior force of Christian exegesis or learning or logic but the movement of Jewish history seems to have been largely responsible for it.

Pelikan's dispassionate judgment on this matter is beyond disputation. Though the Christians were to "save" the Old Testament from those like Marcion who would cast it out completely, that is precisely what they saved—*their* Old Testament. The New Testament is to a considerable extent a reading of that Old Testament, and I would judge it a very mixed reading indeed. Some of it is a strong misreading, and much of it is a weak misreading, but I will concern myself here entirely with strong misreadings, because only strong misreadings work so as to establish lasting enmities between texts. The author of the Gospel of John is an even stronger misreader than St. Paul, and I want to compare John's and Paul's strengths of what I call poetic misprision before I center upon John. But before commencing, I had better declare my own stance.

"Who is the interpreter, and what power does he seek to gain over the text?" That Nietzschean question haunts me always. I am an enemy of the New Testament. My enmity is lifelong, and intensifies as I study its text more closely. But I have no right to assert that my own enmity carries the force of the normative Jewish tradition, because I am not a representative of that tradition. From a normative Jewish perspective, let us say from the stance of the great Akiba, I am one of the minim, the Jewish Gnostic heretics. My own reading of the Hebrew Bible, even if I develop it into a strong misreading, is as unacceptable in its way to the normative tradition as all Christian readings necessarily are. I state this not to posture, but to make clear that I do not pretend to the authority of the normative tradition. In my view, the Judaism that moves in a continuous line from the Academy of Ezra through the Pharisees and on to the religion of my own parents is itself a very powerful misreading of the Hebrew Bible and so of the religion of the Yahwist, whatever we might take that religion to have been. But my subject here is not the text of the Yahwist.

What kind of authority can a literary critic, whose subject is the secular literature of the English language, bring to a reading of the New Testament, particularly to a reading that sees the New Testament as a text in conflict and confrontation with the Hebrew Bible? I cannot speak for other literary critics, as here too I am a sect or party of one, and have no authority other than whatever my ideas and my writings can assert for me. But the central concern of my own literary theory and praxis, for some fifteen years now, has been the crisis of confrontation and conflict between what I have called strong poems, or strong texts. I cannot say that my formulations in this area have met with a very amiable reception, even in the most secular of contexts, and so I do not expect an amiable response as I cross the line into the conflict of scriptures. Still, I have learned a great deal from the response to my work, a response that necessarily has become part of my subject. One lesson has been that there are no purely secular texts, because canonization of poems by the secular academies is not merely a displaced version of Jewish or Christian or Moslem canonization. It is precisely the thing itself, the investment of a text with unity, presence, form, and meaning, followed by the insistence that the canonized text possesses these attributes immutably, quite apart from the interpretive activities of the academies.

If so many partisans of Wordsworth or Whitman or Stevens find the offense of my work unbearable, then clearly I must expect a yet more pained response from the various custodians of the Hebrew Bible or the New Testament. I won't take more space here for unhappy anticipation or personal defense, yet I do want to make the modest observation that several years spent intensely in reading as widely as I can in biblical scholarship have not left me with the impression that much authentic literary criticism of biblical texts has been written. To make a clean sweep of it, little seems to me to have been added by recent overt intercessions by literary critics, culminating in Northrop Frye's *The Great Code*, a work in which the triumph of the New Testament over the Hebrew Bible is quite flatly complete. Frye's code, like Erich Auerbach's *figura*, which I have attacked elsewhere, is only another belated repetition of the Christian appropriation and usurpation of the Hebrew Bible.

But these matters I will argue elsewhere. I come back again to the grand proclamation of John's Jesus: "Before Abraham was, I am." What can an antithetical literary criticism (as I call my work) do with the sublime force of that assertion? Or how should that force be described? It is not the New Testament's antithetical reply to the Yahwist's most sublime moment, when Moses agonizingly stammers: "If I come to the people of Israel and say to them, 'The God of your fathers has sent me to you,' and they ask me, 'What is his name?' what shall I say to them?" God said to Moses, "I AM WHO I AM." This is the Revised Standard Version, and like every other version, it cannot handle Yahweh's awesome, untranslatable play upon his own name: *ehyeh asher ehyeh*. I expand upon a suggestion of Martin Buber's when I render this as "I will be present wherever and whenever I will be present." For that is the Yahwist's vision of *olam* as "a time without boundaries," and of the relation of Yahweh to a dynamics of time that transcends spatial limitations.

The Yahwist's vision of his God certainly would seem to center with a peculiar intensity upon the text of Exodus 3:13–14. But the entire history of ancient Jewish exegesis hardly would lead anyone to believe that this crucial passage was of the slightest interest or importance to any of the great rabbinical commentators. The *Exodus Rabbah* offers mostly midrashim connecting the name of God to his potencies which would deliver Israel from Egypt. But *ehyeh asher ehyeh* as a phrase evidently did not have peculiar force for the great Pharisees. Indeed, Jewish tradition does very little with the majestic proclamation until Maimonides gets to work upon it in *The Guide for the Perplexed*. One of my favorite books, Marmorstein's fascinating *The Old Rabbinic Doctrine of God*, has absolutely not a single reference to Exodus 3 in its exhaustive one-hundred-fifty-page section on "The Names of God." Either we must conclude that *ehyeh asher ehyeh* has very little significance for Akiba and his colleagues, which I think probably was the case, or we must resort to dubious theories of taboo, which have little to do with the strength of Akiba.

This puzzle becomes greater when the early rabbinical indifference to the striking *ehyeh asher ehyeh* text is contrasted to the Christian obsession with Exodus 3, which begins in the New Testament and becomes overwhelming in the church fathers, culminating in Augustine's endless preoccupation with that passage, since for Augustine it was the deepest clue to the metaphysical essence of God. Brevard Childs, in his commentary on Exodus, has outlined the history of this long episode in Christian exegesis. Respectfully, I dissent from his judgment that the ontological aspects of Christian interpretation here really do have any continuity whatsoever either with the biblical text or with rabbinical traditions. These "ontological overtones," as Childs himself has to note, stem rather from the Septuagint's rendering of *ehyeh asher ehyeh* as the very different ἐγώ εἰμι ὁ ὤν and from Philo's very Platonized paraphrase in his *Life of Moses*: "Tell them that I am He Who is, that they may learn the difference between what is and what is not." Though Childs insists that this cannot be dismissed as Greek thinking, it is nothing but that, and explains again why Philo was so crucial for Christian theology and so totally irrelevant to the continuity of normative Judaism.

The continued puzzle, then, is the total lack of early rabbinical interest in the *ehyeh asher ehyeh* text. I labor this point because I read John's greatest subversion of the Hebrew Bible as what I call this transumption of Yahweh's words to Moses in that extraordinary outburst of John's Jesus, "Before Abraham was, I am," which most deeply proclaims: "Before Moses was, I am." To me, this is the acutest manifestation of John's palpable ambivalence toward Moses, an ambivalence whose most perceptive student has been Wayne Meeks. John plays on and against the Yahwist's grand wordplay on Yahweh, and *ehyeh*. However, when I assert even that, I go against the authority of the leading current scholarly commentary upon the Fourth Gospel, and so I must deal with this difficulty before I return to the Johannic ambivalence toward the Moses traditions. And only after examining John's agon with Moses will I feel free to speculate upon the early rabbinic indifference to God's substitution of *ehyeh asher ehyeh* for his proper name.

Both B. Lindars and C.K. Barrett in their standard commentaries on John insist that "Before Abraham was, I am" makes no allusion whatsoever to "I am that I am." A literary critic must begin by observing that New Testament scholarship manifests a very impoverished notion as to just what literary allusion is or can be. But then here is Barrett's flat reading of this assertion of Jesus: "The meaning here is: Before Abraham came into being, I eternally was, as now I am, and ever continue to be." Perhaps I should not chide devoted scholars like Lindars and Barrett for being inadequate interpreters of so extraordinary a trope, because the master modern interpreter of John, Rudolf Bultmann, seems to me even less capable of handling trope. Here is his reading of John 8:57–58:

> The Jews remain caught in the trammels of their own thought. How can Jesus, who is not yet 50 years old, have seen Abraham! Yet the world's conception of time and age is worthless, when it has to deal with God's revelation, as is its conception of life and death. "Before Abraham was, I am." The Revealer, unlike

Abraham, does not belong to the ranks of historical personages. The ἐγώ which Jesus speaks as the Revealer is the "I" of the eternal Logos, which was in the beginning, the "I" of the eternal God himself. Yet the Jews cannot comprehend that the ἐγώ of eternity is to be heard in an historical person, who is not yet 50 years old, who as a man is one of their equals, whose mother and father they knew. They cannot understand, because the notion of the Revealer's "pre-existence" can only be understood in faith.

In a note, Bultmann too denies any allusion to the "I am that I am" declaration of Yahweh. I find it ironical, nearly two thousand years after St. Paul accused the Jews of being literalizers, that the leading scholars of Christianity are hopeless literalizers, which of course the great rabbis never were. I cannot conceive of a weaker misreading of "Before Abraham was, I am" than Bultmann's sneering retreat into "faith," a "faith" in the "pre-existence" of Jesus. If that is all John meant, then John was a weak poet indeed. But John is at his best here, and at his best he is a strong misreader and thus a strong writer. As for Bultmann's polemical point, I am content to repeat a few amiable remarks made by Rabbi David Kimhi almost eight hundred years ago:

> Tell them that there can be no father and son in the Divinity, for the Divinity is indivisible and is one in every aspect of unity unlike matter which is divisible.
>
> Tell them further that a father precedes a son in time and a son is born through the agency of a father. Now even though each of the terms "father" and "son" implies the other ... he who is called the father must undoubtedly be prior in time. Therefore, with reference to this God whom you call Father, Son, and Holy Spirit, that part which you call Father must be prior to that which you call Son, for if they were always coexistent, they would have to be called twin brothers.

I have cited this partly because I enjoy it so much, but also because it raises the true issue between Moses and John, between Abraham and Jesus, which is the agonistic triple issue of priority, authority, and originality. As I read John's trope, it asserts not only the priority of Jesus over Abraham (and so necessarily over Moses), but also the priority, authority, and originality of John over Moses, or as we would say, of John as writer over the Yahwist as writer. That is where I am heading this account of the agon between the Yahwist and John, and so I turn now to some general observations upon the Fourth Gospel—observations by a literary critic, of course, and not by a qualified New Testament believer and/or scholar.

John does seem to me the most anxious in tone of all the gospels, and its anxiety is as much what I would call a literary anxiety as an existential or spiritual one. One sign of this anxiety is the palpable difference between the attitude of Jesus toward himself in the Fourth Gospel as compared to the other three. Scholarly consensus holds that John was written at the close of the first century, and so after the synoptic Gospels. A century is certainly enough time for apocalyptic hope to have ebbed away, and for an acute sense of belatedness to have developed in its place. John's Jesus has a certain obsession with his own glory, and particularly with what that glory ought to be in a Jewish context. Rather like the Jesus of Gnosticism, John's Jesus is much given to saying "I am," and there are Gnostic touches throughout John, though their extent is disputable. Perhaps, as some scholars have surmised, there is an earlier, more Gnostic gospel buried in the Gospel of John. An interesting article by John Meagher of Toronto, back in 1969, even suggested that the original reading of John 1:14 was "And the Word became *pneuma* and dwelt among us," which is a Gnostic formulation, yet curiously more in the spirit and tone of much of the Fourth Gospel than is "And the Word became flesh."

The plain nastiness of the Gospel of John toward the Pharisees is in the end an anxiety as to the spiritual authority of the Pharisees, and it may be augmented by John's Gnostic overtones. A Jewish reader with even the slightest sense of Jewish history, feels threatened when reading John 18:28–19:16. I do not think that this feeling has anything to do with the supposed pathos or problematic literary power of the text. There is a peculiar wrongness about John's Jesus saying, "If my kingship were of this world, my servants would fight, that I might not be handed over to the Jews" (18:36); it implies that Jesus is no longer a Jew, but something else. This unhappy touch is another sign of the pervasive rhetoric of anxiety in the Fourth Gospel. John's vision seemed to be of a small group—his own, presumably—which finds its analogue and asserted origin in the group around Jesus two generations before. In the general judgment of scholars, the original conclusion of the gospel was the parable of doubting Thomas, a manifest trope for a sect or coven undergoing a crisis of faith.

It is within that anxiety of frustrate expectations, perhaps even of recent expulsion from the Jewish world, that John's agon with Moses finds its context. Wayne Meeks has written very sensitively of the Fourth Gospel's ambivalence toward the Moses traditions, particularly those centered upon the image of Moses as prophet-king, a unique amalgam of the two roles that John seeks to extend and surpass in Jesus. My interest in John's handling of Moses is necessarily different in emphasis, for I am going to read a number of John's namings of Moses as being tropes more for the text than for the supposed substance of what the New Testament (following the Septuagint) insists upon calling the Law. I myself will call it not Torah but J or the Yahwist, because that is where I locate the agon. Not theology, not faith, not truth is the issue, but literary power, the scandalous power of J's text, which by synecdoche stands for the Hebrew Bible as the strongest poem that I have ever read in any language I am able to read. John, and Paul before him, took on an impossible precursor and rival, and their apparent victory is merely an illusion. The aesthetic dignity of the Hebrew Bible, and of the Yahwist in particular as its uncanny original, is simply beyond the competitive range of the New Testament as a literary achievement, as it is beyond the range of the only surviving Gnostic texts that have any aesthetic value—a few fragments of Valentinus and the Gospel of Truth that Valentinus may have written. But I will return to the end of this discourse to the issue of rival aesthetic achievements. John's struggle with Moses is at last my direct concern.

There are so many contests with Moses throughout the New Testament that I cannot contrast John in this regard to all of the other texts, but I do want to compare him briefly with Paul, if only because I intend later to consider some aspects of Paul's own struggle with the Hebrew Bible. I think there is still nothing so pungent in all commentary upon Paul as the remarks made by Nietzsche in 1888, in *The Antichrist*:

> Paul is the incarnation of a type which is the reverse of that of the Savior; he is the genius in hatred, in the standpoint of hatred, and in the relentless logic of hatred.... What he wanted was power; with St. Paul the priest again aspired to power,—he could make use only of concepts, doctrines, symbols with which masses may be tyrannised over, and with which herds are formed.

Of course Nietzsche is extreme, but can he be refuted? Paul is so careless, hasty, and inattentive a reader of the Hebrew Bible that he very rarely gets any text right; and in so gifted a person this kind of weak misunderstanding can come only from the dialectics of the power drive, of the will to power over a text, even when the text is as formidable as Torah. There is little agonistic cunning in Paul's misreadings of Torah; many indeed are plain howlers. The most celebrated is his weird exegesis of Exodus 34:29–35, where the text has Moses descending from Sinai, tablets in hand, his face shining with God's glory—a glory so great that Moses must veil his countenance after speaking to the people, and then unveil only when he returns to speak to God. Normative Jewish interpretation, surely known to Paul, was that the shining was the Torah restoration of the *zelem*, the true image of God that Adam had lost, and that the shining prevailed until the death of Moses. But here is 2 Corinthians 3:12–13:

> Since we have such a hope, we are very bold, not like Moses, who put a veil over his face so that the Israelites might not see the end of the fading splendor.

There isn't any way to save this, even by gently calling it a "parody" of the Hebrew text, as Wayne Meeks does. It isn't a transumption or lie against time, which is the Johannine mode; it is just a plain lie against the text. Nor is it uncharacteristic of Paul. Meeks very movingly calls Paul "the Christian Proteus," and Paul is certainly beyond my understanding. Proteus is an apt model for many other roles, but perhaps not for an interpreter of Mosaic text. Paul's reading of what he thought was the Law increasingly seems to me oddly Freudian, in that Paul identifies the Law with the human drive that Freud wanted to call Thanatos. Paul's peculiar confounding of the Law and death presumably keeps him from seeing Jesus as a transcending fulfillment of Moses. Instead, Paul contrasts himself to Moses, hardly to his own disadvantage. Thus, Romans 9:3:

> For I could wish that I myself were accused and cut off from Christ for the sake of my brethren, my kinsmen by race.

It may seem at first an outburst of Jewish pride, of which I would grant the Protean Paul an authentic share, but the Mosaic allusion changes its nature. All exegetes point to Exodus 32:32 as the precursor text. Moses offers himself to Yahweh as atonement for the people after the orgy of the golden calf. "But now, if thou wilt forgive their sin—and if not, blot me, I pray thee, out of thy book which thou hast written." How do the two offers of intercession compare? After all, the people *have* sinned, and Moses would choose oblivion to save them from the consequences of their disloyalty. The allusive force of Paul's offer is turned against both his own Jewish contemporaries and even against Moses himself. Even the Pharisees (for whom Paul, unlike John, has a lingering regard) are worshippers of the golden calf of death, since the Law is death. And all Moses supposedly offered was the loss of his own prophetic greatness, his place in the salvation history. But Paul, out of supposed love for his fellow Jews, offers to lose more than Moses did, because he insists he has more to lose. To be cut off from Christ is to die eternally, a greater sacrifice than the Mosaic offer to be as one who had never lived. This is what I would call the daemonic counter-Sublime of hyperbole, and its repressive force is enormous and very revelatory.

But I return again to John, whose revisionary warfare against Moses is subtler. Meeks has traced the general pattern, and so I follow him here, though of course he would dissent from the interpretation I am going to offer of this pattern of allusion. The allusions begin with John the Baptist chanting a typical Johannine metalepsis, in which the latecomer truly has priority ("John bore witness to him, and cried, 'This was he of whom I said: He who comes after me ranks before me, for he was before me'"), to which the author of the Fourth Gospel adds: "For the law was given through Moses; grace and truth came through Jesus Christ" (John 1:15, 17). Later, the first chapter proclaims: "We have found him of whom Moses in the law and also the prophets wrote, Jesus of Nazareth" (1:45). The third chapter daringly inverts a great Mosaic trope in a way still unnerving for any Jewish reader: "No one has ascended into heaven but he who descended from heaven, the Son of man. And as Moses lifted up the serpent in the wilderness, so must the Son of man be lifted up" (3:13–14). John's undoubted revisionary genius is very impressive here merely from a technical or rhetorical point of view. No heavenly revelations ever were made to Moses, whose function is reduced to a synecdoche, and indeed to its lesser half. To use one of my revisionary ratios, Jesus on the cross will be the *tessera* or antithetical completion of the Mosaic raising of the brazen serpent in the wilderness. Moses was only a part, but Jesus is the fulfilling whole. My avoidance of the language of typology, here and elsewhere, is quite deliberate, and will be defended in my conclusion, where I will say a few unkind words about the Christian and now Auerbachian trope of *figura*.

The same ratio of antithetical completion is invoked when Jesus announces himself as the fulfiller of the sign of manna, as would be expected of the Messiah. But here the gratuitous ambivalence toward Moses is sharper: "Truly, truly, I say to you, it was not Moses who gave you the bread from heaven; my Father gives you the true bread from heaven. For the bread of God is that which comes down from heaven, and gives life to the world" (6:32–33). As the trope is developed, it becomes deliberately so shocking in a Jewish context that even the disciples are shocked; but I would point to one moment in the development as marking John's increasing violence against Moses and all the Jews: "Your fathers ate the manna in the wilderness, and they died.... I am the living bread ... if any one eats of this bread, he will live for ever; and the bread which I shall give for the life of the world is my flesh" (6:49, 51). It is, after all, gratuitous to say that our fathers ate the manna and died; it is even misleading, since had they not eaten the manna, they would not have lived as long as they did. But John has modulated to a daemonic counter-Sublime, and his hyperbole helps to establish a new, Christian sublimity, in which Jews die and Christians live eternally.

Rather than multiply instances of John's revisionism, I want to conclude my specific remarks on the Fourth Gospel by examining in its full context the passage with which I began: "Before Abraham was, I am." I am more than a little unhappy with the sequence I will expound, because I find in it John at nearly his most unpleasant and indeed anti Jewish, but the remarkable rhetorical strength of "Before Abraham was, I am" largely depends upon its contextualization, as John undoes the Jewish pride in being descended from Abraham. The sequence, extending through most of the eighth chapter, begins with Jesus sitting in the temple, surrounded both by Pharisees and by Jews who are in the process of becoming his believers. To those he has begun to persuade, Jesus now says what is certain to turn them away:

> "If you continue in my word, you are truly my disciples, and you will know the truth, and the truth will make you free." They answered him, "We are descendants of Abraham, and have never been in bondage to any one. How is it that you say, 'You will be made free'?"
> (8:31–32)

It seems rather rhetorically weak that Jesus should then become aggressive, with a leap into murderous insinuations:

> "I know that you are descendants of Abraham; yet you seek to kill me, because my word finds no place in you. I speak of what I have seen with my Father, and you do what you have heard from your father."
> (8:37–38)

As John's Jesus graciously is about to tell them, the Jews' father is the devil. They scarcely can be blamed for answering, "Abraham is our father," or for assuming that their accuser has a demon. I look at the foot of the page of the text I am using, *The New Oxford Annotated Bible, Revised Standard Version* (1977), and next to verse 48, on having a demon, the editors helpfully tell me, "*The Jews* turn to insult and calumny." I reflect upon how wonderful a discipline such scholarship is, and I mildly rejoin that by any dispassionate reading John's Jesus has made the initial "turn to insult and calumny." What matter, since the Jews are falling neatly into John's rhetorical trap? Jesus has promised that his believers "will never see death" and the astonished children of Abraham (or is it children of the devil?) protest:

> "Abraham died, as did the prophets; and you say, 'If any one keeps my word, he will never taste death.' Are you greater than our father Abraham, who died?"
> (8:52–53)

Jesus responds by calling them liars, again surely rather gratuitously, and then by ensnaring them in John's subtlest tropological entrapment, which will bring me full circle to where I began:

> "Your father Abraham rejoiced that he was to see my day; he saw it and was glad." The Jews then said to him, "You are not yet fifty years old, and have you seen Abraham?" Jesus said to them, "Truly, truly, I say to you, before Abraham was, I am."
> (8:57–58)

It is certainly the most remarkable transumption in the New Testament, though I had better explain what I mean by transumption, which is a little exhausting for me, since I have been explaining the term endlessly in eight books published over the last nine years. Very briefly, transumption or metalepsis is the traditional term in rhetoric for the trope that works to make the late seem early, and the early seem late. It lies against time, so as to accomplish what Nietzsche called the will's revenge against time, and against time's assertion, "It was." Uniquely among figures of speech, transumption works to undo or reverse anterior tropes. It is therefore the particular figure that governs what we might call "interpretive allusion." Ultimately, it seeks to end-stop allusiveness by presenting its own formulation as the last word, which insists upon an ellipsis rather than a proliferation of further allusion.

When John's Jesus says, "Before Abraham was, I am," the ultimate allusion is not to Abraham but to Moses, and to Yahweh's declaration made to Moses, "I am that I am." The transumption leaps over Abraham by saying also, "Before Moses was, I am," and by hinting ultimately: "I am that I am"—because I am one with my father Yahweh. The ambivalence and agonistic intensity of the Fourth Gospel achieves an apotheosis with this sublime introjection of Yahweh, which simultaneously also is a projection or repudiation of Abraham and Moses. I am aware that I seem to be making John into a Gnostic Christian, but that is the transumptive force of his rhetoric, as opposed perhaps to his more overt dialectic. His Gospel, as it develops, does seem to me to become as Gnostic as it is Christian, and this is the kind of Gnosticism that indeed was a kind of intellectual or spiritual anti-Semitism. Obviously, I believe that there are Gnosticisms and Gnosticisms, and some I find considerably more attractive than others. Just as obviously, the Gnostic elements in John, and even in St. Paul, seem to me very shadowed indeed.

Earlier in this discourse, I confessed my surprise at the normative rabbinical indifference, in ancient days, to Yahweh's sublime declaration, *ehyeh asher ehyeh*. If the great Rabbi Akiba ever speculated about that enigmatic phrase, he kept it to himself. I doubt that he made any such speculations, because I do not think that fearless sage was in the habit of hoarding them, and I am not enough of a Kabbalist to think that Akiba harbored forbidden or esoteric knowledge. To the normative mind of the Judaism roughly contemporary with Jesus, there was evidently nothing remarkable in Yahweh's declining to give his name, and instead almost playfully asserting: "Tell them that I who will be when and where I will be am the one who has sent you." That is how Yahweh talked, and how he was. But to the belated author of the Fourth Gospel, as to all our belated selves, "I am that I am" was and is a kind of *mysterium tremendum*, to use Rudolf Otto's language. That mystery John sought to transcend and transume with the formulation "Before Abraham was, I am." Prior to the text of Exodus was the text that John was writing, in which the Jews were to be swept away into the universe of death, while Jesus led John on to the universe of life.

This transformation is an instance of just how the New Testament reduced the Hebrew Bible to that captive work, the Old Testament. Though the reduction is necessarily of great theological influence, it of course does not touch the Hebrew Bible. I have read the Hebrew Bible since I was a child, and the New Testament since I first took a course in New Testament Greek as an undergraduate. Clearly, I am not a dispassionate reader of the New Testament, though I do not read the Hebrew Bible as the normative Jewish tradition had read it, either. I come back to the issue of the interpreter's authority. When I read, I read as a literary critic, but my concerns have little in common with those of any contemporary critic. Idealizations of any text, however canonical, or of the reading process itself are not much to my taste. Emerson said he read for the lustres. I follow him, but I emphasize even more that the lustres arise out of strife, competition, defense, anxiety, and the author's constant need for survival *as an author*. I don't see how any authentic literary critic could judge John as anything better than a very flawed revisionist of the Yahwist, and Paul as something less than that, despite the peculiar pathos of his protean personality. In the aesthetic warfare between the Hebrew Bible and the New Testament, there is just no contest, and if you think otherwise, then bless you.

But surely the issue is not aesthetic, I will be reminded. Well, we are all trapped in history, and the historical triumph of Christianity is brute fact. I am not moved to say anything about it. But I am moved to reject the idealized modes of interpretation it has stimulated, from early typology on to the revival of *figura* by Erich Auerbach and the Blakean Great Code of Northrop Frye. No text, secular or religious, fulfills another text, and all who insist otherwise merely homogenize literature. As for the relevance of the aesthetic to the issue of the conflict between sacred texts, I doubt finally that much else is relevant to a strong reader who is not dominated by extraliterary persuasions or convictions. Reading *The Book of Mormon*, for instance, is a difficult aesthetic experience, and I would grant that not much in the New Testament subjects me to rigors of quite that range. But then John and Paul do not ask to be read against *The Book of Mormon*.

Can the New Testament be read as less polemically and destructively revisionary of the Hebrew Bible than it actually is? Not by me, anyway. But don't be too quick to shrug off a reading informed by an awareness of the ways of the antithetical, of the revisionary strategies devised by those latecomers who seek strength, and who will sacrifice truth to get strength even as they proclaim the incarnation of the truth beyond death. Nietzsche is hardly the favorite sage of contemporary New Testament scholars, but perhaps he still has something vital to teach them.

What do Jews and Christians gain by refusing to see that the revisionary desperation of the New Testament has made it permanently impossible to identify the Hebrew Bible with the Christian Old Testament? Doubtless there are social and political benefits in idealizations of "dialogue," but there is nothing more. It is not a contribution to the life of the spirit or the intellect to tell lies to one another or to oneself in order to bring about more affection or cooperation between Christians and Jews. Paul is hopelessly equivocal on nearly every subject, but to my reading he is clearly not a Jewish anti-Semite; yet his misrepresentation of Torah was absolute. John is evidently a Jewish anti-Semite, and the Fourth Gospel is pragmatically murderous as an anti Jewish text. Yet it is theologically and emotionally central to Christianity. I give the last word to the sage called Radak in Jewish tradition, that David Kimhi whom I cited earlier. He quotes as proof text Ezekiel 16:53: "I will turn their captivity, the captivity of Sodom and her daughters." And then Radak comments, rightly dismissing from his perspective all Christians as mere heretics from Judaism: "This verse is a reply to the Christian heretics who say that the future consolations have already been fulfilled. *Sodom is still overturned as it was and is still unsettled.*"

THE REVELATION OF SAINT JOHN THE DIVINE

The first Christians evidently were apocalyptic Jews who expected the return of Jesus and an end to time within the span of their own lives. "Uncovering" is the meaning of the Greek *apocalypsis*, or, in American, "taking off the lid." The Book of Daniel, composed during the rebellion of the Maccabeans against Hellenistic Syria, is the archetype for all later apocalypses, including the Revelation of St. John the Divine. Christian tradition holds that the emperor Domitian exiled St. John to the island of Patmos in the Aegean in 95 C.E. Two years later, Nerva was emperor and John returned from his rocky exile to the churches of Asia Minor.

Though some scholars have identified John of Patmos with the author of the Fourth Gospel, a close reading of Revelation and the Gospel of John in the original will show such a contention to be highly unlikely. The Gospel of John, unhappy as it may make a Jewish critic like myself, is powerfully composed, but Revelation is poorly written in the original, with its author rather awkwardly trying to get his Aramaic syntax into a Greek vocabulary. No other work in the New Testament benefits so enormously from translation.

The overt genre of Revelation is the Pauline epistle, but the true patterns for John of Patmos are set by the authors of Daniel and Ezekiel and Zechariah, since Revelation is a jigsaw puzzle in which nearly all the pieces are torn away from their contexts in those three books of the Hebrew Bible. This accounts for the odd detachment of Revelation from the rest of the New Testament. The precursor texts for John of Patmos are in Hebrew and Aramaic, not in Greek. Yet the books of Daniel and the prophets do not contextualize Revelation; it is nowhere close to being as coherent or sane as the works that inspired it.

The influence of Revelation is out of all proportion to its literary strength or spiritual value. Not only has it engrossed the quacks and cranks of all ages down to the present moment, but it has haunted the greatest poets, from Dante and Spenser through Milton to Blake and Shelley. The apocalyptic genre in Western literature always returns to Revelation rather than to Daniel and Zechariah. From Melville to Pynchon, American visionaries are shadowed by Revelation, and any student of English poetry or American fiction needs to achieve some sense of the peculiar rhapsody attributed to John of Patmos.

The Epistle to the Hebrews seems to hover in John's consciousness as his interpretive model for how to read the Hebrew Bible, or, rather, not so much the Hebrew Bible or its Aramaic paraphrase as a curious work still called the "Old Testament" by Christians. The Hebrew Bible ends with Second Chronicles and its great injunction to rebuild Jerusalem: "Let us go up," but the Old Testament concludes with the belated prophet Malachi, whose God urges the hearts of children and of their fathers to turn to one another, "lest I come and smite the earth with a curse." The New Testament strives to accomplish that turning by interpretation or typology, in which every crucial passage in the Old Testament is supposedly "fulfilled" by a passage in the New. Typology is frequently regarded by scholars as a benign or even technical matter, but it is the most extreme instance I know of the exercise of the will to power over a text. Nietzsche's question is precisely relevant to every author of the New Testament: "Who is the interpreter and what power does he seek to gain over the text?"

Typology, as discussed by many of our most eminent critics—Erich Auerbach, Northrop Frye, Charles Singleton, John Freccero—takes on a positive aura, but it is polemical in the extreme. Here is Frye introducing it as though it were amiable indeed:

> Everything that happens in the Old Testament is a "type" or adumbration of something that happens in the New Testament, and the whole subject is therefore called typology, though it is typology in a special sense. Paul speaks in Romans 5:14 of Adam as a *typos* of Christ; the Vulgate renders *typos* here as "forma," but the Authorized Version's "figure" reflects the fact that "figura" had come to be the standard Latin equivalent of *typos*. What happens in the New Testament constitutes an "antitype," a realized form, of something foreshadowed in the Old Testament.

The Hebrew Bible thus becomes a giant *typos* or *figura*, a mere foreshadowing that achieves realized form in the New Testament. But no text actually "fulfills" another text, particularly if the earlier text is stronger. Dante is so strong a poet that he persuades us his Virgil is the fulfillment of which the actual Virgil is the *figura*, but John of Patmos is a weak if hysterical poet, and his Daniel, his Ezekiel, and his Zechariah are travesties of the actual prophetic texts. Still, we do not read Revelation, even in the Authorized Version, for spiritual insight unless we are believers. If you believe that Revelation is the literal truth, then the aesthetic or even the spiritual insights are of course not issues at all. But *literary* criticism of the Bible, still in its infancy, needs to ask evaluative questions, *pace* Northrop Frye. Austin Farrer, Revelation's classic exegete, views typology as "a rebirth of images," but such a judgment is an act of faith, not of criticism:

> Since the process is of the rebirth of images, it is to the matrix of images, the Old Testament, that the Spirit continually leads: for here are the images awaiting rebirth; all this is Christ, could we but see how and why; the Spirit will teach us. The work of reinterpretation may include much hard and close intellectual effort, there is nothing dreamy or sentimental about it; but it is obvious that the calculative reason alone can do nothing here. The images must live again in the mind, with the life of the image of Christ: that is inspiration.
>
> The rebirth of images can be studied everywhere in the New Testament, but nowhere can we get so deep into the heart of the process as we can in St John's Apocalypse. For nowhere else have we a writing which is so simply devoted to the liberation of the images as this is. The Evangelists clothe their history with the images, but they are restricted by the historical actuality upon which they fit them. The Epistles find their inspiration in the images, but they express them only in so far as serves the purpose of instruction or exhortation. But the Apocalypse writes of heaven and things to come, that is, of a realm which has no shape at all but that which the images give it. In this room the image may grow to the fulness of its inborn nature, like a tree in a wide meadow.
> (*A Rebirth of Images*)

If this were said of Dante's *Paradiso*, it would be said to some purpose. My point is not to quarrel with Farrer's distinguished study, but is to suggest that the issue indeed is aesthetic. Since no text fulfills but rather revises another, the question of Revelation's relation to its precursors becomes the agonistic triple query that always marks the Sublime: more? equal to? less than? Any good reader free of extra-aesthetic beliefs would have no difficulty in measuring Revelation's images against those of its prophetic precursors.

Religious history and its contingencies allow us no choice; St. John's Apocalypse is a permanent part of our literary culture. Lurid and inhumane, its influence has been pernicious, yet inescapable. Frye calls it one of the "nightmares of anxiety and triumph," and one may wonder whether this is either an achieved anxiety or an achieved triumph:

And there came one of the seven angels which had the seven vials, and talked with me, saying unto me, Come hither; I will skew unto thee the judgment of the great whore that sitteth upon many waters:

With whom the kings of the earth have committed fornication, and the inhabitants of the earth have been made drunk with the wine of her fornication.

So he carried me away in the spirit into the wilderness: and I saw a woman sit upon a scarlet coloured beast, full of names of blasphemy, having seven heads and ten horns.

And the woman was arrayed in purple and scarlet colour, and decked with gold and precious stones and pearls, having a golden cup in her hand full of abominations and filthiness of her fornication:

And upon her forehead was a name written, MYSTERY, BABYLON THE GREAT, THE MOTHER OF HARLOTS AND ABOMINATIONS OF THE EARTH.

And I saw the woman drunken with the blood of the saints, and with the blood of the martyrs of Jesus: and when I saw her, I wondered with great admiration.
(Rev. 17:1–6)

I cannot reread this without remembering the judgment upon it of a great Protestant sensibility, D.H. Lawrence: "The Apocalypse does not worship power. It wants to murder the powerful, to seize power itself, the weakling." Nietzsche's pale ascetic priest exalting resentment could not be better exemplified than he is by John of Patmos. Resentment and not love is the teaching of the Revelation of St. John the Divine. It is a book without wisdom, goodness, kindness, or affection of any kind. Perhaps it is appropriate that a celebration of the end of the world should be not only barbaric but scarcely literate. Where the substance is so inhumane, who would wish the rhetoric to be more persuasive, or the vision to be more vividly realized?

Michel de Montaigne

(1533-1592)

Montaigne, until the advent of Shakespeare, is the great figure of the European Renaissance, comparable in cognitive power and in influence to Freud in our century. His mordant essay "Of Books" is marked by a genial irony that is profoundly skeptical of the Humanist program that ostensibly (and rather off-handedly) is endorsed:

> Let people see in what I borrow whether I have known how to choose what would enhance my theme. For I make others say what I cannot say so well, now through the weakness of my language, now through the weakness of my understanding. I do not count my borrowings, I weigh them. And if I had wanted to have them valued by their number, I should have loaded myself with twice as many. They are all or very nearly all, from such famous and ancient names that they seem to identify themselves enough without me. In the reasonings and inventions that I transplant into my soil and confound with my own, I have sometimes deliberately not indicated the author, in order to hold in check the temerity of those hasty condemnations that are tossed at all sorts of writings, notably recent writings of men still living, and in the vulgar tongue, which invites everyone to talk about them and seems to convict the conception and design of being likewise vulgar. I want them to give Plutarch a fillip on my nose and get burned insulting Seneca in me. I have to hide my weakness under these great authorities. I will love anyone that can unplume me, I mean by clearness of judgment and by the sole distinction of the force and beauty of the remarks. For I who, for lack of memory, fall short at every turn in picking

them out by knowledge of their origin, can very well realize, by measuring my capacity, that my soil is not at all capable of producing certain too rich flowers that I find sown there, and that all the fruits of my own growing could not match them.

This hardly seems a matter of classical courage but rather of cunning, humor, skill, and a deliciously bland disarming of one's critics. It is also rather clearly a knowingly defensive irony, directed against a literary anxiety that Montaigne insists is universal, and not merely individual. Montaigne at this time (1578–80) is well underway to his final stance, where he forsakes the high Humanist doctrine in favor of the common life, so as to affirm the exuberance of natural existence, and the enormous virtue of being the *honnête homme*, thus establishing a new norm against which Pascal would rebel, or perhaps an influence that Pascal could neither escape nor accept. What "Of Books" subverts most audaciously is the Humanist scheme of benign displacement by imitation. When Montaigne writes of his unsavory critics, "I want them to give Plutarch a fillip on my nose and get burned insulting Seneca in me," he not only accurately names his prime precursors, but he asserts his own power of contamination. In contrast, consider Ben Jonson, more truly Thomas Greene's hero of "classical courage":

> The third requisite in our poet or maker is imitation, *imitatio*, to be able to convert the substance or riches of another poet to his own use. To make choice of one excellent man above the rest, and so to follow him till he grow very he, or so like him as the copy may be mistaken for the principal. Not as a creature that swallows what it takes in, crude, raw, or undigested; but that feeds with an appetite, and hath a stomach to concoct, divide, and turn all into nourishment. Not to imitate servilely, as Horace saith, and catch at vices for virtue, but to draw forth out of the best and choicest flowers, with the bee, and turn all into honey, work it into one relish and savour; make our imitation sweet; observe how the best writers have imitated, and follow them: how Virgil and Statius have imitated Homer; how Horace, Archilochus; how Alcæus, and the other lyrics; and so of the rest.

Here one imitates precisely as the precursors imitated, which seems to me an apt reduction of the Humanist argument. It is no surprise that Jonson goes on to say of reading that it "maketh a full man," borrowing from his truest precursor Sir Francis Bacon in the essay "Of Studies." Admirable essayist in his narrow mode, Bacon is about as adequate to compete with Montaigne as Jonson was to challenge Shakespeare. It takes a singular perversity to prefer Bacon's essays to Montaigne's, and yet Jonson could insist persuasively that he was being loyal to the Humanist doctrine of imitation:

> Some that turn over all books, and are equally searching in all papers; that write out of what they presently find or meet, without choice. By which means it happens that what they have discredited and impugned in one week, they have before or after extolled the same in another. Such are all the essayists, even their master Montaigne. These, in all they write, confess still what books they have read last, and therein their own folly so much, that they bring it to the stake raw and undigested; not that the place did need it neither, but that they thought themselves furnished and would vent it.

Bacon's essays certainly do not "confess still what books they have read last," and Montaigne is anything but formalist in his use of quite immediate reading. Thomas Greene is wiser, I think, when he recognizes that ambivalence and the antithetical haunt all imitation, however Humanist:

> The process called imitation was not only a technique or a habit; it was also a field of ambivalence, drawing together manifold, tangled, sometimes antithetical attitudes, hopes, pieties, and reluctances within a concrete locus.

At the heart of Humanism was an ambivalence, even an antithetical will, that perhaps still makes the phrase "Christian Humanist" something of an oxymoron. Most simply, Humanism entailed a love of Greek and Latin wisdom and humane letters, a desire to know qualities uniquely available in antiquity. Christianity, in the early Renaissance, indeed became Greek and Latin in its culture, at a certain cost. The morality of the Christian Bible is scarcely Greek or Latin, and the God of Christianity remained the God of Abraham, Isaac, and Jacob, rather than the gods of Achilles, Odysseus, and Aeneas. Imitation or mimesis, whether of nature or of a precursor, is a Greek notion, rather than an Hebraic postulate. We cannot image an ancient Greek or Latin author confronting the stark text of the Second Commandment.

Erich Auerbach, in his *Mimesis: The Representation of Reality in Western Literature*, finds in Rabelais and Montaigne an early Renaissance freedom of vision, feeling, and thought produced by a perpetual playing with things, and hints that this freedom began to decline not so much in Cervantes as in Shakespeare, the two writers who by paradox may be the only Western authors since antiquity clearly surpassing the powers of even Rabelais and Montaigne. As Auerbach emphasizes:

> In Rabelais there is no aesthetic standard; everything goes with everything. Ordinary reality is set within the most improbable fantasy, the coarsest jobs are filled with erudition, moral and philosophical enlightenment flows out of obscene expressions and stories.

This extraordinary freedom of representation in Rabelais is matched by Montaigne in Auerbach's description of his emancipation not only from the Christian conceptual schema but from the cosmological view of his precursors Cicero, Seneca, and Plutarch:

> His newly acquired freedom was much more exciting, much more of the historical moment, directly connected with the feeling of insecurity. The disconcerting abundance of phenomena which now claimed the attention of men seemed overwhelming. The world—both outer world and inner world—seemed immense, boundless, incomprehensible.

Shakespeare, "more consciously aristocratic than Montaigne" in Auerbach's view, grants the aesthetic dignity of the tragic only to princes, commanders, and eminent figures in Roman history. To the Humanist heritage Auerbach attributes Shakespeare's sense that there is more than a temporal gap between contemporary life and the heroic past:

> With the first dawn of humanism, there began to be a sense that the events of classical history and legend and also those of the Bible were not separated from the present simply by an extent of time but also by completely different conditions of life. Humanism with its program of renewal of antique forms of life and expression creates a historical perspective in depth such as no previous epoch known to us possessed.

Of Cervantes Auerbach beautifully remarks: "So universal and multilayered, so noncritical and nonproblematic a gaiety in the portrayal of everyday reality has not been attempted again in European letters." It is as though Humanist perspectivism—not yet developed in the rambunctious Rabelais, a powerful shadow in Shakespeare, forsaken for the common life by Montaigne—had been set aside by a genial power of acceptance of the mundane in Cervantes. But these in any case are the Renaissance writers as strong as Homer, Dante, and Chaucer. With lesser writers (lesser only as compared with these), the opening to the past carried with it a perspectivism that generated anxieties both of influence and of representation. Paradoxically, humanism both exalted and burdened writers by proclaiming that the vernacular could achieve what the ancients had achieved, by the aid of an antique greatness that carried its own implicit force of inhibition.

II

The literary criticism of the sixteenth century, since it is so entirely part of what can be called a Humanist manifesto, now demands to be read in a certain spirit of affectionate deidealization. The greatest writers of the century accomplish this deidealization by themselves, and if such an activity be considered criticism (and it is), then Montaigne, rather than Du Bellay or Sidney or Tasso, becomes the great critic of the early Renaissance. To call the *Essays* a vast work of literary criticism is a revisionary act of judgment, but only in the sense of seeing now that Sigmund Freud, who died in 1939, appears in 1987 to have been the crucial critic of the twentieth century. Montaigne's defense of the self is also an analysis of the self, and Montaigne appears now to have been the ancestor not only of Emerson and Nietzsche, both of whom acknowledged him, but also of Freud, who did not.

Returning to Montaigne then, in a wider compass than just the essay "Of Books," is to encounter a poetics of the self that is also a relentless (for all its casual mode) critique of the Humanist, idealized poetics of the self. Petrarch, Du Bellay, even the more pragmatic Sidney, and most of all the tormented Tasso—all of them idealize their stance in relation to vernacular precursors, and also in regard to ancient wisdom. Montaigne, once past his Humanist first phase, and his skeptical transition, does not deceive either himself or others when it comes to the problems of writing:

> I have not had regular dealings with any solid book, except Plutarch and Seneca, from whom I draw like the Danaids, incessantly filling up and pouring out. Some of this sticks to this paper; to myself, little or nothing.

This, from near the start of the 1579–80 essay "Of the Education of Children," is one of the most astonishing sentences even in Montaigne. Terence Cave, in *The Cornucopian Text*, reads this sentence in the manner of Derrida and Barthes:

> The fullness of two model-texts is here designated, it would seem, as a source; the labour of the Danaides would thus represent the activity of transmission or exchange ("commerce"), by which the textual substance of Plutarch and Seneca is displaced into a discourse bearing the signature "Montaigne." But this sentence is marked from the beginning by a negation. Plutarch and Seneca appear in a concessive phrase made possible only by the absence of any "livre solide": a characteristically Montaignian insistence on the emptiness of discourse (particularly the written discourses of pedagogy) allows provisional access to certain privileged texts whose unsystematic, open-ended form endorses that of the *Essais* themselves. The negation is not, however, limited to the unnamed texts Montaigne claims to have neglected. The Danaides are, after all, not a wholly reassuring figure of plenitude. Rabelais cites them as a counterexample of cornucopian productivity, a sign of despair, and the uselessness of their labours is made explicit in the following sentence: "J'en attache quelque chose a ce papier; à moy, si peu que rien." The *locus* is closed, as it began, in negation. The *moi*, in a place outside discourse, is scarcely touched by the language even of Plutarch and Seneca; its integrity is preserved, as at the beginning of the passage, by a repudiation of books. Alien discourse cannot be "attached" to the self, is external to it. Hence the gesture of transference, endlessly repeated, appears as an empty mime. The only thing to which fragments of another text may be attached is "ce papier," a mediate domain which clearly concerns the *moi* (since the sentences inscribed on it have a habit of beginning with "je"), but is no less clearly different from it. The paper on which the text of the *Essais* appears is, indeed, a place of difference: it allows the rewriting and naturalization of foreign texts; it thereby permits the search for the identity of a *moi* in contra-distinction from what is "other"; but at the same time it defers any final access to the goal of the search, since the self is expressly an entity dissociated from the activity of writing.

If read in that deconstructionist manner, then Montaigne is achieving an awareness that the experiential fullness he seeks outside language, and which he hopes to represent in his own language, is no more a true presence in Plutarch and Seneca than in his own pages, or in his own self. Like the Danaids, all writers are condemned to carry the waters of experience in the sieve of language. But Montaigne (unlike Cave) *does* regard the *Moral Essays* of Plutarch and the *Epistles* of Seneca as "solid books." They are not merely privileged texts or sources, but pragmatically, experientially, they have, *for Montaigne*, a different status than his own writing possesses. They are the fathers, true authors and authorities; they do augment because they do not go back to the foundations, but for Montaigne they *are* the foundations. And some of their reality does stick to Montaigne's manuscript and printed page, even if some does not. Montaigne's self is as formidable as the selves of Plutarch and Seneca; his self repels influences. Yet he does grant priority to the text of the fathers, because his text, as opposed to his self, cannot have authority without some transference from the fathers.

Cave concludes his very useful study of Montaigne by turning to the text of the culminating essay, the magnificent "Of Experience" (1587–88). After observing that there is envy and jealousy between our pleasures, so that they clash and interfere with one another, Montaigne opposes himself to those who therefore would abandon natural pleasures:

> I, who operate only close to the ground, hate that inhuman wisdom that would make us disdainful enemies of the cultivation of the body. I consider it equal injustice to set our heart against natural pleasures and to set our heart too much on them. Xerxes was a fool, who, wrapped in all human pleasures, went and offered a prize to anyone who would find him others. But hardly less of a fool is the man who cuts off those that nature has found for him. We should neither pursue them nor flee them, we should accept them. I accept them with more gusto and with better grace than most, and more willingly let myself follow a natural inclination. We have no need to exaggerate their inanity; it makes itself felt enough and evident enough. Much thanks to our sickly, kill-joy mind, which disgusts us with them as well as with itself. It treats both itself and all that it takes in, whether future or past, according to its insatiable, erratic, and versatile nature.
>
> Unless the vessel's pure, all you pour in turns sour.

HORACE

I, who boast of embracing the pleasures of life so assiduously and so particularly, find in them, when I look at them thus minutely, virtually nothing but wind. But what of it? We are all wind. And even the wind, more wisely than we, loves to make a noise and move about, and is content with its own functions, without wishing for stability and solidity, qualities that do not belong to it.

Cave deconstructs this:

Full experience is always absent; presence is unattainable. All that the *Essais* can do, with their ineradicable self-consciousness, is to posit paradigms of wholeness as features of a discourse which, as it pours itself out, celebrates its own inanity. The Montaignian text represents the emptying of the cornucopia by the very gesture of extending itself indefinitely until the moment of ultimate *egressio* or elimination: the figures of abundance play a prominent part in the closing pages of "De l'experience." Whatever plenitude seems to have been proper to the past, whatever festivity is assigned to these terminal moments, Montaigne's writing is both the only place in which they can be designated, and a place from which they remain inexhaustibly absent.

The plenitude of the textual past, of Plutarch, and of Seneca, and of Horace, is certainly present here, but so is the pragmatic presence of an achieved text, a newness caught in its annunciation. If we are all wind, and Montaigne's *Essays* nothing but wind, why then let us be as wise as the wind? The text, like ourselves, makes a noise and moves about. Like the wind, we and our texts ought not to seek for qualities not our own. But an unstable and fluid text, always metamorphic, can be viewed as positively as a mobile self. If Montaigne declares limitation, he also asserts a freedom, both for his text and for himself.

Montaigne, like the characters of Shakespeare's plays, changes because he listens to what he himself has said. Reading his own text, he becomes Hamlet's precursor, and represents reality in and by himself. His power of interpretation over his own text is also a power over the precursors' texts, and so makes of his own belatedness an earliness. What Petrarch and Du Bellay and Tasso longed for vainly, what Sidney urbanely courted, is what Rabelais first possessed in the Renaissance, and is what culminates in Montaigne's "Of Experience," before it goes on to triumph again in Don Quixote, Falstaff, and Hamlet. Call it a Humanist reality rather than a Humanist idealization: an exaltation of the vernacular that authentically carried representation back to its Homeric and biblical strength. In that exaltation, the writer makes us see regions of reality we could not have seen without him. As Wallace Stevens said of the poet, the enterprise of the Renaissance Humanist author:

> tries by a peculiar speech to speak
>
> The peculiar potency of the general,
> To compound the imagination's Latin with
> The lingua franca et jocundissima.

Blaise Pascal

(1623-1662)

PASCAL NEVER LOSES HIS CAPACITY TO OFFEND AS WELL AS TO EDIFY. CONTRAST his very different effects upon Paul Valéry and T.S. Eliot. Here is Valéry:

> I hate to see a man using artifice to turn others against their lot, when they are in it in spite of themselves and are doing what they can to make the best of it; to see a man trying to persuade others that they must expect the worst, must always keep in mind the most intolerable notion of their predicament, and be alert to whatever is most unbearable in it—which is precisely the notion of suffering and risk, and anxiety about the risk— using the notion of eternity as an almighty weapon, and developing it by the artifice of repetition.

This is to accuse Pascal of being an obscurantist rhetorician, rather resembling the T.S. Eliot of the religious prose writings. Here is Eliot on Pascal:

> But I can think of no Christian writer, not Newman even, more to be commended than Pascal to those who doubt, but who have the mind to conceive, and the sensibility to feel, the disorder, the futility, the meaninglessness, the mystery of life and suffering, and who can only find peace through a satisfaction of the whole being.

I suspect that Valéry and Eliot are saying much the same thing, the difference being the rival perspectives towards Pascal of a secular intellectual and a Christian polemicist. Pascal essentially is a polemicist, rather than a religious or meditative writer. The *Pensées* ultimately are not less tendentious than the *Provincial Letters*. A Christian polemicist in our time ought to find his true antagonist in Freud, but nearly all do not; they either evade Freud, or self-defeatingly seek to appropriate him. Pascal's Freud was Montaigne, who could not be evaded or appropriated, and who scarcely can be refuted. But Pascal's case of influence-anxiety, in regard to Montaigne, was hopelessly overwhelming. Eliot, putting the best case for Pascal, insisted that Montaigne simply had the power to embody a universal skepticism, in which Pascal necessarily shared, though only to a limited degree. Doubtless Eliot attributed to Montaigne one of the essayist's plethora of authentic powers, but a secretly shared (and overcome) skepticism hardly can account for the full scandal of Montaigne's influence upon Pascal. Tables of parallel passages demonstrate an indebtedness so great, extending to figuration, examples, syntax, actual repetition of phrases, that Pascal would be convicted of plagiarism in any American school or university, with their rather literal notions of what constitutes plagiarism. The frequent effect in reading Pascal is that he begins to seem an involuntary parody of his precursor. This is particularly unfortunate whenever Pascal overtly denounces Montaigne, since sometimes we hear the pious son castigating the unbelieving father in the father's inescapable accents.

It has been surmised that Pascal jotted down his *Pensées* with his copy of Montaigne's *Essays* always lying open before him. Whether this was literally true or not, we may say that Montaigne was for Pascal quite simply a presence never to be put by. Eliot speaks of Montaigne's readers as being "thoroughly infected" by him, and certainly Pascal must have known inwardly the anguish of contamination. What are we to do with Pensée 358, one example out of many:

> Man is neither angel nor brute, and the unfortunate thing is
> that he who would act the angel acts the brute.

That would have been admirable, had it not been lifted from the best essay ever written, Montaigne's "Of Experience," where it is expressed with rather more force and insight:

> They want to get out of themselves and escape from the man.
> That is madness: instead of changing into angels, they change
> into beasts; instead of raising themselves, they lower them-
> selves.

It is an ancient commonplace, but Montaigne plays variations upon his sources, since his sense of self is his own. What is distressing is that Pascal does not evade or revise Montaigne but simply repeats him, presumably unaware of his bondage to his skeptical precursor. Since Pascal's mode is polemic, and Montaigne's is rumination and speculation, the rhetorical edge is different; Pascal emphasizes moral action, while Montaigne centers upon moral being. Yet the reader is made uncomfortable, not because Pascal has appropriated Montaigne but because Pascal has manifested a paucity of invention. Voltaire and Valéry would seem to be confirmed. Pascal writes as a pragmatic enemy of Montaigne, and this necessarily makes Pascal, as Valéry said, into an enemy of humankind. We are in a difficult situation enough, without being castigated by Pascal merely for being what we have to be. Do we still need Pascal? We read Montaigne as we read Shakespeare and Freud. How can we read Pascal?

Nietzsche insisted upon finding in Pascal an antithetical precursor, and shrewdly located Pascal's major error in the famous "wager":

> He supposes that he proves Christianity to be true because it is necessary. This presupposes that a good and truthful providence exists which ordains that everything necessary shall be true. But there can be necessary errors!

Later Nietzsche observed: "One should never forgive Christianity for having destroyed such men as Pascal." Yet Nietzsche also remarked, in a letter to Georg Brandes, that he almost loved Pascal for having been "the only logical Christian." The true link between the two was in their greatness as moral psychologists, a distinction they share with Montaigne and with Kierkegaard, and in another mode with Swift. Pascal's strong swerve away from Montaigne, which transcends his guilt of obligation to a naturalistic and skeptical master, is manifested in the development of a new kind of religious irony. Montaigne urges relativism because we are opaque to ideas of order other than our own, but this is precisely Pascal's motivation for our necessary surrender to God's will. Since God is hidden, according to Pascal, our condition is not less than tragic. A hidden God is doubly an incoherence for us; intolerable if he exists, and equally intolerable if he does not. We are thus reduced to an ironic quietism, in which we are best off doing nothing in regard to worldly realities. We reject the order of society so thoroughly that pragmatically we can accept it totally.

The extraordinary ironies of the *Provincial Letters* are founded upon this Pascalian stance, that allows him to chastise the Jesuits for worldliness while defending society against them:

What will you do with someone who talks like that, and how will you attack me, since neither my words nor my writings afford any pretext for your accusation of heresy and I find protection against your threats in my own obscurity? You feel the blows of an unseen hand revealing your aberrations for all to see. You try in vain to attack me in the persons of those whom you believe to be my allies. I am not afraid of you either on behalf of myself or of anyone else, as I am attached to no community and no individual whatsoever. All the credit you may enjoy is of no avail as far as I am concerned. I hope for nothing from the world; I fear nothing from it, I desire nothing of it; by God's grace I need no one's wealth or authority. Thus, Father, I entirely escape your clutches. You cannot get hold of me however you try. You may well touch Port-Royal, but not me. Some have indeed been evicted from the Sorbonne, but that does not evict me from where I am. You may well prepare acts of violence against priests and doctors, but not against me who am without such titles. You have perhaps never had to deal with anyone so far out of your range and so well fitted to attack your errors, by being free, without commitments, without allegiance, without ties, without connexions, without interests; sufficiently acquainted with your precepts and determined to drive them as far as I may believe myself obliged by God to do, without any human consideration being able to halt or check my pursuit.

Implicit in this superbly polemical paragraph is the unassailable rhetorical position of the ironic quietist, beyond this world yet its only true defender. One calls this "unassailable" in Pascal's stance, because his rhetoric and psychology are so intimately related to his cosmology, and the three indeed are one. We have fallen into figuration, psychic division, and the eternal silence of the infinite spaces, and all these ought to terrify us equally. Sara Melzer usefully emphasizes Pascal's difference from negative theology, to which I would add Gnosticism, as the most negative of all theologies. God's otherness, the Pascalian version of which is hiddenness, has nothing in common with the alien God of the Gnostics and the hermeticists. For Pascal, the hiddenness leads to the wager of faith, rather than to a negation of all tropes, terms for order, and scientific postulates.

If this is error, it is at least one of the necessary errors, psychologically speaking. Pascal never found his way out of the shadow of Montaigne, not I think because Montaigne spoke also for Pascal's own skepticism, but because Montaigne was too authentic a self and too strong a writer to need wagers of any kind. A paragraph like this, from the *Apology for Raymond Sebond*, must have been a permanent reproach to Pascal:

> Furthermore, it is here in us, and not elsewhere, that the powers and actions of the soul should be considered. All the rest of its perfections are vain and useless to it; it is for its present state that all its immortal life is to be paid and rewarded, and for man's life that it is solely accountable. It would be an injustice to have cut short its resources and powers; to have disarmed it, and to pass judgment and a sentence of infinite and perpetual duration upon it, for the time of its captivity and imprisonment, its weakness and illness, the time when it was forced and constrained; and to stop at the consideration of so short a time, perhaps one or two hours, or at worst a century, which is no more in proportion to infinity than an instant; in order, from this moment of interval, to decide and dispose definitively of its whole existence. It would be an inequitable disproportion to receive eternal compensation in consequence of so short a life.

Against this, Pascal's eloquence and psychic intensity must fall short, even in the most notorious of the *Pensées*:

> 205
> When I consider the short duration of my life, swallowed up in the eternity before and after, the little space which I fill, and even can see, engulfed in the infinite immensity of spaces of which I am ignorant, and which know me not, I am frightened, and am astonished at being here rather than there; for there is no reason why here rather than there, why now rather than then. Who has put me here? By whose order and direction have this place and time been allotted to me? *Memoria hospitis unius diei proetereuntis.*

> 206
> The eternal silence of these infinite spaces frightens me.

"It is here in us, and not elsewhere, that the powers and actions of the soul should be considered." Montaigne remains in our mind, Pascal in our heart. Freud, the Montaigne of our era, reminded us that the voice of reason was not loud but would not rest until it gained a hearing. Montaigne's

voice is never-resting, while Pascal's voice is restless. As Montaigne's involuntary and perpetual ephebe, Pascal always knew which voice was stronger.

John Dryden
(1631–1700)

Bᴀᴄᴏɴ, Jᴏɴsᴏɴ, ᴀɴᴅ Mɪʟᴛᴏɴ sᴇᴇᴍ ᴛᴏ ᴍᴇ ᴛʜᴇ ᴘʀɪɴᴄɪᴘᴀʟ ᴄʀɪᴛɪᴄᴀʟ consciousnesses of the later Renaissance, but none of them, not even Jonson, can be regarded as a literary critic in our sense. John Dryden, who leaps the gap between the later Renaissance and the Enlightenment, is surely a crucial literary critic in the Longinian tradition. He is also the resolution of the later Renaissance's debate between and about Ancients and Moderns, though the nature of that resolution is not entirely clear. Paul Fry, in his *The Reach of Criticism*, attempts to clarify Dryden's complex stance:

> Dryden is neither an Ancient nor a Modern, finally, because his belief in the priority of sense to language—of Homer's having exhausted invention, for example—is more or less evenly balanced by his unswerving faith in the progress or "refinement" of language, with the help of which he has "improved" Chaucer. It is too readily assumed that all Dryden's contemporaries shared his belief in the continued progress of language. Dryden himself admits that they did not: "Many are of a contrary opinion, that the English tongue [in Jonson's time] was in the height of its perfection" ("Defence of the Epilogue," 1, 171). It may well be asked, then, why it is so important for Dryden to insist that English is improving, that Denham and Waller are new benchmarks, and so on.
>
> These opinions constitute Dryden's last formalism and serve, like the formality with which the *Essay* was composed, to salvage the self-respect of the author and his contemporaries. The equilibrium between the vigor of the past and the refinement of the present is actually very precarious. Dryden reveals the

weakness of his case in the difficulty he has maintaining it. He insists, for example, that Chaucer will not scan (II, 281), despite Speght's warning in the 1602 edition that probably Chaucer would scan if only we understood his system. By expressing this conviction, Dryden commits himself to the lame idea that a person whom he credits with the highest intelligence and with proficiency in all the arts and sciences (II, 277, 287) is unable to count feet or to invent a means of doing so. Dryden has no choice but to find Chaucer wanting in this respect; otherwise there would be nothing left to say for modernity, and in that case the reciprocity of benefit between past and present souls, on the strength of which Dryden justifies his own election to the symposium of his "Preface," could no longer be demonstrated. Thus the assertion that "our numbers were in their nonage" until Waller and Denham appeared (II, 281) must be made by any handy means to seem stronger and more conclusive than it is.

It is not only a matter of saving some few scraps of honor for the Moderns, but of affirming what the Hobbesian Dryden had always helplessly denied: the freedom of the will. Having yielded priority in invention, characterization, and copiousness of thought—all draughts of dead-coloring that can only be retouched once they are laid down—Dryden then retrenches and maintains that his own authority, his originative exercise of will, is directed toward the refinement of the heroic couplet. But if this refinement is a worthwhile accomplishment, why not praise other sorts of refinement as well? Dryden boasts of having improved a system of versification, yet disparages Virgil for having *merely* improved Homer's plot. In every respect—and there would be no harm in this if the stakes were lower—the secondariness of the Moderns is elaborative, interpretive in nature. It is an art of variation within limits prescribed, not prescribed in this case by an Almighty Poet but by the poetic tradition, a "third" of yet another kind that keeps one from going astray even when one hopes to do so.

Fry catches an underlying sadness, perhaps even a creative desperation, in the cheerful and hardworking Dryden. On this reading, the Moderns have been defeated despite the positive program of Bacon and the Sublime example of Milton. Dryden stands midway between Jonson and the Swift of *The Battle of the Books*, for whom precious few scraps of honor remain upon the tattered ragamuffin Moderns. Whether Dryden's literary pessimism was deeply informed by his uneasy belief in a cyclic view of history, we cannot be certain. Skepticism was endemic in Dryden's era, but that also cannot account for Dryden's curious sense of defeat. It was not so much that the faith in progress was waning, but that Milton, like Shakespeare before him, had closed out many of the apparent possibilities for the imagination.

It may be that the war between Ancients and Moderns throughout the seventeenth century was a mock epic only, since in such a literary war the precursors must always win unless the terms of the contest are changed once and for all. No poet ever could hope to usurp Homer, so long as invention was understood as an external struggle of gods and men. From Homer to Goethe, there is a continuous tradition, because the subject of literature had not changed and evidently could not change. What we have learned to call Romanticism, or a last stage of the Enlightenment, finally worked that change. Dr. Samuel Johnson, not only the greatest Enlightenment literary critic, but still the strongest critic in the Western tradition, yet allows himself to think of invention as being Homeric, with all subsequent figures falling away. But a great Romantic critic like Hazlitt knows that a giant older contemporary had begun anew, and had made of poetry a *tabula rasa*: Wordsworth. After Wordsworth, there are neither Ancients nor Moderns, but only strong or weak poets.

What the Western world calls literary criticism and literary theory has little to do now either with the ancient world or with the whole of the European Renaissance. By critical theory and *praxis* we mean Dr. Samuel Johnson and Samuel Taylor Coleridge, and those who came after, down to our present day. But in the long movement from Aristotle to the pragmatic Dryden, an inevitable prelude was enacted without which we could not be as we are. Are we Ancients? Are we Moderns? These questions, stimulated by Dryden's skepticism, are as darkly vital now as ever they were.

II

"The mind creates no order of its own," in Martin Price's reading of Dryden's view, "but the mind can give shape to whatsoever of the order of charity can be made the world's concern." Pascal's order of charity transcends the orders of body and of mind, and rebukes philosophers and poets who would substitute their own cleverness for sacred wisdom. Dryden, Ancient and Modern, quested for both orders, mind and charity, and longed always for the spiritual authority he found at last in the Roman Catholic Church. His religious poems, though not the equal of his masterpieces, the political satire *Absalom and Achitophel* and the mock-heroic satire *Mac Flecknoe*, haunt us with a singular intensity, partly because they suggest that there is no such genre as the religious poem. Dryden teaches us, implicitly, that literature is both secular and sacred, either all secular or all sacred, with the supposed distinction being founded only upon social or political dialectics. The underlying sadness of Dryden's pro-fessedly religious poems is akin to his somewhat concealed literary pes-simisms. What we hear in the celebrated opening of *Religio Laici* is an ulti-mate sense of spiritual loss:

> Dim as the borrowed beams of moon and stars
> To lonely, weary, wandering travelers,
> Is Reason to the soul; and, as on high
> Those rolling fires discover but the sky,
> Not light us here, so Reason's glimmering ray
> Was lent, not to assure our doubtful way,
> But guide us upward to a better day.
> And as those nightly tapers disappear
> When day's bright lord ascends our hemisphere;
> So pale grows Reason at Religion's sight;
> So dies, and so dissolves in supernatural light.
> Some few, whose lamp shone brighter, have been led
> From cause to cause, to nature's secret head;
> And found that one first principle must be:
> But what, or who, that universal He;
> Whether some soul incompassing this ball,
> Unmade, unmoved, yet making, moving all;
> Or various atoms' interfering dance
> Leapt into form (the noble work of chance);
> Or this great all was from eternity;
> Not even the Stagirite himself could see,
> And Epicurus guessed as well as he:
> As blindly groped they for a future state;
> As rashly judged of providence and fate:
> But least of all could their endeavours find
> What most concerned the good of humankind;
> For happiness was never to be found,
> But vanished from 'em like enchanted ground.
> One thought content the good to be enjoyed;
> This every little accident destroyed:
> The wiser madmen did for virtue toil,

A thorny or at best a barren soil;
In pleasure some their glutton souls would steep,
But found their line too short, the well too deep,
And leaky vessels which no bliss could keep.
Thus anxious thoughts in endless circles roll,
Without a centre where to fix the soul;
In this wild maze their vain endeavours end:
How can the less the greater comprehend?
Or finite reason reach Infinity?
For what could fathom God were more than He.

The poet Walter Savage Landor remarked to the diarist Crabb Robinson that "nothing was ever written in hymn equal to the beginning of Dryden's *Religio Laici*,—the first eleven lines." What Landor caught was the curiously hymn-like harmony of Dryden's opening, a harmony somewhat at variance with the *dianoia* or thought-content of those first eleven lines. Dryden's faith is movingly revealed as a yearning for revelation, rather than as the revelation itself. The burden of the opening is to mediate between the Deists, who discard revelation, and the Fideists, who reject reason. Metaphorically, Dryden's Reason dissolves into the supernatural sun whose beams it has borrowed, but the tonal affect of the passage suggests a darker skepticism. The hymn-like strain rises to lament "our doubtful way," and yet rises so strongly as to make equivocal Dryden's professed aim to keep to a middle way in religion.

How much, imagistically speaking, can Reason do for us, according to this passage? The moon and the planets together help little enough those "lonely, weary, wandering travelers," who do not seem to be traversing the best of all possible worlds. What reveals the sky does not illuminate us. "Dim," the poem's first word, sets the key for a cosmos where Aristotle himself cannot see the truths of creation, since here the philosophers are condemned to blind gropes and rash judgments. Reason perhaps stands in this passage like that proverbial glass we call half-full or half-empty depending upon our temperaments and circumstances.

Dryden will end his *Layman's Faith* with the dangerously bland assurances that "the things we must believe are few and plain," and that "points obscure are of small use to learn, / But common quiet is mankind's concern." Critically, we can acknowledge that the poem's opening was so mysteriously strong that no ending would have sufficed, but still no one ever has preferred the amiable close of *Religio Laici* to its illustrious opening. Something rich and strange in Dryden returns from repression in that immense beginning, and that something has one of its origins in Milton's

Paradise Lost, particularly in the great invocation to book 3, where the blind prophet addresses the Holy Light:

> So much the rather thou Celestial Light
> Shine inward, and the mind through all her powers
> Irradiate, there plant eyes, all mist from thence
> Purge and disperse, that I may see and tell
> Of things invisible to mortal sight.

It is this inwardness that is deliberately lacking in Dryden, whose dim celestial light shines as an external image. What refreshes us in Dryden, the lack of prophetic election or an egotistical sublime, at last estranges him from us also. He appeals to all varieties of historicism—old and new—but perhaps not to the deepest reader in each of us. And yet his limitations were knowing ones, wisely maintained at every point. Consider his famous lines on Milton, printed under the prophetic engraved portrait of the greatest modern epic writer in Tonson's folio edition of *Paradise Lost* in 1688.

> Three poets, in three distant ages born,
> Greece, Italy, and England, did adorn.
> The first in loftiness of thought surpass'd,
> The next in majesty, in both the last:
> The force of Nature could no farther go;
> To make a third she join'd the former two.

The cognitive superiority of Homer, joined to the stylistic eminence of Virgil, compels Nature to drive beyond her limits in making Milton, who is a more-than-natural force. Dryden knows himself to be in the unenviable position of being the first major and representative post-Miltonic poet. Milton has usurped the kingdom of poetry, more powerfully because more permanently than Cromwell, his chief of men, usurped the kingdom of Britain. Greatest of Ancients *and* of Moderns, Milton leaves Dryden only the middle way, and the middle voice:

> All, all of a piece throughout:
> Thy chase had a beast in view;
> Thy wars brought nothing about;
> Thy lovers were all untrue.
> 'Tis well an old age is out,
> And time to begin a new.

Samuel Johnson

(1709-1784)

There lurks, perhaps, in every known heart a desire of distinction which inclines every man first to hope, and then to believe, that Nature has given him something peculiar to himself. This vanity makes one mind nurse aversions and another actuate desires, till they rise by art much above their original state of power and as affectation, in time, improves to habit, they at last tyrannize over him who at first encouraged them only for show.

—JOHNSON, in a letter to Boswell, 8 December 1763

DR. SAMUEL JOHNSON, IN THE JUDGMENT OF MANY (MYSELF INCLUDED), is the strongest critic in the varied history of Western literary culture. In the Anglo-American tradition, his only near rival would seem to be William Hazlitt, who has something like Johnson's energy, intellect, and knowledge, but lacks the full compass of Johnson's human sympathies, and is simply not as wise. Johnson shows us that criticism, as a literary art, joins itself to the ancient genre of wisdom writing, and so is descended from Koheleth (Ecclesiastes) and Jesus Ben Sirach (Ecclesiasticus). If you search for Johnson's precursor, turn from Aristotle or even from Ben Jonson, father of English neoclassicism, and find the forerunner of *Rasselas* and *The Rambler* in Koheleth:

Whatsoever thy hand findeth to do, do it with thy might; for there is no work, nor device, nor knowledge, nor wisdom, in the grave, whither thou goest.

The mind of Johnson, confronting the Biblical Preacher's words, was altered permanently. Indeed, Johnson is so strong a writer, that he nearly achieves the metaleptic reversal of making us believe that the author of Ecclesiastes has read deeply in Samuel Johnson. Sometimes I find myself reading Ecclesiastes aloud, and become confused, believing that I am read-ing *Rasselas*:

> It is better to hear the rebuke of the wise, than for a man to hear the song of fools.
>   For as the crackling of thorns under a pot, so is the laugh-ter of the fool: this also is vanity.

Johnson teaches us that the authority of criticism as a literary genre depends upon the human wisdom of the critic, and not upon the rightness or wrongness of either theory or praxis. Hazlitt observed that the arts, including literature, are not progressive, and this includes criticism as a branch of the literary art. There always will be those setting rules for crit-icism, down to current Gallic versions of formalism, linguistic skepticism, and even psycholinguistics, but they have not given and will not give us lit-erary criticism, which will go on being the wisdom of interpretation and the interpretation of wisdom. Johnson and Hazlitt, Ruskin and Pater, Oscar Wilde and Kenneth Burke, all in different but related ways show us that memorable criticism is experiential criticism, that there is no method except oneself, and most profoundly that it is "objectivity" which turns out to be easy, vulgar, and therefore disgusting. True critical subjectivity or personality is hardly an abandonment to self, but is a difficult achievement, dependent upon learning, intellect, and the mystery of individual vitality. "Objectivity" turns out to be a digest of the opinions of others, whether those opinions mask as philosophy, science, or the social conventions of the academies:

> Minim professes great admiration of the wisdom and munifi-cence by which the academies of the Continent were raised, and often wishes for some standard of taste, for some tribunal, to which merit may appeal from caprice, prejudice, and malignity. (*Idler*) No. 61

Mr. Dick Minim we have in abundance these bad days; he pours forth tomes denouncing interpretation, and calling for rules, principles, methods that will turn Anglo-American criticism into a Germano-Gallic "human science." "Rigor, Rigor!" cries our contemporary Minim, while he keeps reminding us that poems and stories are written in and by language. Dr. Samuel Johnson, who had not the benefits of the Hegelian philosophy and its Franco-Heideggerian revisionists, did what he could with what he had, as here on Shakespeare's *Henry IV* plays:

> But *Falstaff* unimitated, unimitable *Falstaff*, how shall I describe thee? Thou compound of sense and vice; of sense which may be admired but not esteemed, of vice which may be despised, but hardly detested.... Yet the man thus corrupt, thus despicable, makes himself necessary to the prince that despises him, by the most pleasing of all qualities, perpetual gaiety, by an unfailing power of exciting laughter, which is the more freely indulged, as his wit is not of the splendid or ambitious kind, but consists in easy escapes and sallies of levity, which make sport but raise no envy.

That the balance of this judgment is admirable, and unmatched, is palpable. But the critical magnificence surpasses mere balance, and is a crucial insight into Shakespearean representation. Falstaff is "unimitated"; he is not a mimesis, but a supermimesis of essential nature. He is also "unimitable," because he is a form more real than living man; he contains us, not we him. His "perpetual gaiety," his wit of "easy escapes and sallies of levity," a wit that exempts him from envy, testify to his unique nature as a person without a superego. Without a superego to admonish the ego to forsake its aggressivities (while punishing the ego all the more each time it abandons an aggressive drive), we would be as Falstaff, in a condition of perpetual gaiety, because our death drive, like Falstaff's, would have been subsumed by play, by easy escapes and sallies of levity. What Nietzsche failed to represent by his frequently bathetic Zarathustra, and what Freud assumed was beyond representation, Johnson shows us that Shakespeare triumphantly had accomplished in Sir John Falstaff. Johnson, greatest of critics, can teach the rest of us that the essence of poetry is *invention*. Invention is how meaning gets started, and Johnson implicitly demonstrates that Shakespeare, more even than Homer or the Bible, was the work most abundant in original invention.

Yet that is only part of how superbly suggestive Johnson upon Shakespeare is. Falstaff's admirable if not estimable sense makes itself necessary to us as well as to Hal, Bolingbroke's son, because we too lack perpetual gaiety, because we all of us, like Samuel Johnson, are too much punished by our superegos. Falstaff's sense, his unfailing power, is the sense and power of how meaning gets started, of how invention is accomplished. In the terms of Freudian reductiveness, meaning gets started rather than repeated when the superego is overcome, but in the Freudian reduction the superego cannot be overcome. Shakespeare, the most inventive and original of all writers, ever, is able to generate an almost totally fresh meaning through the exuberance of Falstaff's triumphant will to power over language. Such a will, whether in writing or speaking, can work its way only through diction, through a choice of words that pragmatically amounts to a series of choices in language. Johnson was both a critic of power (invention) and of the will to diction, and he understood the reflection of power by choice of language better than any critic has been able to convey since.

II

Johnson's greatest work as a critic is *The Lives of the Poets*, written between 1777 and 1781. Yet everything about this work is peculiar, since the *Lives* are introductions to a very odd collection of the British poets, chosen for the most part not by Johnson, but by the booksellers. Fifty poets are represented, with Oliver Goldsmith, Johnson's close friend, excluded and such bards as Roscommon, Pomfret, Dorset, Stepney, Sprat, Fenton, Yalden, and Lyttelton included, as though they were canonical. Johnson mostly shrugs them off, even when he had suggested them, remarking amiably enough in his *Life of Yalden*:

> Of his poems, many are of that irregular kind, which, when he formed his poetical character, was supposed to be Pindarick. Having fixed his attention on Cowley as a model, he has attempted in some sort to rival him, and has written a *Hymn to Darkness*, evidently as a counterpart to Cowley's *Hymn to Light*.

Alas, poor Yalden! He is remembered now, if at all, only for that remark, and for the rather grand Johnsonian sentence that concludes his *Life*:

> Of his other poems it is sufficient to say that they deserve perusal, though they are not always exactly polished, though the rhymes are sometimes very ill sorted, and though his faults seem rather the omissions of idleness than the negligence of enthusiasm.

A bit earlier, Johnson had quoted Yalden's unfortunate line in which Jehovah contemplates the new created Light:

> A while th'Almighty wondering stood.

Alas, poor Yalden! We can never forget the Johnsonian observation upon this:

> He ought to have remembered that Infinite Knowledge can never wonder. All wonder is the effect of novelty upon Ignorance.

That last sentence is an epitome of the neoclassic critical stance, and could be Ben Jonson deprecating the followers of Spenser, or Samuel Johnson himself dismissing the poetry of Sensibility, the swerve away from Pope and back to Milton, in Gray, Collins, and the Wartons. In his *Life of Gray*, Johnson is superbly honest and direct in admitting his lack of pleasure in the poetry, and particularly in the two great Pindarics, *The Bard* and *The Progress of Poesy*. Boswell, in the *Life of Johnson*, reports the critic as dismissing Gray's Odes: "they are but cucumbers after all." The dismissal is especially hurtful if an American remembers that Johnson means the British cucumber, an ungainly and rough vegetable whose baroque outlines do suggest the shape of a Gray Pindaric upon the page.

The masterpiece of the *Lives* is the long and beautiful meditation upon Pope. Pope and Dryden, Johnson had by heart; he seems to have had total recall of their work. Swift was a profound problem for Johnson. Despite their intellectual affinities, or perhaps because of them, Johnson was unnerved by Swift. *A Tale of a Tub*, much as I myself am frightened by it, is certainly the most powerful discursive prose work in the English language. Johnson seems to have been even more frightened by it. He called it "this wild work" and wrote of it with a kind of traumatic response:

> of this book charity may be persuaded to think that it might be written by a man of a peculiar character, without ill intention; but it is certainly of dangerous example.

Scholars have surmised that Johnson feared joining Swift in madness. That seems to me a little too simple. Certainly Johnson, like many men and many women, feared dying badly:

> But few there are whom hours like these await,
> Who set unclouded in the gulfs of fate.
> From Lydia's monarch should the search descend,
> By Solon cautioned to regard his end,
> In life's last scene what prodigies surprise,
> Fears of the brave, and follies of the wise?

From Marlborough's eyes the streams of dotage flow,
And Swift expires a driveller and a show.

Swift's terrible irony, savage beyond measure, is antithetical to Johnson's empirical and humane stance. Neoclassical literary theory, which culminated in Johnson, emphasizes the virtues of moral instruction, imitation, and refinement, in the sense of improving the tradition without necessarily revising it. But Swift, though he agreed with this in the abstract, hardly possessed an Horatian temperament. His ferocity, perhaps unparalleled among the great writers, emerges fully only in *A Tale of a Tub*, as Johnson carefully notes:

> It exhibits a vehemence and rapidity of mind, a copiousness of images, and vivacity of diction, such as he afterwards never possessed or never exerted. It is of a mode so distinct and peculiar that it must be considered by itself....

That is to say, in Johnson's own terms, Swift's extraordinary nightmare of a book exhibits supreme invention, and the essence of poetry is invention, according to Johnson himself. We all of us have a favorite writer; as I grow older, Johnson is mine, as Pope was Johnson's. We tend to confederate Swift and Pope in our minds; they were close friends, political and literary allies, and they divide the glory of the British Augustans between them, in an age of satire. But Johnson was at ease with Pope, and uncomfortable with Swift. As a wisdom writer, he knew the difference between them. Pope, like Addison, has a link to Francis Bacon, as does Johnson. Swift is not a wisdom writer, but something darker and stronger.

III

Johnson, in my judgment, remains Shakespeare's best critic, precisely because Shakespeare compels Johnson to retreat from neoclassicism and to stand upon the common sense of British naturalism in order to accept and admire Shakespeare's mimetic triumphs. In his *Preface to Shakespeare*, Johnson gives us the inevitable starting point for thinking about Shakespearean representation:

> There is a vigilance of observation and accuracy of distinction which books and precepts cannot confer; from this almost all original and native excellence proceeds. *Shakespeare* must have looked upon mankind with perspicacity, in the highest degree

curious and attentive. Other writers borrow their characters from preceding writers, and diversify them only by the accidental appendages of present manners; the dress is a little varied, but the body is the same. Our authour had both matter and form to provide; for except the characters of *Chaucer*, to whom I think he is not much indebted, there were no writers in *English*, and perhaps not many in other modern languages, which shewed life in its native colours.

Probably Johnson underestimated Shakespeare's indebtedness to Chaucer. *A Midsummer Night's Dream* and *Troilus and Cressida* owe much to Chaucer, and possibly *Romeo and Juliet* does also. More crucially, there is a complex link between Chaucer's strongest figures, the Pardoner and the Wife of Bath, and the magnificent Falstaff. Chaucer may well have given Shakespeare something of that greatest gift they share: they are the first writers whose personages change *by listening to themselves speak*. But I add little to Johnson here, since he so massively indicates that only Chaucer and Shakespeare represent reality in reality's own colors, and one of the most essential of those colors or tropes is the effect of our words upon ourselves. It is on the central issue of Shakespeare's greatest strength, which is his mode of so representing reality as to compel aspects of reality, that otherwise we could not know, to appear, that Johnson achieves his most useful insight:

> Though he had so many difficulties to encounter, and so little assistance to surmount them, he has been able to obtain an exact knowledge of many modes of life, and many casts of native dispositions; to vary them with great multiplicity; to mark them by nice distinctions; and to skew them in full view by proper combinations. In this part of his performances he had none to imitate, but has himself been imitated by all succeeding writers; and it may be doubted, whether from all his successors more maxims of theoretical knowledge, or more rules of practical prudence, can be collected, than he alone has given to his country.

Johnson splendidly recognizes that Shakespeare's legacy is both in cognitive awareness or theoretical knowledge, and in wisdom or practical prudence. Shakespeare attained "exact knowledge," and represented it in full view; he therefore surpassed the metaphysicians in epistemological certainty, and the moralists in pragmatic measurement. An original who established a contingency that governs all writers since, Shakespeare clearly sets the standard for representation itself. This is Johnson's most complex realization about Shakespeare, and therefore about imaginative literature. To know many modes of life, and so many casts of native dispositions, is here very much a knowing indistinguishable from representation, from the allied acts of varying with multiplicity, marking by nice distinctions, and showing in full view. To vary, mark, and show is not apart from the knowing, but is the knowing. Shakespeare, Johnson implies, creates representations so original that conceptually *they contain us*, and continue to shape our psychology of motivation. To have created the modern representation of the mind was the achievement neither of Montaigne nor (belatedly) of Freud, but of Shakespeare alone. What Johnson teaches us is that Shakespeare invented our psychology, to an astonishing degree.

IV

Johnson's great achievement was his criticism. It is accurate to remark that *The Vanity of Human Wishes, Rasselas,* and the more general essays essentially are memorable as extensions of Johnsonian literary criticism or wisdom literature. Of Boswell, we might remark that his two greatest works were Johnson and himself, or the *Life of Johnson* and *Tour to the Hebrides,* and the *London Journal.* Frank Brady's genial observation that Boswell was the Norman Mailer of his day reminds us that "Norman Mailer," the hero of *Advertisements for Myself* and *The Armies of the Night,* probably is Norman Mailer's greatest work, surpassing *The Executioner's Song* and *Ancient Evenings.* That Boswell's "Johnson" is not quite the author of *The Lives of the Poets* is clear enough, whereas Boswell's "Boswell," like Mailer's "Mailer," leaves us in a state of wonder, which we will remember Johnson (in the *Life* of the wretched Yalden) deprecating as the effect of novelty upon ignorance.

One can prefer "Johnson without Boswell" (as I tend to do) and still reread the *Life of Johnson* endlessly as the finest literary biography in English. Boswell's own *Journal,* even the *London Journal,* seems to me not of the aesthetic eminence either of the *Life of Samuel Johnson* or the scarcely inferior *Journal of a Tour to the Hebrides,* but that is only to say that Boswell's "Johnson" is a grander fiction than Boswell's "Boswell." Still, one cannot dispute Frank Brady as to the extraordinary flexibility of style in the *Journal*; it indeed "can accommodate a wide range of material and a high degree of complexity." Brady's summary of Boswell's strengths and limitations in the *Journal* seems to me definitive:

Boswell kept his journal compulsively, and it makes compulsive reading. The reader of journals is greedy for the actual: how do other people live, think, and feel? Of all literary forms, the journal comes closest to answering these questions directly: at its best, it realizes dramatically for the reader events and feelings in a way that seems spontaneous and true to immediate experience. Characters shift and shade off into obscurity; events are discontinuous, become prominent and disappear: even the form of the journal is comparable to living, as a day-to-day process whose outcome is unknown. But, unlike life, the journal is a written record, which in Boswell's case strings together all the unpredictable sequences of an important career, full of sharply portrayed incidents and dramatic reversals. Its length in itself draws the reader into an increasingly familiar group of figures, and a narrative which may extend a theme over many years or tell a tiny story in one or two entries.

Subjectivity is both the prime value and the limitation of the journal; interest and creativity are its crucial issues. Biography interposes the biographer between reader and subject; autobiography is liable to the corrective pull of hindsight. The journal draws the reader into another's mind without mediation or distortion. Prejudices, conscious or unconscious, the reader allows for as automatically as he does for the prejudices of the actual people he knows; whatever theoretical issues it may raise, bias is seldom a problem in practice.

But there are problems. It is at least a superficial paradox that the journal, apparently the most artless of literary forms, requires great skill to hold the reader's attention over a long stretch. It must compensate for lack of coherent narrative and character presentation by descriptive or thematic interest that depends directly on the writer's having an interesting, unusual, or powerful mind and some sense of what will entertain or involve a reader. At the same time, skill must never diminish the effect of credibility. The reader may enjoy the tall tales of Casanova more than the sober accounts of a reliable narrator, but he discounts Casanova's memoirs as in part fiction masquerading as fact.

It is possible to take the sophisticated attitude that whatever the journalist says, true or false, is revealing; but a reader is more likely to feel comfortable if he thinks he is reading a true story. And if the narrative is based on verifiable fact he is apt to think better of it; like Johnson he believes that "the value of every story depends on its being true." Boswell emphasizes circumstantial accuracy, the literal truth of matter-of-fact detail; and the credibility this gives his journal carries over to his attempts to register exact states of mind. Here inconsistency plays its part: it would be difficult to invent such vivid variations of character.

The journalist's final advantage is that, other factors being equal, the reader tends to empathize more quickly and fully with real than with fictional characters simply because they are real. For the same reason, the reader's attitude may shift sharply against a journalist, especially when, as in Boswell's case, he is extending the limits of what is permissible to say. On reading Boswell's journal after his death, his respectable executor Sir William Forbes repeatedly wrote "reprehensible passage." Often true enough, but is this the comment of inherent decorum or protective hypocrisy? Or both? Johnson paraphrases an observation in William Law's *Serious Call to a Devout and Holy Life* as, "Every man knows something worse of himself than he is sure of in others." And it is obvious that the reader who says, "Thank God, I am not like him," may be suppressing the unwelcome insight that they have a good deal in common.

But even the most sympathetically disposed can get impatient with vanity or self-pity, very likely elements in a journal since the writer so often uses it as a vent for the feelings he must repress in social life. And the unremitting subjectivity of the journal may in itself become stifling. Finally, the journalist runs the likely risk that the reader will see something in his story other than what he sees himself.

In the end, to recur to Johnson, the only way to determine literary merit is "length of duration and continuance of esteem." Like his biographies, Boswell's journal shows every sign that it will stand the test of time. But its extent and brilliance necessarily distort our perception of him because of the way in which they situate the reader within what Amiel described as "that molecular whirlwind which we call individual existence." We apprehend Boswell from inside, as we do ourselves. He is diffusive as we are; he lacks the solidity we attribute to others. The gain in intimacy is enormous, but it is easy to lose a grasp on how his contemporaries perceived him.

I have quoted all of this long judgment because it is so remarkably Johnsonian, and likely would have been accepted by Boswell himself. Brady, like his great mentor (and mine), Frederick A. Pottle, shows us implicitly that the power of the *Life of Samuel Johnson* and of the *Tour to the Hebrides* is finally the power of love, of Boswell's more-than-filial love for the capacious soul of Samuel Johnson.

Jean-Jacques Rousseau

(1712-1778)

William Hazlitt, in my judgment still Rousseau's best critic, insisted that the Genevan moralist's sensibility was far more vital than either his Enlightened reason or his Romantic imagination. Finding less Negative Capability in Rousseau than in any comparable figure, Hazlitt cheerfully praised him for the gusts of his Egotistical Sublime. Rousseau's intense passion for himself was seen by Hazlitt as the necessary prelude to the French Revolution, carried out by men and women who had learned from Rousseau to give their self-love primacy over the claims of society, history, and tradition. In Hazlitt's shrewd insight, the Jacobin sensibility, which transformed societal tyranny into personal insult, owed everything to the tormented sensibility of that unique individual, Rousseau.

Praising the *Confessions* as a veritable Bible of revolution, Hazlitt saw in Rousseau the Romantic Prometheus, kindler of revolt against the sky-gods of Europe. With an English Dissenter's irony, Hazlitt wrote in praise of Rousseau, yet with distaste for a temperament both heroic and "morbid." Hazlitt's ambivalence towards Rousseau is roughly akin to his attitude towards Wordsworth. Each seemed to Hazlitt a true Original and so a prophet of literary rebellion, but both were judged to be egomaniacs, though only Wordsworth had betrayed the Revolution.

Rousseau to this day reads very differently to Anglo-American critics than he does to Continental exegetes. Except for the *Confessions*, he is read neither widely nor deeply in the contemporary English-speaking world. Allan Bloom, attempting to revive *Émile*, compares it to Plato's *Republic* as a survey of the entire human condition. These, he says, are "books for philosophers," but since we live now in a literary culture, not a philosophic one, I surmise that *Émile* is not likely to be revived. The *Nouvelle Héloïse* is more available to our sensibility, and I am surprised it receives so little attention these days. The *Confessions*, though, are a crucial element in our literary culture, and have established the mode for modern autobiography.

Rousseau's *Confessions* indeed seem to me the inevitable link between Montaigne and our Montaigne, Freud, who has systemized self-reflection for us. J.H. Van den Berg, in his *The Changing Nature of Man*, says of Rousseau that "he was the first to view the child as a child, and to stop treating the child as an adult," but remarks of him also that he was culpable for "pushing the child away." Van den Berg locates in *Émile* the invention of the trope of psychic "maturation," and so ascribes to Rousseau the authorship of adolescence as such. That may be partly an ironic tribute on Van den Berg's part, yet to me it seems accurate. Before Rousseau, where are we to find representations of adolescence? If we combine Hazlitt and Van den Berg on Rousseau, then there is a close relation between the new sensibility of a rebellious self-love, and the new crossing or transition of adolescence, and it seems plausible that one consciousness should have invented both. Psychosexually, the Rousseau of the *Confessions* never does make it out of adolescence, while the universalizing of his Egotistical Sublime is necessarily at the center of his autobiography.

"Such were the errors and faults of my youth. I have related the story of them with a fidelity that brings pleasure to my heart." That beginning of the final paragraph of *The First Part* of the *Confessions* is not exactly Rousseau at his worst but it does indicate his splendidly outrageous tendency to forgive himself everything, once he has confessed his guilt. John Calvin's reaction to his fellow Genevan's Romanticized sense of election would have been strenuous, and I delight to imagine Calvin and Rousseau confronting one another at the tomb of Farinata in Dante's *Inferno*, where the earlier heretic stands upright and proud, "as if of Hell he had a great disdain." But not even Farinata or Calvin is as massively self-assured as Rousseau. Here is a grandly outrageous moment from Book Twelve of the *Confessions*:

> I must leave nothing unsaid. I have never concealed my poor Mamma's vices or my own, and I must show no greater favour to Thérèse. However warm a pleasure I take in honouring a person who is dear to me, I still do not wish to disguise her faults, if an involuntary change in the heart's affection is truly a fault. For a long while I had observed a cooling off on her part. I was aware that she no longer felt for me as she had done in our good days; and I was the more conscious of the fact because I was as fond of her as ever. I was once more in the predicament which I had found so uncomfortable with Mamma; and in

Thérèse's case it was no less uncomfortable. Let us not look for supernatural perfection; the case would be the same with any woman upon earth. The attitude I had taken with regard to my children, logical though it had seemed to me, had not always left me easy in my mind. While thinking out my *Treatise upon Education*, I felt that I had neglected some duties from which nothing could excuse me. So strong did my remorse finally grow that it almost drew from me a public confession of my fault at the beginning of *Émile*. The allusion, indeed, is so clear that after such a passage it is surprising that anyone had the courage to reproach me. My situation was, however, at that time still the same, or even worse, because of the animosity of my enemies, who wanted nothing better than to catch me at fault. I was afraid that I might repeat the offence and, not wishing to run the risk, preferred to condemn myself to abstinence rather than expose Thérèse to the risk of finding herself in the same condition once more. I had noticed besides that intercourse with women sensibly aggravated my complaint. The compensatory vice, of which I have never been able entirely to cure myself, seemed to me less deleterious. For this dual reason, therefore, I had formed resolutions which I had sometimes only imperfectly kept, but in which I had been persisting with more success during the last three or four years. It was from the beginning of that time that I had noticed a cooling in Thérèse. She persisted in her attachment to me, but it was out of duty, not out of love. This naturally diminished the pleasure in our relations, and I imagined that, relying as she could on my continuing to look after her, she might perhaps have preferred to stay in Paris rather than wander about the world with me. However she had shown such grief at our separation, had extracted such emphatic promises from me that we should come together again, and had expressed her desire so strongly since my departure both to the Prince de Conti and M. de Luxembourg, and far from daring to speak to her of separation I scarcely had the courage to think of it myself; and once my heart had told me how impossible it would be to do without her my only thought was to call her back at the earliest possible moment. I wrote to her to start, and she came. It was scarcely two months since I had left her, but this was our first separation for many years. We had felt it most cruelly, both of us. How violent was our first embrace! Oh, how sweet are the tears of

joy and affection, and how my heart feasts on them! Why have
I been permitted to shed them so seldom?

I hardly know which to prefer, Rousseau's "Let us not look for supernatural perfection," in regard to poor Thérèse, of whom he was "as fond
... as ever," or his surprise "that anyone had the courage to reproach" him
for abandoning his own children, once he had almost confessed his "fault."
How intensely his heart feasted upon "the tears of joy and affection" we
need not doubt. The great Rousseau was certainly no hypocrite; he was
merely a sacred monster, peculiarly pernicious for his women. For literary
power in self-representation, for originality in sensibility, for strength of
influence upon what came after—for all of these, the *Confessions* are beyond
comparison with any possible rival in eighteenth-century literature, whatever any of us may choose to think of Rousseau as an individual.

Shelley, who revered Rousseau above any other writer between
Milton and Wordsworth, nevertheless rendered a Dantesque judgment
upon the author of the *Confessions* in his great death-poem, "The Triumph
of Life." Rousseau appears with the grand disdain for Hell of Farinata, but
also with a pride wholly his own, the pride of a sensibility that knew itself
to be absolutely original and inevitably epochal:

> Before thy memory
> I feared, loved, hated, suffered, did, & died,
> And if the spark with which Heaven lit my spirit
> Earth had with purer nutriment supplied
>
> Corruption would not now thus much inherit
> Of what was once Rousseau—nor this disguise
> Stained that within which still disdains to wear it.—
> If I have been extinguished, yet there rise
> A thousand beacons from the spark I bore.—

James Boswell

(1740-1795)

Boswell's *Life of Johnson* begins with a dedicatory letter to Sir Joshua Reynolds, which includes a paragraph of acutely defensive self-consciousness remarkable even for Boswell:

> In one respect, this Work will, in some passages, be different from the former. In my *Tour*, I was almost unboundedly open in my communications; and from my eagerness to display the wonderful fertility and readiness of Johnson's wit, freely skewed to the world its dexterity, even when I was myself the object of it. I trusted that I should be liberally understood, as knowing very well what I was about, and by no means as simply unconscious of the pointed effects of the satire. I own, indeed, that I was arrogant enough to suppose that the tenour of the rest of the book would sufficiently guard me against such a strange imputation. But it seems I judged too well of the world; for, though I could scarcely believe it, I have been undoubtedly informed, that many persons, especially in distant quarters, not penetrating enough into Johnson's character, so as to understand his mode of treating his friends, have arraigned my judgement, instead of seeing that I was sensible of all that they could observe.

Doubtless, Boswell remembered too well certain attacks upon his *Tour to the Hebrides with Samuel Johnson*. Mrs. Hester Lynch Piozzi, formerly Mrs. Henry Thrale, had accused Boswell of misrepresenting her judgments, while Sir John Hawkins had allowed only a single reference to Boswell in his authorized biography of Johnson, which like Mrs. Piozzi's

Anecdotes of Johnson, appeared in 1786, five years before Boswell's *Life*. Hawkins disposed of Boswell in one suave sentence: "He had long been solicited by Mr. James Boswell, a native of Scotland, and one that highly valued him, to accompany him in a journey to the Hebrides."

Determined to provoke no more such slights, Boswell disarmingly concludes his dedication to Reynolds with two remarkable sentences: "I have, therefore, in this Work been more reserved; and though I tell nothing but the truth, I have still kept in my mind that the whole truth is not always to be exposed. This, however, I have managed so as to occasion no diminution of the pleasure which my book should afford; though malignity may sometimes be disappointed of its gratifications."

Let us test the "whole truth" in the *Tour* with the "nothing but the truth" of the *Life*. First, from the *Tour*:

> It grew dusky; and we had a very tedious ride for what was called five miles; but I am sure would measure tell. We had no conversation. I was riding forward to the inn at Glenelg, on the shore opposite to Sky, that I might take proper measures, before Dr. Johnson, who was now advancing in dreary silence, Hay leading his horse, should arrive. Vass also walked by the side of his horse, and Joseph followed behind: as therefore he was thus attended, and seemed to be in deep meditation, I thought there could be no harm in leaving him for a little while. He called me back with a tremendous shout, and was really in a passion with me for leaving him. I told him my intentions, but he was not satisfied, and said, 'Do you know, I should as soon have thought of picking a pocket, as doing so.'— *Boswell*. 'I am diverted with you, sir.' *Johnson*. 'Sir, I could never be diverted with incivility. Doing such a thing, makes one lose confidence in him who has done it, as one cannot tell what he may do next.'—His extraordinary warmth confounded me so much, that I justified myself but lamely to him; yet my intentions were not improper. I wished to get on, to see how we were to be lodged, and how we were to get a boat; all which I thought I could best settle myself, without his having any trouble. To apply his great mind to minute particulars, is wrong: it is like taking an immense balance, such as is kept on quays for weighing cargoes of ships,—to weigh a guinea. I knew I had neat little scales, which would do better; and that his attention to every thing which falls in his way, and his uncommon desire to be always in the right, would make him weigh, if he knew of

the particulars: it was right therefore for me to weigh them, and let him have them only in effect. I however continued to ride by him, finding he wished I should do so.

To spare Johnson the "minute particulars" of lodging and travel, poor Boswell has stumbled into the fundamental error of exposing the great critic to the madness of solitude, peculiarly unendurable in the waste-lands of Scotland, yet always terribly hard upon the sociable Johnson, with his precarious balance. Yet this seems a mild provocation when contrasted with a characteristic moment in the *Life*:

When we were alone, I introduced the subject of death, and endeavoured to maintain that the fear of it might be got over. I told him that David Hume said to me, he was no more uneasy to think he should *not be* after this life, than that he *had not been* before he began to exist. JOHNSON. 'Sir, if he really thinks so, his perceptions are disturbed; he is mad: if he does not think so, he lies. He may tell you, he holds his finger in the flame of a candle, without feeling pain; would you believe him? When he dies, he at least gives up all he has.' BOSWELL. 'Foote. Sir told me, that when he was very ill he was not afraid to die.' JOHNSON. 'It is not true, Sir. Hold a pistol to Foote's breast, or to Hume's breast, and threaten to kill them, and you'll see how they behave.' BOSWELL. 'But may we not forti-fy our minds for the approach of death?' Here I am sensible I was in the wrong, to bring before his view what he ever looked upon with horrour; for although when in a celestial frame, in his 'Vanity of human Wishes', he has supposed death to be 'kind Nature's signal for retreat,' from this state of being to 'a happier seat,' his thoughts upon this aweful change were in general full of dismal apprehensions. His mind resembled the vast amphitheatre, the Colisaeum at Rome. In the centre stood his judgement, which, like a mighty gladiator, combated those apprehensions that, like the wild beasts of the *Arena*, were all around in cells, ready to be let out upon him. After a conflict, he drove them back into their dens; but not killing them, they were still assailing him. To my question, whether we might not fortify our minds for the approach of death, he answered, in a passion, 'No, Sir, let it alone. It matters not how a man dies, but how he lives. The act of dying is not of importance, it lasts so short a tine.' He added, (with an earnest look,) 'A man knows it must be so, and submits. It will do him no good to whine.'

I attempted to continue the conversation. He was so provoked, that he said, 'Give us no more of this;' and was thrown into such a state of agitation, that he expressed himself in a way that alarmed and distressed me; shewed an impatience that I should leave him, and when I was going away, called to me sternly, 'Don't let us meet to-morrow.'

Johnson, a brave man, feared neither death nor dying, yet dreaded judgment, dreaded being damned for having failed to develop all his gifts. Comparison of the two episodes perhaps reveals more circumstantial detail in the *Tour* than in the *Life*, but this is the "whole truth" only in an uninteresting sense. The "nothing but the truth" in the episode from the *Life* may conceal Boswell's experimental meddling with his friend's fears. Boswell, as outrageous a literary figure as Norman Mailer, certainly was capable of goading Johnson deliberately, in order to garner fresh material. In one peculiar moment, Boswell infuriates Johnson by formulating the phantasmagoria of the great man locked up in the Tower, by his enemies, in the company of a newborn babe. Would the Doctor nurture the infant? Would he educate him? Johnson rightly is exasperated, but we, the readers, are rightly charmed. Boswell, on one level, really does want Johnson to play the part of Johnson all the time, almost as though Johnson were the Falstaff of reality.

II

Boswell's "Johnson" is of course, a fiction, but so is Boswell's "Boswell" in the *London Journal*, and so, in a related sense, is Johnson's "Johnson," the Ecclesiastes-like wisdom writer of *The Rambler*, *Rasselas*, *The Vanity of Human Wishes*, the *Preface to Shakespeare*, and the *Lives of the Poets*. When we read the *Life of Johnson*, we begin with the assumption that Dr. Samuel Johnson is not of the company of Sir John Falstaff, even though we delight to imagine them both as monarchs of conversation enthroned in their proper context, the tavern. Yet there is a sense in which Johnson is not only a conversational genius in himself, but the cause of grand conversation in other men and women just as Falstaff is the cause of wit in others. Witness Boswell's delicious account of the meeting between Johnson and an old college acquaintance, Edwards, after a separation of some forty-nine years. Nothing could be more memorable than a famous observation by the amiable Edwards: "You are a philosopher, Dr. Johnson.

I have tried too in my time to be a philosopher; but, I don't know how, cheerfulness was always breaking in!"

Whether this truly was Edwards's, or is Boswell's own superb invention, we cannot know. What we do know is that Johnson was his own invention, and not Boswell's. Johnson without Boswell has rather a smaller audience now than Boswell without Johnson, but it is fit audience though few. "Boswell with Johnson" might be a proper description for the authorship of the *Life of Johnson*. It may even be divided thus; if *ethos* is the *daimon*, or character is fate, then Johnson is the author of the deepest portion of the *Life*, because Johnson's character is anything but Boswell's creation. The *ethos* of the greatest English writer of wisdom literature is as clearly recognizable in the *Life of Johnson* as it is in the *Life of Savage* or the *Life of Pope*. But if *pathos* is the swerve away from overdetermination, or personality is freedom, then the personality of Johnson, in the *Life of Johnson*, truly is Boswell's creation. So endearing is that personality, so vital is it to us as readers, that Boswell's Johnson, like Shakespeare's Falstaff, has become a permanent image of human freedom. Freedom from what, in Johnson's case? Falstaff is free of the superego, while Johnson is tormented by that psychic agency. Johnson, I think, has so strong an ego that paradoxically he is free of the ego, free of the ego's narcissistic investment in a self, which becomes its own self. Johnson, particularly in Boswell, though uncannily dark, and shadowed by presentiments, does not manifest either of Kierkegaard's two inevitable despairs: the despair of having failed to become oneself, or the still greater despair of having become oneself. It may be Boswell's greatest triumph that he gives us Dr. Johnson as a hero of consciousness, a man strong enough to live without illusions and without deceit.

Boswell's Johnson is eminently a humorist, and though a moralist, he is generally too wise to present his wisdom without humor. There are hundreds of instances in the *Life*, but I have a special fondness for a breakfast conversation between Johnson and Boswell on June 5, 1781, when the doctor was already seventy-two years in age:

> On Tuesday, June 5, Johnson was to return to London. He was very pleasant at breakfast; I mentioned a friend of mine having resolved never to marry a pretty woman. JOHNSON. 'Sir, it is a very foolish resolution to resolve never to marry a pretty woman. Beauty is of itself very estimable. No, Sir, I would prefer a pretty woman, unless there are objections to her. A pretty woman may be foolish; a pretty woman may be wicked; a pretty woman may not like me. But there is no such danger in mar-

rying a pretty woman as is apprehended; she will not be persecuted if she does not invite persecution. A pretty woman, if she
has a mind to be wicked, can find a readier way than another;
and that is all.'

"And that is all," but as always with Boswell's Johnson, that is a great deal.

III

Boswell's greatest achievement, in the *Life*, is that he persuades us
that his Johnson is *the* Johnson, which many incessant readers of Johnson
(myself included) do not like to admit. Yet so strong is Boswell's imagination of Johnson that we tend to read it into Johnson whenever we read the
sage, so that we never can be free of Boswell, once we have read the *Life of
Johnson*. Even the greatest of modern scholar-critics of Johnson, my
teacher W.K. Wimsatt Jr., who was certainly the most Johnsonian personality I will ever know, is pervaded by Boswell, consciously and unconsciously, throughout his magnificent *The Prose Style of Johnson*. Wimsatt
powerfully conveys Johnson's dislike of mere history and related love of
biography, which is based upon a dislike of the plainness of fact, not as
opposed to fiction, but as opposed to elaboration and its possibilities. On
this account, Boswell in the *Life of Johnson* is more Johnsonian than even
Johnson could have been. The true test for Boswell's masterpiece would
thus be set by Johnson himself, in *Rambler* No. 3:

> The task of an author is, either to teach what is not known, or
> to recommend known truths by his manner of adorning them;
> either to let new light in upon the mind, and open new scenes
> to the prospect, or to vary the dress and situation of common
> objects, so as to give them fresh grace and more powerful
> attractions, to spread such flowers over the regions through
> which the intellect has already trade its progress, as may tempt
> it to return, and take a second view of things hastily passed over
> or negligently regarded.

This task of elaboration by adornment, variation, refinement is the
project of both Pope in his poetry and Boswell in the *Life of Johnson*. What
Johnson praised in Pope, we must praise in Boswell: if Boswell be not a
biographer, where is biography to be found? Boswell is both neoclassical,
as suits a follower of Johnson, and an apostle of sentiment, of sensibility
and the Sublime, as was inevitable for a literary consciousness in Boswell's

own generation. Johnson, though far shrewder and more humane in praxis than in critical theory, was something of a cultural reactionary. This
hardly matters, since Shakespeare and even Milton (despite Johnson's
strong prejudice against Milton) caused Johnson to overthrow his own
critical speculations. Boswell is most Johnson's disciple when he is most
empirical. He reimagines Johnson by adopting Johnson's own realism.
Johnson is a biographical literary critic, and M.J.C. Hodgart was accurate
when he observed that "Johnson's short lines are the model for Boswell's
concept of 'total' biography. Johnson has the ability to relate everything to
his own experience of life, and to identify himself closely with the men he
writes about, sharing their problems and emotions."

Boswell too has this ability, even if his close identification was primarily only with Johnson. That identification, an act of love, is at the center of the *Life of Johnson*. In the many-sided Boswell, this identification is
necessarily dialectical, and yet it remains an identification. Every kind of
high literary art comes together in the *Life of Johnson*, but the coming
together is conditioned and refined by a human love. What finally persuades us in the *Life* is not technique and not even the defense of culture,
though Johnson himself exalted both. What persuades us is the elaboration, through adornment, variation, and refinement, of Boswell's surpassing admiration and reverence, of his love for Johnson.

William Hazlitt

(1778-1830)

DAVID BROMWICH, HAZLITT'S BEST CRITIC, SHREWDLY SAYS OF HAZLITT'S key word *gusto* that it "accords nicely with the belief that taste adds to our nature instead of correcting it." I take it that Hazlitt's gusto is an aesthetic displacement of the Dissenting Protestant version of grace, which corrects our nature without abolishing it. The son of a radical Dissenting Minister, Hazlitt himself was always a Jacobin with a faith in Napoleon as the true heir of the Revolution. Unswerving in his politics, Hazlitt also remained an unreconstructed early Wordsworthian, unlike Wordsworth himself, a difference that Hazlitt bitterly kept in mind, as here in his observations on Wordsworth's *The Excursion*:

> In the application of these memorable lines, we should, per-
> haps, differ a little from Mr. Wordsworth; nor can we indulge
> with him in the fond conclusion afterwards hinted at, that one
> day *our* triumph, the triumph of humanity and liberty, may be
> complete. For this purpose, we think several things necessary
> which are impossible. It is a consummation which cannot hap-
> pen till the nature of things is changed, till the many become as
> united as the *one*, till romantic generosity shall be as common as
> gross selfishness, till reason shall have acquired the obstinate
> blindness of prejudice, till the love of power and of change shall
> no longer goad man on to restless action, till passion and will,
> hope and fear, love and hatred, and the objects proper to excite
> them, that is, alternate good and evil, shall no longer sway the
> bosoms and businesses of men. All things move, not in progress,
> but in a ceaseless round; our strength lies in our weakness; our
> virtues are built on our vices; our faculties are as limited as our

being; nor can we lift man above his nature more than above
the earth he treads. But though we cannot weave over again the
airy, unsubstantial dream, which reason and experience have
dispelled,

> What though the radiance, which was once so bright,
> Be now for ever taken from our sight,
> Though nothing can bring back the hour
> Of glory in the grass, of splendour in the flower:

yet we will never cease, nor be prevented from returning on the
wings of imagination to that bright dream of our youth; that
glad dawn of the day-star of liberty; that spring-time of the
world, in which the hopes and expectations of the human race
seemed opening in the same gay career with our own; when
France called her children to partake her equal blessings
beneath her laughing skies; when the stranger was met in all
her villages with dance and festive songs, in celebration of a
new and golden era; and when, to the retired and contemplative student, the prospects of human happiness and glory were
seen ascending like the steps of Jacob's ladder, in bright and
never-ending succession. The dawn of that day was suddenly
overcast; that season of hope is past; it is fled with the other
dreams of our youth, which we cannot recall, but has left
behind it traces, which are not to be effaced by Birthday and
Thanksgiving odes, or the chaunting of *Te Deums* in all the
churches of Christendom. To those hopes eternal regrets are
due; to those who maliciously and wilfully blasted them, in the
fear that they might be accomplished, we feel no less what we
owe—hatred and scorn as lasting!

In effect, the aesthetic loss of Wordsworth's visionary gleam is associated here with the spiritual loss of revolutionary hope. All loss, for the
critic Hazlitt, is ultimately a loss of gusto, since *gusto* is Hazlitt's version of
Blake's "exuberance," as in: "Exuberance is Beauty." One sees this clearly
when he transfers the term *gusto* from painters to writers:

> The infinite quantity of dramatic invention in Shakespeare
> takes from his gusto. The power he delights to shew is not
> intense, but discursive. He never insists on any thing as much
> as he might, except a quibble. Milton has great gusto. He

repeats his blow twice; grapples with and exhausts his subject. His imagination has a double relish of its objects, an inveterate attachment to the things he describes, and to the words describing them.

> ————Or where Chineses drive
> With sails and wind their *cany* waggons light.

> Wild above rule or art, *enormous* bliss.

There is a gusto in Pope's compliments, in Dryden's satires, and Prior's tales; and among prose-writers, Boccaccio and Rabelais had the most of it. We will only mention one other work which appears to us to be full of gusto, and that is the *Beggar's Opera*. If it is not, we are altogether mistaken in our notions on this delicate subject.

Shakespeare's gusto is in his exuberance of invention, Milton's in his exhaustive tenacity at battering the object, as it were. An aesthetic category comprehensive enough to include also Pope, Dryden, and Prior, on the one side, and Boccaccio, Rabelais, and John Gay, on the other, is perhaps too broad to be of use to practical criticism. Hazlitt's own gusto or critical exuberance proved capable of overcoming this difficulty, and he gave us a poetics of power still unsurpassed in its potential:

The language of poetry naturally falls in with the language of power. The imagination is an exaggerating and exclusive faculty: it takes from one thing to add to another: it accumulates circumstances together to give the greatest possible effect to a favourite object. The understanding is a dividing and measuring faculty, it judges of things not according to their immediate impression on the mind, but according to their relations to one another. The one is a monopolising faculty, which seeks the greatest quantity of present excitement by inequality and disproportion; the other is a distributive faculty, which seeks the greatest quantity of ultimate good, by justice and proportion. The one is an aristocratical, the other a republican faculty. The principle of poetry is a very anti-levelling principle. It aims at effect, it exists by contrast. It admits of no medium. It is everything by excess. It rises above the ordinary standard of sufferings and crimes. It presents a dazzling appearance. It shows its head turretted, crowned, and crested. Its front is gilt and bloodstained. Before it "it carries noise, and behind it leaves tears." It has its altars and its victims, sacrifices, human sacrifices. Kings, priests, nobles, are its train-bearers, tyrants and slaves its executioners.—"Carnage is its daughter."—Poetry is right-royal. It puts the individual for the species, the one above the infinite—many, might before right. A lion hunting a flock of sheep or a herd of wild asses is a more poetical object than they; and we even take part with the lordly beast, because our vanity or some other feeling makes us disposed to place ourselves in the situation of the strongest party. So we feel some concern for the poor citizens of Rome when they meet together to compare their wants and grievances, till Coriolanus comes in and with blows and big words drives this set of "poor rats," this rascal scum, to their homes and beggary before him. There is nothing heroical in a multitude of miserable rogues not wishing to be starved, or complaining that they are like to be so; but when a single man comes forward to brave their cries and to make them submit to the last indignities, from mere pride and self-will, our admiration of his prowess is immediately converted into contempt for their pusillanimity. The insolence of power is stronger than the plea of necessity. The tame submission to usurped authority or even the natural resistance to it has nothing to excite or flatter the imagination: it is the assumption of a right to insult or oppress others that carries an imposing air of superiority with it. We had rather be the oppressor than the oppressed. The love of power in ourselves and the admiration of it in others are both natural to man: the one makes him a tyrant, the other a slave.

This is from Hazlitt's discussion of Coriolanus in his *Characters of Shakespeare's Plays*. The quality of excess is central to Hazlitt's insight here, which tells us that meaning gets started (rather than being merely repeated) by excess, by overflow, and by a sense of potential, a sense of something evermore about to be. The dialectic of this poetics of power depends upon an interplay of Shakespearean and Wordsworthian influences upon Hazlitt. From Shakespeare, Hazlitt takes an awareness that character may be fate, yet only personality bestows some measure of freedom. From Wordsworth, Hazlitt received a new consciousness of how a writer could begin again despite the strength and persistence of cultural traditions. The freedom of personality, in Falstaff, *is* freedom because ego ceases to be persecuted by superego. The originality of writing, in Wordsworth, is the disappearance of subject matter, and its replacement by subjectivity. Taken together, the ego of free wit and the triumph of a fresh subjectivity make up the manner and matter of Hazlitt's characteristic achievement, an essay at once familiar and critical, firmly literary yet also discursive and speculative.

In his loving meditation, "On the Periodical Essayists," Hazlitt lists his precursors: Montaigne, Steele (rather than Addison), Johnson (despite Hazlitt's dislike of his style), Goldsmith. Had Edmund Burke been a familiar essayist rather than an orator, Burke certainly would be Hazlitt's nearest ancestor. Instead, Hazlitt makes a second to Johnson in a great procession of critical essayists that goes on to Carlyle, Emerson, Ruskin, Pater, and Wilde. (I omit Coleridge because of his obsession with method, and Arnold because of his authentic incompetence.) The procession ceases in our century because the mode now seems inadequate, not so much to the apparent complexities of modernist literature (after all, many of those now resolve themselves into more complications), but to the waning of the self, with all the perplexities attendant upon that waning. A curious irony of modern literature made Freud, the analyst of such waning, also the only twentieth-century essayist worthy to be the coda of the long tradition that went from Montaigne on through Johnson, Hazlitt, and Emerson until it culminated in Freud's older contemporaries, Ruskin, Nietzsche, and Pater.

II

Hazlitt's poetics of power seems to me more Freudian than any of the psychopoetics—orthodox or Lacanian—that currently drift uselessly in Freud's wake. Like Freud, Hazlitt knows that the poets—Shakespeare, Milton, Wordsworth—were there before him, which is a very different realization than any that penetrate the blindnesses of what now passes for "Freudian literary criticism." The poets are still there before Freud, better guides to the interpretation of Freud than he could ever be to the reading of consciousnesses even more comprehensive and coherent than his own. Hazlitt, in his best theoretical essay, "On Poetry in General," begins with the fine realization: "Poetry then is an imitation of Nature, but the imagination and the passions are a part of man's nature." Passion, or pathos, or sublimity, or power (the four are rightly one, according to Hazlitt) remove poetry from the domain of all conventional considerations of psychology and morality:

We are as fond of indulging our violent passions as of reading a description of those of others. We are as prone to make a torment of our fears, as to luxuriate in our hopes of good. If it be asked, Why do we do so? the best answer will be, Because we cannot help it. The sense of power is as strong a principle in the mind as the love of pleasure. Objects of terror and pity exercise the same despotic control over it as those of love or beauty. It is as natural to hate as to love, to despise as to admire, to express our hatred or contempt, as our love or admiration.

> Masterless passion sways us to the mood
> Of what it likes or loathes.

Not that we like what we loathe; but we like to indulge our hatred and scorn of it; to dwell upon it, to exasperate our idea of it by every refinement of ingenuity and extravagance of illustration; to make it a bugbear to ourselves, to point it out to others in all the splendour of deformity, to embody it to the senses, to stigmatize it by name, to grapple with it in thought, in action, to sharpen our intellect, to arm our will against it, to know the worst we have to contend with, and to contend with it to the utmost. Poetry is only the highest eloquence of passion, the most vivid form of expression that can be given to our conception of anything, whether pleasurable or painful, mean or dignified, delightful or distressing. It is the perfect coincidence of the image and the words with the feeling we have, and of which we cannot get rid in any other way, that gives an instant "satisfaction to the thought." This is equally the origin of wit and fancy, of comedy and tragedy, of the sublime and pathetic. When Pope says of the Lord Mayor's show,—

> Now night descending, the proud scene is o'er,
> But lives in Settle's numbers one day more!

—when Collins makes Danger, "with limbs of giant mould,"

> —Throw him on the steep
> Of some loose hanging rock asleep:

when Lear calls out in extreme anguish,

> Ingratitude, thou marble-hearted fiend,

How much more hideous shew'st in a child
Than the sea-monster!

—the passion of contempt in the one case, of terror in the
other, and of indignation in the last, is precisely satisfied. We
see the thing ourselves, and shew it to others as we feel it to
exist, and as, in spite of ourselves, we are compelled to think of
it. The imagination, by thus embodying and turning them to
shape, gives an obvious relief to the indistinct and importunate
cravings of the will.—We do not wish the thing to be so; but we
wish it to appear such as it is. For knowledge is conscious
power; and the mind is no longer, in this case, the dupe, though
it may be the victim of vice or folly.

To speak of poetry as giving "an obvious relief to the indistinct and
importunate cravings of the will" is to have more than anticipated Freud.
Hazlitt's quotation from *The Merchant of Venice* is the center of one of
Shylock's great speeches:

Some men there are love not a gaping pig;
Some that are mad if they behold a cat;
And others, when the bagpipe sings i' th' nose,
Cannot contain their urine; for affection,
Mistress of passion, sways it to the mood
Of what it likes or loathes.

"Masterless passion" is as likely a reading as "Mistress of passion,"
the text being uncertain, and better suits Hazlitt's emphasis upon the cravings of the will. Hazlittian exuberance, *gusto*, teaches us to admire Shylock
even as we admire Coriolanus. Few passages even in Hazlitt are as superbly
memorable as when he shows us how the grandest poetry can be the most
immoral, here in *Coriolanus*:

This is but natural, it is but natural for a mother to have more
regard for her son than for a whole city; but then the city
should be left to take some care of itself. The care of the state
cannot, we here see, be safely entrusted to maternal affection,
or to the domestic charities of high life. The great have private
feelings of their own, to which the interests of humanity and
justice must courtesy. Their interests are so far from being the
same as those of the community, that they are in direct and

necessary opposition to them; their power is at the expense of our weakness; their riches of our poverty; their pride of our degradation; their splendour of our wretchedness; their tyranny of our servitude. If they had the superior knowledge ascribed to them (which they have not) it would only render them so much more formidable; and from Gods would convert them into Devils. The whole dramatic moral of *Coriolanus* is that those who have little shall have less, and that those who have much shall take all that others have left. The people are poor; therefore they ought to be starved. They are slaves; therefore they ought to be beaten. They work hard; therefore they ought not to be treated like beasts of burden. They are ignorant; therefore they ought not to be allowed to feel that they want food, or clothing, or rest, that they are enslaved, oppressed, and miserable. This is the logic of the imagination and the passions; which seek to aggrandize what excites admiration, and to heap contempt on misery, to raise power into tyranny, and to make tyranny absolute; to thrust down that which is low still lower, and to make wretches desperate; to exult magistrates into kings, kings into gods; to degrade subjects to the rank of slaves, and slaves to the condition of brutes. The history of mankind is a romance, a mask, a tragedy, constructed upon the principles of *poetical justice*; it is a noble or royal hunt, in which what is sport to the few is death to the many, and in which the spectators halloo and encourage the strong to set upon the weak, and cry havoc in the chase though they do not share in the spoil. We may depend upon it that what men delight to read in books, they will put in practice in reality.

Though Hazlitt is an intellectual of the permanent Left, of the French Revolution, he is too great a critic not to see that poetry worships power without regard to the morality of power. Indeed, his poetics of power compels us to see more than that, which is that Plato was right in fearing Homer's effect upon society. Poetical justice is antithetical to societal justice, and the noble or royal hunt of the imagination does not make us better citizens or better human beings, and very likely may make us worse.

III

Hazlitt, like Johnson before him, and the great progression of

Carlyle, Emerson, Ruskin, Pater, and Wilde after him, teaches us several unfashionable truths as to the nature of authentically literary criticism. It must be experiential; it must be at least somewhat empirical or pragmatic; it must be informed by love for its subject; above all it must follow no method except the personality of the critic himself. Coleridge never ceased to quest for method, and lost the critical gift in consequence, while Matthew Arnold drowned what gift he had by assuring himself that they handled these matters better on the Continent. Hazlitt is a literary critic; our contemporary imitators of Continental philosophy may be human scientists or ideological rebels or what they will, but they are not literary critics. Hume's philosophy teaches the critic to fall back upon personality because every other possibility has been collapsed by skepticism. German thought persuaded Coleridge to posit an "organic" unity in imaginative works, but such organicism and its resultant unities can be seen now as banal fictions. Hazlitt, like Johnson, refuses to carry philosophical aesthetics into the pragmatic realms of criticism. I read Coleridge when and as I have to, but I read Hazlitt for pleasure and insight. Whether he writes on "The Indian jugglers" or "On Going a Journey" or "On a Sun-Dial," Hazlitt reminds us always that life and literature are, for him, the one interpenetrated reality.

I remember "The Indian Jugglers" partly for its vivid celebration of the jugglers' skill:

> Coming forward and seating himself on the ground in his white dress and tightened turban, the chief of the Indian jugglers begins with tossing up two brass balls, which is what any of us could do, and concludes with keeping up four at the same time, which is what none of us could do to save our lives, nor if we were to take our whole lives to do it in. Is it then a trifling power we see at work, or is it not something next to miraculous? It is the utmost stretch of human ingenuity, which nothing but the bending the faculties of body and mind to it from the tenderest infancy with incessant, ever-anxious application up to manhood, can accomplish or make even a slight approach to. Man, thou art a wonderful animal, and thy ways past finding out! Thou canst do strange things, but thou turnest them to little account!—To conceive of this effort of extraordinary dexterity distracts the imagination and makes admiration breathless. Yet it costs nothing to the performer, any more than if it were a mere mechanical deception with which he had nothing to do but to watch and laugh at the astonishment of the

spectators. A single error of a hair's-breadth, of the smallest conceivable portion of time, would be fatal: the precision of the movements must be like a mathematical truth, their rapidity is like lightning. To catch four balls in succession in less than a second of time, and deliver them back so as to return with seeming consciousness to the hand again, to make them revolve round him at certain intervals, like the planets in their spheres, to make them chase one another like sparkles of fire, or shoot up like flowers or meteors, to throw them behind his back and twine them round his neck like ribbons or like serpents, to do what appears an impossibility, and to do it with all the ease, the grace, the carelessness imaginable, to laugh at, to play with the glittering mockeries, to follow them with his eye as if he could fascinate them with its lambent fire, or as if he had only to see that they kept time with the music on the stage—there is something in all this which he who does not admire may be quite sure he never really admired anything in the whole course of his life. It is skill surmounting difficulty, and beauty triumphing over skill.

Remarkable as descriptive writing, this acquires hidden power when subsequently it is revealed as a literary paradigm, leading Hazlitt to the profound observation: "No act terminating in itself constitutes greatness." The act of writing *Paradise Lost* is precisely one that does not terminate in itself. Hazlitt's insight is that the canon is constituted by works that engender further works that do not terminate in themselves. "On Going a Journey" begins by advising that "the soul of a journey is liberty, perfect liberty, to think, feel, do just as one pleases." A few pages later the essay achieves perceptions into our involuntary perspectivism that both anticipate and correct Nietzsche:

There is hardly anything that shows the short-sightedness or capriciousness of the imagination more than travelling does. With change of place we change our ideas; nay, our opinions and feelings. We can by an effort indeed transport ourselves to old and long-forgotten scenes, and then the picture of the mind revives again, but we forget those that we have just left. It seems that we can think but of one place at a time. The canvas of the fancy has only a certain extent, and if we paint one set of objects upon it, they immediately efface every other. We cannot enlarge our conceptions; we only shift our point of view.

The landscape bares its bosom to the enraptured eye; we take our fill of it; and seem as if we could form no other image of beauty or grandeur. We pass on, and think no more of it; the horizon that shuts it from our sight also blots it from our memory like a dream. In travelling through a wild barren country, I can form no idea of a woody and cultivated one. It appears to me that all the world must be barren, like what I see of it. In the country we forget the town, and in town we despise the country. "Beyond Hyde Park," says Sir Fopling Flutter, "all is a desert." All that part of the map that we do not see before us is a blank. The world in our conceit of it is not much bigger than a nutshell. It is not one prospect expanded into one another, county joined to county, kingdom to kingdom, lands to seas, making an image voluminous and vast; the mind can form no larger idea of space than the eye can take in at a single glance. The rest is a name written on a map, a calculation of arithmetic. For instance, what is the true signification of that immense mass of territory and population, known by the name of China to us? An inch of paste-board on a wooden globe, of no more account than a China orange! Things near us are seen of the size of life: things at a distance are diminished to the size of the understanding. We measure the universe by ourselves, and even comprehend the texture of our own being only piecemeal.

"On a Sun-Dial" is a nostalgic reverie explaining why Hazlitt has never bothered to own a watch or a clock. In the midst of this brief study of the nostalgias, we are suddenly given a memorable theory of romance, as applicable to Hawthorne as to Wordsworth:

Surely, if there is anything with which we should not mix up our vanity and self-consequence, it is with Time, the most independent of all things. All the sublimity, all the superstition that hang upon this palpable mode of announcing its flight, are chiefly attracted to this circumstance. Time would lose its abstracted character, if we kept it like a curiosity or a jack-in-a-box: its prophetic warnings would have no effect, if it obviously spoke only at our prompting, like a paltry ventriloquism. The clock that tells the corning, dreaded hour—the castle bell, that "with its brazen throat and iron tongue, sounds one unto the drowsy ear of night"—the curfew, "swinging slow with sullen roar" o'er wizard stream or fountain, are like a voice from other worlds, big with unknown events. The last sound, which is still kept up as an old custom in many parts of England, is a great favourite with me. I used to hear it when a boy. It tells a tale of other times. The days that are past, the generations that are gone, the tangled forest glades and hamlets brown of my native country, the woodsman's art, the Norman warrior armed for the battle or in his festive hall, the conqueror's iron rule and peasant's lamp extinguished, all start up at the clamorous peal, and fill my mind with fear and wonder. I confess, nothing at present interests me but what has been—the recollection of the impressions of my early life, or events long past, of which only the dim traces remain in a smouldering ruin or half-obsolete custom. That *things should be that are now no more*, creates in my mind the most unfeigned astonishment. I cannot solve the mystery of the past, nor exhaust my pleasure in it.

One sees, after reading this, why Wordsworth's "Ode: Intimations of Immortality" was Hazlitt's poem-of-poems, as it was Emerson's and Ruskin's. Hazlitt's regret is hardly for actual immortality, which he dismisses with splendid vigor in his "On the Fear of Death." It is rather what he adumbrates in his superb "On the Feeling of Immortality in Youth":

Objects, on our first acquaintance with them, have that singleness and integrity of impression that it seems as if nothing could destroy or obliterate them, so firmly are they stamped and rivetted on the brain. We repose on them with a sort of voluptuous indolence, in full faith and boundless confidence. We are absorbed in the present moment, or return to the same point—idling away a great deal of time in youth, thinking we have enough and to spare. There is often a local feeling in the air, which is as fixed as if it were of marble; we loiter in dim cloisters, losing ourselves in thought and in their glimmering arches; a winding road before us seems as long as the journey of life, and as full of events. Time and experience dissipate this illusion; and by reducing them to detail, circumscribe the limits of our expectations. It is only as the pageant of life passes by and the masques turn their backs upon us, that we see through the deception, or believe that the train will have an end. In many cases, the slow progress and monotonous texture of our lives, before we mingle with the world and are embroiled in its affairs, has a tendency to aid the same feeling. We have a difficulty, when left to ourselves, and without the resource of books or some more lively pursuit, to "beguile the slow and creeping hours of time," and argue that if it moves on always at this tedious snail's-pace, it can never come to an end. We are willing to skip over certain portions of it that separate us from favourite objects, that irritate ourselves at the unnecessary delay. The young are prodigal of life from a superabundance of it; the old are tenacious on the same score, because they have little left, and cannot enjoy even what remains of it.

As a commentary upon our common experience, both when young and when old, this compels the chill of a self-recognition beyond illusion and delusion alike. But it is also a powerfully implicit commentary upon Wordsworth's Great Ode, and upon very nearly everything else in Wordsworth that truly matters. Hazlitt's strength, matched among critics in the language only by Johnson and by Ruskin, is that he never allows us to forget the dark and antithetical relationship between the power of the imagination and the power of human experience. Imaginative gain and experiential loss are identical in Hazlitt, who, unlike Wordsworth, understands that there is no knowledge that is not purchased by the loss of power, no power that is not purchased at the expense both of others and of the self.

Thomas Carlyle

(1795-1881)

IN HIS EARLY ESSAY "SIGNS OF THE TIMES" (1829), CARLYLE PROPHESIED
the rise of our own literary culture. A culture becomes literary, for better
and for worse, when religion, philosophy, and science accelerate the long
process of losing their authority. Carlyle, seer of transcendental possibilities, began as a rebel against the main tradition of British speculation, the
empirical line from Bacon to Bentham, and yet his rebellion was more
equivocal than he seems to have realized. Protesting the Mechanical Age,
Carlyle remained what Nietzsche in *The Twilight of the Gods* mocked him
for being, an English atheist who, merely upon principle, declined to be
what he truly was.

This hardly damages Carlyle as a writer; perhaps it might yet revive
him if his scholars would cease emulating his rhetorical descents into the
bathos of High German Transcendentalism. Goethe was for Carlyle a mask
and a shield, without which Carlyle would have been a belated British poet,
Byronic in verse, Coleridgean in prose. Reading Carlyle's poems of 1823–33
is a gleeful experience for those who seek revenge upon his later prose:

> What is Life? A thawing iceboard
> On a sea with sunny shore;—
> Gay we sail; it melts beneath us;
> We are sunk, and seen no more.

Carlyle's famous portrait of Coleridge in his *Life of John Sterling*
(1851) goes back to an 1824 call upon Coleridge in London. Nothing could
be more brilliantly unfair than Carlyle's summing-up of his truest precursor, and nothing could be more revelatory, of Carlyle himself:

To the man himself Nature had given, in high measure, the
seeds of a noble endowment; and to unfold it had been forbidden him. A subtle lynx-eyed intellect, tremulous pious sensibility to all good and all beautiful; truly a ray of empyrean light;
but imbedded in such weak laxity of character, in such indo-
lences and esuriences as had made strange work with it. Once
more, the tragic story of a high endowment with an insufficient
will. An eye to discern the divineness of the Heaven's splen-
dours and lightnings, the insatiable wish to revel in their god-
like radiances and brilliances; but no heart to front the scathing
terrors of them, which is the first condition of your conquering
an abiding place there. The courage necessary for him, above
all things, had been denied this man. His life, with such ray of
the empyrean in it, was great and terrible to him; and he had
not valiantly grappled with it, he had fled from it; sought refuge
in vague day-dreams, hollow compromises, in opium, in theo-
sophic metaphysics. Harsh pain, danger, necessity, slavish har-
nessed toil, were of all things abhorrent to him. And so the
empyrean element, lying smothered under the terrene, and yet
inextinguishable there, made sad writhings. For pain, danger,
difficulty, steady slaving toil, and other highly disagreeable
behests of destiny, shall in no wise be shirked by any brightest
mortal that will approve himself loyal to his mission in this
world; nay precisely the higher he is, the deeper will be the dis-
agreeableness, and the detestability to flesh and blood, of the
tasks laid on him; and the heavier too, and more tragic, his
penalties if he neglect them.

Carlyle is the courageous titan with the heart to front pain, danger,
difficulty, and steady slaving toil. Poor Coleridge attempted to steal into
heaven, and Carlyle, too canny to believe in an outworn logos, mocks his
precursor's pieties of self-deception:

What the light of your mind, which is the direct inspiration of the
Almighty, pronounces incredible,—that, in God's name, leave
uncredited; at your peril do not try believing that. No subtlest
hocus-pocus of "reason" versus "understanding" will avail for that
feat;—and it is terribly perilous to try it in these provinces!

These provinces are empirical, the lands of Bacon and Locke, Hume
and Bentham, and the Mills. Carlyle's anxiety is that he may become

irresolute or self-deceived, that he may become Coleridge. Carlyle has no Supreme Fiction, but only what in his early "Corn-Law Rhymes" (1832) he calls the knowing that comes through his work, a knowing that is strength, force, seeing, and "a certain Originality." The ultimate instance of this knowing is Shakespeare, about whom Carlyle writes with rare insight in *On Heroes and Hero-Worship* (1841). Far better than the entire history of formal Shakespeare criticism is Carlyle's fundamental realization that Shakespeare's true power is cognitive:

> For, in fact, I say the degree of vision that dwells in a man is a correct measure of the man. If called to define Shakspeare's faculty, I should say superiority of Intellect, and think I had included all under that. What indeed are faculties? We talk of faculties as if they were distinct, things separable; as if a man had intellect, imagination, fancy, etc., as he has hands, feet, and arms. That is a capital error. Then again, we hear of a man's "intellectual nature," and of his "moral nature," as if these again were divisible, and existed apart. Necessities of language do perhaps prescribe such forms of utterance; we must speak, I am aware, in that way, if we are to speak at all. But words ought not to harden into things for us. It seems to me, our apprehension of this matter is, for the most part, radically falsified thereby. We ought to know withal, and to keep for ever in mind, that these divisions are at bottom but *names*; that man's spiritual nature, the vital Force which dwells in him, is essentially one and indivisible; that what we call imagination, fancy, understanding, and so forth, are but different figures of the same Power of Insight, all indissolubly connected with each other, physiognomically related; that if we knew one of them, we might know all of them. Morality itself, what we call the moral quality of a man, what is this but another *side* of the one vital Force whereby he is and works? All that a man does is physiognomical of him. You may see how a man would fight, by the way in which he sings; his courage, or want of courage, is visible in the word he utters, in the opinion he has formed, no less than in the stroke he strikes. He is *one*; and preaches the same Self abroad in all these ways.

What Carlyle teaches us is that Shakespeare's cognitive originality has altered every mode available to us for representing cognition in language, including the one we now ascribe to Freud. Reading Carlyle on

Shakespeare, we see that Freud's map of the mind codifies and rationaliz-es Shakespeare's. An extraordinary further outburst of Carlyle's rhetoric is evocative of Shakespeare's deepest influence upon us:

> If I say therefore, that Shakspeare is the greatest of Intellects, I have said all concerning him. But there is more in Shakspeare's intellect than we have yet seen. It is what I call an unconscious intellect; there is more virtue in it than he himself is aware of. Novalis beautifully remarks of him, that those Dramas of his are Products of Nature too, deep as Nature herself. I find a great truth in this saying. Shakspeare's Art is not Artifice; the noblest worth of it is not there by plan or precontrivance. It grows-up from the deeps of Nature, through this noble sincere soul, who is a voice of Nature. The latest generations of men will find new meanings in Shakspeare, new elucidations of their own human being; "new harmonies with the infinite structure of the Universe; concurrences with later ideas, affinities with the higher powers and senses of man." This well deserves med-itating. It is Nature's highest reward to a true simple great soul, that he get thus to be *a part of herself.* Such a man's works what-soever he with utmost conscious exertion and forethought shall accomplish, grow up withal unconsciously, from the unknown deeps in him;—as the oak tree grows from the Earth's bosom, as the mountains and waters shape themselves; with a symme-try grounded on Nature's own laws, conformable to all Truth whatsoever. How much in Shakspeare lies hid; his sorrows, his silent struggles known to himself; much that was not known at all, not speakable at all: like *roots,* like sap and forces working underground! Speech is great; but Silence is greater.

By "unconscious intellect" Carlyle primarily means mind at its least tendentious, or as he says later, at its most prophetic. Attempting prophe-cy, Carlyle himself became wholly tendentious. Too strong to admit the reproach he felt in Shakespeare, Carlyle was also too honest not to be made uneasy. For him, Shakespeare was religious writing, a new Bible to replace Old and New Testament alike. We can learn from Carlyle also that the distinction between religious and secular writing is merely political and not critical. Critically, all writing is religious, or all writing is secular; Carlyle sees that Shakespeare has abolished the distinction, and has become the second Bible of the West.

II

What in the nineteenth and twentieth centuries is religious writing? What can it be? Which of these passages, setting their polemics aside, is better described as religious writing?

> People say to me, that it is but a dream to suppose that Christianity should regain the organic power in human society which once it possessed. I cannot help that; I never said it could. I am not a politician; I am proposing no measures, but exposing a fallacy, and resisting a pretence. Let Benthamism reign, if men dare no aspirations; but do not tell them to be romantic, and then solace them with glory; do not attempt by philosophy what was once done by religion. The ascendancy of Faith may be impracticable, but the reign of Knowledge is incomprehensible.

> He that has done nothing has known nothing. Vain is it to sit scheming and plausibly discoursing: up and be doing! If thy knowledge be real, put it forth from thee: grapple with real Nature; try thy theories there, and see how they hold out. *Do* one thing, for the first time in thy life do a thing; a new light will rise to thee on the doing of all things whatsoever.

I have taken these passages randomly enough; they lay near by. The distinguished first extract is both truly religious and wonderfully written, but the second is religious writing. Newman, in the first, from *The Tamworth Reading Room* (1841), knows both the truth and his own mind, and the relation between the two. Carlyle, in the second, from "Corn-Law Rhymes" (1832), knows only his own knowing, and sets that above both Newman's contraries, religion and philosophy. "Corn-Law Rhymes" became a precursor text for Emerson because he could recognize what had to be religious writing for the nineteenth century, and to that recognition, which alone would not have sufficed, Emerson added the American difference, which Carlyle could not ever understand. Subtle as this difference is, another intertextual juxtaposition can help reveal it:

> "But it is with man's Soul as it was with Nature: the beginning of Creation is—Light. Till the eye have vision, the whole members are in bonds. Divine moment, when over the tempest-tost Soul, as once over the wild-weltering Chaos, it is spoken: Let there be Light! Ever to the greatest that has felt such moment,

is it not miraculous and God-announcing; even as, under simpler figures, to the simplest and least. The mad primeval Discord is hushed; the rudely-jumbled conflicting elements bind themselves into separate Firmaments: deep silent rock-foundations are built beneath; and the skyey vault with its everlasting Luminaries above: instead of a dark wasteful Chaos, we have a blooming, fertile, heaven-encompassed World."

"Nature is not fixed but fluid. Spirit alters, moulds, makes it. The immobility or bruteness of nature, is the absence of spirit; to pure spirit, it is fluid, it is volatile, it is obedient. Every spirit builds itself a house; and beyond its house a world; and beyond its world, a heaven. Know then, that the world exists for you. For you is the phenomenon perfect. What we are, that only can we see.... Build, therefore, your own world. As fast as you conform your life to the pure idea in your mind, that will unfold its great proportions.... The kingdom of man over nature, which cometh not with observation,—a dominion such as now is beyond his dream of God,—he shall enter without more wonder than the blind man feels who is gradually restored to perfect sight."

This juxtaposition is central, because the passages are. The first rhapsody is Carlyle's Teufelsdröckh uttering his Everlasting Yea in *Sartor Resartus*; the second is Emerson's Orphic poet chanting the conclusion of *Nature*. Carlyle's seeing soul triumphs over the Abyss, until he can say to himself: "Be no longer a Chaos, but a World, or even Worldkin. Produce! Produce!" The Abyss is bondage, the production is freedom, somehow still "in God's name!" Emerson, despite his supposed discipleship to Carlyle in *Nature*, has his seeing soul proclaim a world so metamorphic and beyond natural metamorphosis that its status is radically *prior* to that of the existent universe. For the earth is only part of the blind man's "dream of God." Carlyle's imagination remains orthodox, and rejects Chaos. Emerson's seeing, beyond observation, is more theosophical than Germanic Transcendental. The freedom to imagine "the pure idea in your mind" is the heretical absolute freedom of the Gnostic who identified his mind's purest idea with the original Abyss. American freedom, in the context of Emerson's American religion, indeed might be called "Abyss-radiance."

I return to the question of what, in the nineteenth century, makes writing *religious*. Having set Carlyle in the midst, between Newman and Emerson, I cite next the step in religious writing beyond even Emerson:

we have an interval, and then our place knows us no more. Some spend this interval in listlessness, some in high passions, the wisest, at least among "the children of this world," in art and song. For our one chance lies in expanding that interval, in getting as many pulsations as possible into the given time.

Pater, concluding *The Renaissance*, plays audaciously against Luke 16:8, where "the children of this world are in their generation wiser than the children of light." Literalizing the Gospel's irony, Pater insinuates that in his generation the children of this world are the only children of light. Light expands our fiction of duration, our interval or place in art, by a concealed allusion to the Blakean trope that also fascinated Yeats; the pulsation of an artery in which the poet's work is done. Pater sinuously murmurs his credo, which elsewhere in *The Renaissance* is truly intimated to be "a strange rival religion" opposed to warring orthodoxies, fit for "those who are neither for Jehovah nor for His enemies."

To name Emerson and Pater as truly "religious writers" is to call into question very nearly everything that phrase usually implies. More interestingly, this naming also questions that mode of displacement M.H. Abrams analyzes in his strong study *Natural Supernaturalism*: "not ... the deletion and replacement of religious ideas but rather the assimilation and reinterpretation of religious ideas." I believe that the following remarks of Abrams touch their limit precisely where Carlyle and Emerson part, on the American difference, and also where Carlyle and Ruskin part from Pater and what comes after. The story Abrams tells has been questioned by J. Hillis Miller, from a Nietzschean linguistic or Deconstructive perspective, so that Miller dissents from Abrams exactly where Nietzsche himself chose to attack Carlyle (which I cite below). But there is a more ancient perspective to turn against Abrams's patterns-of-displacement, an argument as to whether poetry did not inform religion before religion ever instructed poetry. And beyond this argument, there is the Gnostic critique of creation-theories both Hebraic and Platonic, a critique that relies always upon the awesome trope of the primal Abyss.

Abrams states his "displacement" thesis in a rhetoric of continuity:

> Much of what distinguishes writers I call "Romantic" derives from the fact that they undertook, whatever their religious creed or lack of creed, to save traditional concepts, schemes, and values which had been based on the relation of the Creator to his creature and creation, but to reformulate them within the prevailing two-term system of subject and object, ego and non-

ego, the human mind or consciousness and its transactions with nature. Despite their displacement from a supernatural to a natural frame of reference, however, the ancient problems, terminology, and ways of thinking about human nature and history survived, as the implicit distinctions and categories through which even radically secular writers saw themselves and their world.

Such "displacement" is a rather benign process, as though the incarnation of the Poetic Character and the Incarnation proper could be assimilated to one another, or the former serve as the reinterpretation of the latter. But what if poetry as such is always a counter-theology, or Gentile Mythus, as Vico believed? Abrams, not unlike Matthew Arnold, reads religion as abiding in poetry, as though the poem were a saving remnant. But perhaps the saving remnant *of poetry* is the only force of what we call theology? And what can theology be except what Geoffrey Hartman anxiously terms it: "a vast, intricate domain of psychopoetic events," another litany of evasions? Poems are the original lies-against-time, as the Gnostics understood when they turned their dialectics to revisionary interpretations not only of the Bible and Plato, but of Homer as well. Gnosticism was the inaugural and most powerful of Deconstructions because it undid all genealogies, scrambled all hierarchies, allegorized every microcosm/macrocosm relation, and rejected every representation of divinity as non-referential.

Carlyle, though he gave Abrams both the scheme of displacement and the title-phrase of "natural supernaturalism," seems to me less and less self-deceived as he progressed onwards in life and work, which I think accounts for his always growing fury. Here I follow Nietzsche, in the twelfth "Skirmish" of *Twilight of the Idols* where he leaves us not much of the supposedly exemplary life of Carlyle:

this unconscious and involuntary farce, this heroic-moralistic interpretation of dyspeptic states. Carlyle: a man of strong words and attitudes, a rhetor from *need*, constantly lured by the craving for a strong faith and the feeling of his incapacity for it (in this respect, a typical romantic!). The craving for a strong faith is no proof of a strong faith, but quite the contrary. If one has such a faith, then one can afford the beautiful luxury of skepticism; one is sure enough, firm enough, has ties enough for that. Carlyle drugs something in himself with the fortissimo of his veneration of men of strong faith and with his rage against the less simple minded: he *requires* noise. A constant passionate dishonesty against himself—that is his *proprium*; in this respect he is and remains interesting. Of course, in England he is admired precisely for his honesty. Well, that is English; and in view of the fact that the English are the people of consummate cant, it is even as it should be, and not only comprehensible. At bottom, Carlyle is an English atheist who makes it a point of honor not to be one.

It seems merely just to observe, following Nietzsche's formidable wit, that Carlyle contrived to be a religious writer without being a religious man. His clear sense of the signs and characteristics of the times taught him that the authentic nineteenth-century writer had to be religious *qua* writer. The burden, as Carlyle knew, was not so much godlessness as belatedness, which compels a turn to Carlyle (and Emerson) on history.

III

Carlyle, with grim cheerfulness, tells us that history is an unreadable text, indeed a "complex Manuscript, covered over with formless inextricably—entangled unknown characters,—nay, which is a *Palimpsest*, and had once prophetic writing, still dimly legible there...." We can see emerging in this dark observation the basis for *The French Revolution*, and even for *Past and Present*. But that was Carlyle "On History" in 1830, just before the advent of Diogenes Teufelsdröckh, the author of "On History Again" in 1833, where the unreadable is read as Autobiography repressed by all Mankind: "a like unconscious talent of remembering and of forgetting again does the work here." The great instance of this hyperbolic or Sublime repression is surely Goethe, whose superb self-confidence breathes fiercely in his couplet cited by Carlyle as the first epigraph to *Sartor Resartus*:

> Mein Vermachtniss, wie herrlich weir und breit!
> Die Zeit ist mein Vermachtniss, mein Acker ist die Zeit.

> [My inheritance, how splendidly wide and broad!
> Time is my inheritance, my seed-field is time.]

Goethe's splendid, wide, and broad inheritance is time itself, the seed-field that has the glory of having grown Goethe! But then, Goethe had no precursors in his own language, or none at least that could make him anxious. Carlyle trumpets his German inheritance: Goethe, Schiller, Fichte, Novalis, Kant, Schelling. His English inheritance was more troublesome to him, and the vehemence of his portrait of Coleridge reveals an unresolved relationship. This unacknowledged debt to Coleridge, with its too-conscious swerve away from Coleridge and into decisiveness and overt courage, pain accepted and work deified, may be the hidden basis for the paradoxes of Carlyle on time, at once resented with a Gnostic passion and worshipped as the seed-bed of a Goethean greatness made possible for the self. It is a liberation to know the American difference again when the reader turns from Carlyle's two essays on history to "History," placed first of the *Essays* (1841) of Emerson:

> This human mind wrote history, and this must read it. The Sphinx must solve her own riddle. If the whole of history is in one man, it is all to be explained from individual experience....
>
> Property also holds of the soul, covers great spiritual facts, and instinctively we at first hold to it with swords and laws, and wide and complex combinations. The obscure consciousness of this fact is the light of all our day, the claim of claims; the plea for education, for justice, for charity, the foundation of friendship and love, and of the heroism and grandeur which belong to acts of self-reliance. It is remarkable that involuntarily we always read as superior beings....
>
> The student is to read history actively and not passively; to esteem his own life the text, and books the commentary.

So much then for Carlyle on history; so much indeed for history. The text is not interpretable? But there is no text! There is only your own life, and the Wordsworthian light of all our day turns out to be: self-reliance. Emerson, in describing an 1847 quarrel with Carlyle in London, gave a vivid sense of his enforcing the American difference, somewhat at the expense of a friendship that was never the same again:

> Carlyle ... had grown impatient of opposition, especially when talking of Cromwell. I differed from him ... in his estimate of Cromwell's character, and he rose like a great Norse giant from his chair—and, drawing a line with his finger across the table, said, with terrible fierceness: "Then, sir, there is a line of separation between you and me as wide as that, and as deep as the pit.

Hardly a hyperbole, the reader will reflect, when he reads what two years later Carlyle printed as "The Nigger Question." This remarkable performance doubtless was aimed against "Christian Philanthropy" and related hypocrisies, but the abominable greatness of the tract stems from its undeniable madness. The astonished reader discovers not fascism, but a terrible sexual hysteria rising up from poor Carlyle, as the repressed returns in the extraordinary trope of black pumpkin-eating:

> far over the sea, we have a few black persons rendered extreme-
> ly "free" indeed. Sitting yonder with their beautiful muzzles up
> to the ears in pumpkins, imbibing sweet pulps and juices; the
> grinder and incisor teeth ready for ever new work, and the
> pumpkins cheap as grass in those rich climates: while the sugar-
> crops rot round them uncut, because labour cannot be hired, so
> cheap are the pumpkins.... and beautiful Blacks sitting there up
> to the ears in pumpkins, and doleful Whites sitting here with-
> out potatoes to eat....
>
> The fortunate Black man, very swiftly does he settle his
> account with supply and demand: not so swiftly the less fortu-
> nate White man of those tropical localities. A bad case, his, just
> now. He himself cannot work; and his black neighbour, rich in
> pumpkin, is in no haste to help him. Sunk to the ears in pump-
> kin, imbibing saccharine juices, and much at his ease in the
> Creation, he can listen to the less fortunate white man's
> "demand" and take his own time in supplying it....
>
> An idle White gentleman is not pleasant to me; though I
> confess the real work for him is not easy to find, in these our
> epochs; and perhaps he is seeking, poor soul, and may find at
> last. But what say you to an idle Black gentleman, with his rum-
> bottle in his hand (for a little additional pumpkin you can have
> red-herrings and rum, in Demerara),—rum-bottle in his hand,
> no breeches on his body, pumpkin at discretion....
>
> Before the West Indies could grow a pumpkin for any
> Negro, how much European heroism had to spend itself in
> obscure battle; to sink, in mortal agony, before the jungles, the
> putrescences and waste savageries could become arable, and the
> Devils be in some measure chained there! ... A bit of the great
> Protector's own life lies there; beneath those pumpkins lies a bit
> of the life that was Oliver Cromwell's.

I have cited only a few passages out of this veritable procession of pumpkins, culminating in the vision of Carlyle's greatest hero pushing up the pumpkins so that unbreeched Blacks might exercise their potent teeth. Mere racism does not yield so pungent a phantasmagoria, and indeed I cannot credit it to Carlyle's likely impotence either. This pumpkin litany is Carlyle's demi-Gnosticism at its worst, for here time is no fair seed-bed but rather devouring time, Kronos chewing us up as so many pumpkins, the time of "Getting Under Way" in *Sartor Resartus*:

> "Me, however, as a Son of Time, unhappier than some others, was Time threatening to eat quite prematurely; for, strive as I might, there was no good Running, so obstructed was the path, so gyved were the feet."

IV

Sartor Resartus, rather than *Past and Present* or *The French Revolution*, seems now to be Carlyle's great accomplishment, though alas it seems fated also to lack readers, now and in the future. A little application of Carlyle to current American society would do wonders. Envision a House of Representatives and a Senate required to deliberate absolutely naked (presumably in a sufficiently heated Capitol). Clearly the quality of legislation would rise, and the quantity of rhetoric would fall. Envision professors, quite naked, instructing equally naked classes. The intellectual level might not be elevated, but the issue of authority would be clarified. Envision our president, naked on television, smilingly charming us with his customary amiable incoherence. We might be no less moved, but reality would have a way of breaking in upon him, and even upon us.

Teufelsdröckh's Theorem, "Society founded upon cloth," is sublimely illustrated in one of Carlyle's happiest conceits:

> "What would Majesty do, could such an accident befall in reality; should the buttons all simultaneously start, and the solid wool evaporate, in very Deed, as here in Dream? *Ach Gott!* How each skulks into the nearest hiding-place; their high State Tragedy (*Haupt- und Staats-Action*) becomes a Pickleherring-Farce to weep at, which is the worst kind of Farce; *the tables* (according to Horace), and with them, the whole fabric of Government, Legislation, Property, Police, and Civilised Society, *are dissolved*, in wails and howls."

Lives the man that can figure a naked Duke of Windlestraw addressing a naked House of Lords? Imagination, choked as in mephitic air, recoils on itself, and will not forward with the picture. The Woolsack, the Ministerial, the Opposition Benches—*infandum! infandum!* And yet why is the thing impossible? Was not every soul, or rather every body, of these Guardians of our Liberties, naked, or nearly so, last night; "a forked Radish with a head fantastically carved"? And why might he not, did our stern fate so order it, walk out to St. Stephen's, as well as into bed, in that no-fashion; and there, with other similar Radishes, hold a Bed of Justice? "Solace of those afflicted with the like!" Unhappy Teufelsdröckh, had man ever such a "physical or psychical infirmity" before? And now how many, perhaps, may thy unparalleled confession (which we, even to the sounder British world, and goaded-on by Critical and Biographical duty, grudge to reimpart) incurably infect therewith! Art thou the malignest of Sansculottists, or only the maddest?

"It will remain to be examined," adds the inexorable Teufelsdröckh, "in how far the SCARECROW, as a Clothed Person, is not also entitled to benefit of clergy, and English trial by jury: nay perhaps, considering his high function (for is not he too a Defender of Property, and Sovereign armed with the terrors of the Law?), to a certain royal Immunity and Inviolability; which, however, misers and the meaner class of persons are not always voluntarily disposed to grant him." * * * * "O my friends, we are (in Yorick Sterne's words) but as 'turkeys driven, with a stick and red clout, to the market': or if some drivers, as they do in Norfolk, take a dried bladder and put peas in it, the rattle thereof terrifies the boldest!"

Carlyle is in the tradition of Rabelais, Voltaire, and Swift, so far as his genre (or non-genre) can be determined, but he is less a satirist than the seer of a grotesque phantasmagoria. *Sartor Resartus* is an outrageous and excessive fiction, and requires a very active reading. Its enigma is the paradox that Nietzsche superbly attacked, Carlyle's faithless faith, which is expounded in book 3, chapter 8, "Natural Supernaturalism":

"O Heaven, it is mysterious, it is awful to consider that we not only carry each a future Ghost within Him; but are, in very deed, Ghosts! These Limbs, whence had we them; this stormy Force; this life-blood with its burning Passion? They are dust and shadow; a Shadow-system gathered round our ME;

wherein, through some moments or years, the Divine Essence is to be revealed in the Flesh. The warrior on his strong war-horse, fire flashes through his eyes; force dwells in his arm and heart: but warrior and war-horse are a vision; a revealed Force, nothing more. Stately they tread the Earth, as if it were a firm substance: fool! the Earth is but a film; it cracks in twain, and warrior and war-horse sink beyond plummet's sounding. Plummet's? Fantasy herself will not follow them. A little while ago, they were not; a little while, and they are not, their very ashes are not.

"So has it been from the beginning, so will it be to the end. Generation after generation takes to itself the Form of a Body; and forth-issuing from Cimmerian Night, on Heaven's mission APPEARS. What Force and Fire is in each he expends: one grinding in the mill of Industry; one hunter-like climbing the giddy Alpine heights of Science; one madly dashed in pieces on the rocks of Strife, in war with his fellow:—and then the Heaven-sent is recalled; his earthly Vesture falls away, and soon even to sense becomes a vanished Shadow. Thus, like some wild-flaming, wild-thundering train of Heaven's Artillery, does this mysterious MANKIND thunder and flame, in long-drawn, quick-succeeding grandeur, through the unknown Deep. Thus, like a God-created, fire-breathing Spirit-host, we emerge from the Inane; haste stormfully across the astonished Earth; then plunge again into the Inane. Earth's mountains are levelled, and her seas filled up, in our passage: can the Earth, which is but dead and a vision, resist Spirits which have reality and are alive? On the hardest adamant some footprint of us is stamped-in; the last Rear of the host will read traces of the earliest Van. But whence?—O Heaven, whither? Sense knows not; Faith knows not; only that it is through Mystery to Mystery, from God and to God.

> 'We are *such stuff*
> As dreams are made of, and our little Life
> Is rounded with a sleep!'

Carlyle's "Natural Supernaturalism" has the presumed merit of rendering our lives into so many dramatic poems, but is there any cognitive force in his passionate assertions? Lionel Trilling called Natural Supernaturalism a new form of belief or "a secular spirituality." It is however an outcropping, as I have indicated, of the most ancient of heresies, Gnosticism. Its one originality surpasses all paradox, because it is a pantheistic gnosis, and every ancient Gnosticism posited an alien God, wholly cut off from our cosmos. Weirdly, Carlyle imports the alien God into nature, while estranging mankind from itself. This rather dubiously gives us just the reverse of Blake's apocalyptic humanism; we become an almost unredeemable entity confronting an already more-than-redeemed nature.

Carlyle's later decline is prefigured in his characteristic valorization of nature over what Blake had called "the Human Form Divine." In his profound anxiety to overturn the empirical view of the cosmos as a vast machine, Carlyle divinized nature and debased man. It is Carlyle, and not his critic Nietzsche, who is the true forerunner of twentieth-century Fascism, with its mystical exaltation of the state and its obliteration of compassion and the rights of the individual. That shadow cannot be removed from the later Carlyle, author of such efforts as "The Nigger Question" (1849) and "Shooting Niagara: and After?" (1867), and uncritical idolator of those iron men, Oliver Cromwell and Frederick the Great. It is the Carlyle who wrote during the fifteen years from 1828 to 1843 who still matters to us. The author of "Signs of the Times" (1829) and "Characteristics" (1831), of *Sartor Resartus* (completed 1831) and *Past and Present* (1843) remains the sage who fathered Ruskin, inspired Emerson, and stimulated the social prophecy of William Morris. If time has darkened Carlyle, it has shown also that there is a perpetual remnant of value in him, a voice that still rises out of the wilderness.

Ralph Waldo Emerson

(1803-1882)

EMERSON IS AN EXPERIENTIAL CRITIC AND ESSAYIST, AND NOT A Transcendental philosopher. This obvious truth always needs restating, perhaps now more than ever, when literary criticism is so overinfluenced by contemporary French heirs of the German tradition of Idealist or Transcendental philosophy. Emerson is the mind of our climate, the principal source of the American difference in poetry, criticism and pragmatic post-philosophy. That is a less obvious truth, and it also needs restating, now and always. Emerson, by no means the greatest American writer, perhaps more an interior orator than a writer, is the inescapable theorist of all subsequent American writing. From his moment to ours, American authors either are in his tradition, or else in a counter-tradition originating in opposition to him. This continues even in a time when he is not much read, such as the period from 1945 to 1965 or so. During the last twenty years, Emerson has returned, burying his undertakers. "The essays of Emerson," T.S. Eliot remarked, "are already an encumbrance," one of those judicial observations that governed the literary academy during the Age of Eliot, but that now have faded into an antique charm.

Other judicial critics, including Yvor Winters and Allen Tate, sensibly blamed Emerson for everything they disliked in American literature and even to some extent in American life. Our most distinguished living poet, Robert Penn Warren, culminated the counter-traditional polemic of Eliot and Tate in his lively sequence, "Homage to Emerson, on Night-Flight to New York." Reading Emerson's essays in the "pressurized gloom" of the airliner, Warren sees the glowing page declare: "There is / No sin. Not even error." Only at a transcendental altitude can Warren's heart be abstract enough to accept the Sage of Concord, "for / At 38,000 feet Emerson / Is dead right." At ground level, Emerson "had forgiven God everything" because "Emerson thought that significance shines through everything."

Sin, error, time, history, a God external to the self, the visiting of the crimes of the fathers upon the sons: these are the topoi of the literary cosmos of Eliot and his Southern followers, and these were precisely of no interest whatsoever to Ralph Waldo Emerson. Of Emerson I am moved to say what Borges said of Oscar Wilde: he was always right. But he himself always says it better:

> That is always best which gives me to myself. The sublime is excited in me by the great stoical doctrine, obey thyself. That which shows God in me, fortifies me. That which shows God out of me, makes me a wart and wen. There is no longer a necessary reason for my being.

One might say that the Bible, Shakespeare and Freud show us as caught in a psychic conflict, in which we need to be everything in ourselves while we go on fearing that we are nothing in ourselves. Emerson dismisses the fear, and insists upon the necessity of the single self achieving a total autonomy, of becoming a cosmos without first ingesting either nature or other selves. He wishes to give us to ourselves, although these days supposedly he preaches to the converted, since it is the fashion to assert that we live in a culture of narcissism, of which our smiling President is the indubitable epitome. Emerson, in this time of Reagan, should be cited upon the limitations of all American politics whatsoever:

> We might as wisely reprove the east wind, or the frost, as a political party, whose members, for the most part, could give no account of their position, but stand for the defence of those interests in which they find themselves.... A party is perpetually corrupted by personality. Whilst we absolve the association from dishonesty, we cannot extend the same charity to their leaders. They reap the rewards of the docility and zeal of the masses which they direct.... Of the two great parties, which, at this hour, almost share the nation between them, I should say, that, one has the best cause, and the other contains the best men. The philosopher, the poet, or the religious man, will, of course, wish to cast his vote with the democrat, for free trade, for wide suffrage, for the abolition of legal cruelties in the penal code, and for facilitating in every manner the access of the young and the poor to the sources of wealth and power. But he

can rarely accept the persons whom the so-called popular party propose to him as representatives of these liberalities.

Emerson writes of the Democrats and of the Whigs (precursors of our modern Republicans) in the early 1840's, when he still believes that Daniel Webster (foremost of "the best men") will never come to advocate the worst cause of the slaveholders. Though his politics have been categorized as "transcendental anarchism," Emerson was at once a believer in pure power and a prophet of the moral law, an apparent self-contradiction that provoked Yvor Winters in an earlier time, and President Giamatti of Yale more recently. Yet this wise inconsistency led Emerson to welcome Whitman in poetry for the same reasons he had hailed Daniel Webster in politics, until Webster's Seventh of March speech in 1850 moved Emerson to the most violent rhetoric of his life. John Jay Chapman, in a great essay on Emerson, remarked that, in his polemic against Webster, Emerson "is savage, destructive, personal, bent on death." Certainly no other American politician has been so memorably denounced in public as Webster was by Emerson:

> Mr. Webster, perhaps, is only following the laws of his blood and constitution. I suppose his pledges were not quite natural to him. He is a man who lives by his memory; a man of the past, not a man of faith and of hope. All the drops of his blood have eyes that look downward, and his finely developed understanding only works truly and with all its force when it stands for animal good; that is, for property.

All the drops of his blood have eyes that look downward; that bitter figuration has outlived every phrase Webster himself ventured. Many modern historians defend Webster for his part in the compromise of 1850, by which California was admitted as a free state while the North pledged to honor the Fugitive Slave Law. This defense maintains that Webster helped preserve the Union for another decade, while strengthening the ideology of Union that culminated in Lincoln. But Emerson, who had given Webster every chance, was driven out of his study and into moral prophecy by Webster's support of the Fugitive Slave Law:

> We are glad at last to get a clear case, one on which no shadow of doubt can hang. This is not meddling with other people's affairs: this is hindering other people from meddling with us. This is not going crusading into Virginia and Georgia after

slaves, who it is alleged, are very comfortable where they are:—that amiable argument falls to the ground: but this is befriending in our own State, on our own farms, a man who has taken the risk of being shot or burned alive, or cast into the sea, or starved to death, or suffocated in a wooden box, to get away from his driver: and this man who has run the gauntlet of a thousand miles for his freedom, the statute says, you men of Massachusetts shall hunt, and catch, and send back again to the dog-hutch he fled from. And this filthy enactment was made in the nineteenth century, by people who could read and write. I will not obey it, by God.

As late as 1843, Emerson's love of Webster as incarnate Power had prevailed: "He is no saint, but the wild olive wood, ungrafted yet by grace." After Webster's defense of the Fugitive Slave Law, even Emerson's decorum was abandoned: "The word *liberty* in the mouth of Mr. Webster sounds like the word *love* in the mouth of a courtezan." I suspect that Emerson's deep fury, so uncharacteristic of him, resulted partly from the violation of his own cheerfully amoral dialectics of power. The extraordinary essay on "Power" in *The Conduct of Life* appears at first to worship mere force or drive as such, but the Emersonian cunning always locates power in the place of crossing over, in the moment of transition:

> In history, the great moment is, when the savage is just ceasing to be a savage, with all his hairy Pelasgic strength directed on his opening sense of beauty:—and you have Pericles and Phidias,—not yet passed over into the Corinthian civility. Everything good in nature and the world is in that moment of transition, when the swarthy juices still flow plentifully from nature, but their astringency or acridity is got out by ethics and humanity.

A decade or so before, in perhaps his central essay, "Self-Reliance," Emerson had formulated the same dialectic of power, but with even more exuberance:

> Life only avails, not the having lived. Power ceases in the instant of repose; it resides in the moment of transition from a past to a new state, in the shooting of a gulf, in the darting to an aim. This one fact the world hates, that the soul *becomes*; for that for ever degrades the past, turns all riches to poverty, all

reputation to a shame, confounds the saint with the rogue, shoves Jesus and Judas equally aside. Why, then, do we prate of self-reliance? Inasmuch as the soul is present, there will be power not confident but agent. To talk of reliance is a poor external way of speaking. Speak rather of that which relies, because it works and is.

Magnificent, but surely even the Webster of 1850 retained his Pelasgic strength, surely even that Webster works and is? Emerson's cool answer would have been that Webster had failed the crossing. I think Emerson remains *the* American theoretician of power—be it political, literary, spiritual, economic—because he took the risk of exalting transition for its own sake. Admittedly, I am happier when the consequence is Whitman's "Crossing Brooklyn Ferry" than when the Emersonian product is the first Henry Ford, but Emerson is canny enough to prophesy both disciples. There is a great chill at the center of his cosmos, which remains ours, both the chill and the cosmos:

> But Nature is no sentimentalist,—does not cosset or pamper us. We must see that the world is rough and surly, and will not mind drowning a man or a woman; but swallows your ship like a grain of dust. The cold, inconsiderate of persons, tingles your blood, benumbs your feet, freezes a man like an apple.

This is from the sublime essay, "Fate," which leads off *The Conduct of Life*, and culminates in the outrageous question: "Why should we fear to be crushed by savage elements, we who are made up of the same elements?" Elsewhere in "Fate," Emerson observes: "The way of Providence is a little rude," while in "Power" he restates the law of *Compensation* as "nothing is got for nothing." Emerson too is no sentimentalist, and it is something of a puzzle how he ever got to be regarded as anything other than a rather frightening theoretician of life or of letters. But then, his personality also remains a puzzle. He was the true American charismatic, and founded the actual American religion, which is Protestant without being Christian. Was the man one with the essayist, or was only the wisdom uncanny in our inescapable sage?

II

A biography of Emerson is necessarily somewhat redundant at best, because Emerson, like Montaigne, is almost always his own subject, though hardly in Montaigne's own mode. Emerson would not have said: "I am myself the matter of my book," yet Emerson on "History" is more Emerson than history. Though he is almost never overtly autobiographical, his best lesson nevertheless is that all true subjectivity is a difficult achievement, while supposed objectivity is merely the failure of having become an amalgam of other selves and their opinions. Though he is in the oral tradition, his true genre was no more the lecture than it had been the sermon, and certainly not the essay, though that is his only formal achievement, besides a double handful of strong poems. His journals are his authentic work, and seem to me poorly represented by all available selections. Perhaps the journals simply ought not to be condensed, because Emerson's reader needs to be immersed in their flow and ebb, their own experience of the influx of insight followed by the perpetual falling back into skepticism. They move endlessly between a possible ecstasy and a probable shrewdness, while knowing always that neither daemonic intensity nor worldly irony by itself can constitute wisdom.

The essential Emerson begins to emerge in the journals in the autumn of 1830, when he was twenty-seven, with his first entry on Self-Reliance, in which he refuses to be "a secondary man" imitating any other being. A year later (October 27, 1831) we hear the birth of Emerson's *reader's Sublime*, the notion that what moves us in the eloquence, written or oral, of another must be what is oldest in oneself, which is not part of the Creation, and indeed is God in oneself:

> Were you ever instructed by a wise and eloquent man? Remember then, were not the words that made your blood run cold, that brought the blood to your cheeks, that made you tremble or delighted you,—did they not sound to you as old as yourself? Was it not truth that you knew before, or do you ever expect to be moved from the pulpit or from man by anything but plain truth? Never. It is God in you that responds to God without, or affirms his own words trembling on the lips of another.

On October 28, 1832, Emerson's resignation from the Unitarian ministry was accepted (very reluctantly) by the Second Church, Boston. The supposed issue was the proper way of celebrating the Lord's Supper, but the underlying issue, at least for Emerson himself, was celebrating the self as God. Stephen Whicher in his superb *Emerson: An Organic Anthology* (still the best one-volume Emerson) gathered together the relevant notebook texts of October 1832. We find Emerson, sustained by daemonic influx, asserting: "It is light. You don't get a candle to see the sun rise," where clearly Jesus is the candle and Emerson is the sunrise (prophetic, like so much else in early Emerson, of Nietzsche's *Zarathustra*). The most outrageous instance of an inrush of God in Emerson is the notorious and still much derided Transparent Eyeball passage in *Nature* (1836), which is based upon a journal entry of March 19, 1835. But I give the final text from *Nature*:

> Crossing a bare common, in snow puddles, at twilight, under a clouded sky, without having in my thoughts any occurrence of special good fortune, I have enjoyed a perfect exhilaration. I am glad to the brink of fear.... There I feel that nothing can befall me in life,—no disgrace, no calamity, (leaving me my eyes,) which nature cannot repair. Standing on the bare ground,—my head bathed by the blithe air, and uplifted into infinite space,—all mean egotism vanishes. I become a transparent eyeball; I am nothing; I see all; the currents of the Universal Being circulate through me; I am part or particle of God.

Nature, in this passage as in the title of the little book, *Nature*, is rather perversely the wrong word, since Emerson does not mean "nature" in any accepted sense whatsoever. He means Man, and not a natural man or fallen Adam, but original man or unfallen Adam, which is to say America, in the transcendental sense, just as Blake's Albion is the unfallen form of Man. Emerson's primal Man, to whom Emerson is joined in this epiphany, is all eye, seeing earliest, precisely as though no European, and no ancient Greek or Hebrew, had seen before him. There is a personal pathos as well, which Emerson's contemporary readers could not have known. Emerson feared blindness more than death, although his family was tubercular and frequently died young. But there had been an episode of hysterical blindness during his college years, and its memory, however repressed, hovers throughout his work. Freud's difficult "frontier concept" of the bodily ego, which is formed partly by introjective fantasies, suggests that thinking can be associated with any of the senses or areas of the body. Emerson's fantastic introjection of the transparent eyeball as bodily ego seems to make thinking and seeing the same activity, one that culminated in self-deification.

Emerson's power as a kind of interior orator stems from this self-deification. Nothing is got for nothing, and perhaps the largest pragmatic consequence of being "part or particle of God" is that your need for other people necessarily is somewhat diminished. The transparent eyeball passage itself goes on to manifest an estrangement from the immediacy of other selves:

> The name of the nearest friend sounds then foreign and acci-
> dental: to be brothers, to be acquaintances, master or servant,
> is then a trifle and a disturbance.

This passage must have hurt Emerson himself, hardly a person for whom "to be brothers" ever was "a trifle and a disturbance." The early death of his brother Charles, just four months before *Nature* was published in 1836, was one of his three terrible losses, the others being the death of Ellen Tucker, his first wife, in 1831, after little more than a year of mar-riage, and the death of his first born child, Waldo, in January 1842, when the boy was only five years old. Emerson psychically was preternaturally strong, but it is difficult to interpret the famous passage in his great essay, "Experience," where he writes of Waldo's death:

> An innavigable sea washes with silent waves between us and the
> things we aim at and converse with. Grief too will make us ide-
> alists. In the death of my son, now more than two years ago, I
> seem to have lost a beautiful estate—no more. I cannot get it
> nearer to me. If tomorrow I should be informed of the bank-
> ruptcy of my principal debtors, the loss of my property would
> be a great inconvenience to me, perhaps, for many years; but it
> would leave me as it found me,—neither better nor worse. So
> is it with this calamity; it does not touch me; something which
> I fancied was a part of me, which could not be torn away with-
> out tearing me nor enlarged without enriching me, falls off
> from me and leaves no scar.

Perhaps Emerson should have written an essay entitled "The Economic Problem of Grief," but perhaps most of his essays carry that as a hidden subtitle. The enigma of grief in Emerson, after all, may be the secret cause of his strength, of his refusal to mourn for the past. Self-reliance, the American religion he founded, converts solitude into a firm stance against history, including personal history. That there is no history, only biography, is the Emersonian insistence, which may be why a valid biography of Emerson appears to be impossible. John McAleer's biography sets out shrewdly to evade the Emersonian entrapment, which is that Emerson knows only biography, a knowledge that makes personal history redundant. What then is the biographer of Emerson to do?

Such worthy practitioners of the mode as Ralph Rusk and Gay Wilson Allen worked mightily to shape the facts into a life, but are evaded by Emerson. Where someone lives so massively from within, he cannot be caught by chroniclers of events, public and private. McAleer instead molds his facts as a series of encounters between Emerson and all his friends and associates. Unfortunately, Emerson's encounters with others—whether his brothers, wives, children, or Transcendental and other literary colleagues, are little more revelatory of his inner life than are his encounters with events, whether it be the death of Waldo or the Civil War. All McAleer's patience, skill and learning cannot overcome the sage's genius for solitude. A biography of Emerson becomes as baffling as a biography of Nietzsche, though the two lives have nothing in common, except of course for ideas. Nietzsche acknowledged Emerson, with affection and enthusiasm, but he probably did not realize how fully Emerson had anticipated him, particularly in unsettling the status of the self while proclaiming simultaneously a greater overself to come.

III

The critic of Emerson is little better off than the biographer, since Emerson, again like Nietzsche and remarkably also akin to Freud, anticipates his critics and does their work for them. Emerson resembles his own hero, Montaigne, in that you cannot combat him without being contaminated by him. T.S. Eliot, ruefully contemplating Pascal's hopeless agon with Montaigne, observed that fighting Montaigne was like throwing a hand grenade into a fog. Emerson, because he appropriated America, is more like a climate than an atmosphere, however misty. Attempting to write the order of the variable winds in the Emersonian climate is a hopeless task, and the best critics of Emerson, from John Jay Chapman and O.W. Firkins through Stephen Whicher to Barbara Packer and Richard Poirier, wisely decline to list his ideas of order. You track him best, as writer and as person, by learning the principle proclaimed everywhere in him: that which you can get from another is never instruction, but always provocation.

But what is provocation, in the life of the spirit? Emerson insisted that he called you forth only to your self, and not to any cause whatsoever. The will to power, in Emerson as afterwards in Nietzsche, is reactive rather than active, receptive rather than rapacious, which is to say that it is a will to interpretation. Emerson teaches interpretation, but not in any of the European modes fashionable either in his day or in our own, modes currently touching their nadir in a younger rabblement celebrating itself as having repudiated the very idea of an individual reader or an individual critic. Group criticism, like group sex, is not a new idea, but seems to revive whenever a sense of resentment dominates the aspiring clerisy. With resentment comes guilt, as though societal oppressions are caused by how we read, and so we get those academic covens akin to what Emerson, in his 1838 journal, called "philanthropic meetings and holy hurrahs," for which read now "Marxist literary groups" and "Lacanian theory circles":

> As far as I notice what passes in philanthropic meetings and holy hurrahs there is very little depth of interest. The speakers warm each other's skin and lubricate each other's tongue, and the words flow and the superlatives thicken and the lips quiver and the eyes moisten, and an observer new to such scenes would say, Here was true fire; the assembly were all ready to be martyred, and the effect of such a spirit on the community would be irresistible; but they separate and go to the shop, to a dance, to bed, and an hour afterwards they care so little for the matter that on slightest temptation each one would disclaim the meeting.

Emerson, according to President Giamatti of Yale, "was as sweet as barbed wire," a judgment recently achieved independently by John Updike. Yes, and doubtless Emerson gave our politics its particular view of power, as Giamatti laments, but a country deserves its sages, and we deserve Emerson. He has the peculiar dialectical gift of being precursor for both the perpetual New Left of student non-students and the perpetual New Right of preacher non-preachers. The American Religion of Self-Reliance is a superb *literary* religion, but its political, economic and social consequences, whether manifested Left or Right, have now helped place us in a country where literary satire of politics is impossible, since the real thing is far more outrageous than even a satirist of genius could invent. Nathanael West presumably was parodying Calvin Coolidge in *A Cool Million*'s Shagpoke Whipple, but is this Shagpoke Whipple or President Reagan speaking?

> America is the land of opportunity. She takes care of the honest and industrious and never fails them as long as they are both. This is not a matter of opinion, it is one of faith. On the day that Americans stop believing it, on that day will America be lost.

Emerson unfortunately believed in Necessity, including "the offence of superiority in persons," and he was capable of writing passages that can help to justify Reagan's large share of the Yuppie vote, as here in "Self-Reliance":

> Then again, do not tell me, as a good man did today, of my obligation to put all poor men in good situations. Are they my poor? I tell thee, thou foolish philanthropist, that I grudge the dollar, the dime, the cent I give to such men as do not belong to me and to whom I do not belong. There is a class of persons to whom by all spiritual affinity I am bought and sold; for them I will go to prison if need be; but your miscellaneous popular charities; the education at college of fools; the building of meeting-houses to the vain end to which many now stand; alms to sots; and the thousand-fold Relief Societies;—though I confess with shame I sometimes succumb and give the dollar, it is a wicked dollar, which by and by I shall have the manhood to withhold.

True, Emerson meant by his "class of persons" men such as Henry Thoreau and Jones Very and the Reverend William Ellery Channing, which is not exactly Shagpoke Whipple, Ronald Reagan and the Reverend Jerry Falwell, but Self-Reliance translated out of the inner life and into the marketplace is difficult to distinguish from our current religion of selfishness, as set forth so sublimely in the recent grand epiphany at Dallas. Shrewd Yankee that he was, Emerson would have shrugged off his various and dubious paternities. His spiritual elitism could only be misunderstood, but he did not care much about being misread or misused. Though he has been so oddly called "the philosopher of democracy" by so many who wished to claim him for the Left, the political Emerson remains best expressed in one famous and remarkable sentence by John Jay Chapman: "If a soul be taken and crushed by democracy till it utter a cry, that cry will be Emerson."

IV

I return with some relief to Emerson as literary prophet, where Emerson's effect, *pace* Yvor Winters, seems to me again dialectical but in the end both benign and inevitable. Emerson's influence, from his day until ours, has helped to account for what I would call the American difference in literature, not only in our poetry and criticism, but even in our novels and stories—ironic since Emerson was at best uneasy about novels. What is truly surprising about this influence is its depth, extent and persistence, despite many concealments and even more evasions. Emerson does a lot more to explain most American writers than any of our writers; even Whitman or Thoreau or Dickinson or Hawthorne or Melville serve to explain *him*. The important question to ask is not "How?" but "Why?" Scholarship keeps showing the "how" (though there is a great deal more to be shown) but it ought to be a function of criticism to get at that scarcely explored "why."

Emerson was controversial in his own earlier years, and then became all but universally accepted (except, of course, in the South) during his later years. This ascendancy faded during the Age of Literary Modernism (*circa* 1915–1945) and virtually vanished, as I remarked earlier, in the heyday of academic New Criticism or Age of Eliot (*circa* 1945–1965). Despite the humanistic protests of President Giamatti, and the churchwardenly mewings of John Updike, the last two decades have witnessed an Emerson revival, and I prophesy that he, rather than Marx or Heidegger, will be the guiding spirit of our imaginative literature and our criticism for some time to come. In that prophecy, "Emerson" stands for not only the theoretical stance and wisdom of the historical Ralph Waldo, but for Nietzsche, Walter Pater and Oscar Wilde, and much of Freud as well, since Emerson's elitist vision of the higher individual is so consonant with theirs. Individualism, whatever damages its American ruggedness continues to inflict on our politics and social economy, is more than ever the only hope for our imaginative lives. Emerson, who knew that the only literary and critical method was oneself, is again a necessary resource in a time beginning to weary of Gallic scientism in what are still called the Humanities.

Lewis Mumford, in *The Golden Day* (1926), still is the best guide as to why Emerson was and is the central influence upon American letters: "With most of the resources of the past at his command, Emerson achieved nakedness." Wisely seeing that Emerson was a Darwinian before Darwin, a Freudian before Freud, because he possessed "a complete vision," Mumford was able to make the classic formulation as to Emerson's strength: "The past for Emerson was neither a prescription nor a burden: it was rather an esthetic experience." As a poem already written, the past was not a force for Emerson; it had lost power, because power for him resided only at the crossing, at the actual moment of transition.

The dangers of this repression of the past's force are evident enough, in American life as in its literature. In our political economy, we get the force of secondary repetition; Reagan as Coolidge out-Shagpoking Nathanael West's Whipple. We receive also the rhythm of ebb and flow that makes all our greater writers into crisis-poets. Each of them echoes, however involuntarily, Emerson's formula for discontinuity in his weird, irrealistic essay, "Circles":

> Our moods do not believe in each other. Today I am full of thoughts and can write what I please. I see no reason why I should not have the same thought, the same power of expression, tomorrow. What I write, whilst I write it, seems the most natural thing in the world; but yesterday I saw a dreary vacuity in this direction in which now I see so much; and a month hence, I doubt not, I shall wonder who he was that wrote so many continuous pages. Alas for this infirm faith, this will not strenuous, this vast ebb of a vast flow! I am God in nature; I am a weed by the wall.

From God to weed and then back again; it is the cycle of Whitman from "Song of Myself" to "As I Ebb'd with the Ocean of Life," and of Emerson's and Whitman's descendants ever since. Place everything upon the nakedness of the American self, and you open every imaginative possibility from self-deification to absolute nihilism. But Emerson knew this, and saw no alternative for us if we were to avoid the predicament of arriving too late in the cultural history of the West. Nothing is got for nothing; Emerson is not less correct now than he was 150 years ago. On November 21, 1834, he wrote in his journal: "When we have lost our God of tradition and ceased from our God of rhetoric then may God fire the heart with his presence." Our God of tradition, then and now, is as dead as Emerson and Nietzsche declared him to be. He belongs, in life, to the political clerics and the clerical politicians and, in letters, to the secondary men and women. Our God of rhetoric belongs to the academies, where he is called by the name of the Gallic Demiurge, Language. That leaves the American imagination free as always to open itself to the third God of Emerson's prayer.

Søren Kierkegaard

(1813-1855)

WHAT KIERKEGAARD CALLED "REPETITION" IS WHAT ANY OF US EXPERIENCES when we will to take yet again a possibility believed to have transcendental aspects. That is dangerously close to the perpetual self-deception most of us call "falling in love," so that you can reduce Kierkegaard's "repetition" to the Freudian repetition-compulsion of the Death Drive, if that reduction pleases you. Like Freud, Kierkegaard is a great erotic ironist, but that is all these two great consciousnesses share. "Irony is an abnormal growth ... it ends by killing the individual." That Kierkegaardian realization divides the two repetitions, and allows the Danish thinker to praise the married man who has been faithful as the true hero of his repetition: "He solves the great riddle of living in eternity and yet hearing the hall clock strike, and hearing it in such a way that the stroke of the hour does not shorten but prolongs his eternity."

Such "repetition" is an ironical revision of the Hegelian trope of "mediation." If Hegel's Christ is the great mediator, then Kierkegaard's Christ is the master of repetition, of a scene in which we are instructed in repetition. Kierkegaard, to me, is less a religious writer than he is a poetic speculator, and one of the crucial areas of his speculation is the process of instruction. I do not mean that Kierkegaard was interested primarily in speculative philosophy, which for him meant Hegel's speculative mediation. Rather, the truly speculative enterprise was the immense difficulty of becoming a Christian in a society ostensibly Christian. Becoming a Christian was for Kierkegaard as perpetual an *agon* as becoming a strong poet was for Keats. For teachers, Keats was found by Wordsworth, Milton, and Shakespeare. Kierkegaard, seeking an even more rugged originality, was found mostly by himself, and by Christ, the only absolute founder of a Scene of Instruction.

I turn to Kierkegaard as the great theorist of the Scene of Instruction, particularly in his brilliantly polemical text, the *Philosophical Fragments* (1844). The title page of this short book asks the splendid triple question: "Is an historical point of departure possible for an eternal consciousness; how can such a point of departure have any other than a merely historical interest; is it possible to base an eternal happiness upon historical knowledge." Kierkegaard's intent is to refute Hegel by severely dividing Christianity from Idealist philosophy, but his triple question is perfectly applicable to the secular paradox of poetic incarnation and poetic influence. For the anxiety of influence stems from the ephebe's assertion of an eternal, divinating consciousness that nevertheless took its historical point of departure in an intratextual encounter, and most crucially in the interpretative moment or act of misprision contained in that encounter. How indeed, the ephebe must wonder, can such a point of departure have more than merely historical rather than poetic interest? More anxiously, even, how is the strong poet's claim to poetic immortality (the only eternal happiness that is relevant) to be founded upon an encounter trapped belatedly in time?

Two sections of the *Fragments* are closest to the dilemmas of the poetic Scene of Instruction. These are the essay of the imagination called "The God as Teacher and Savior," and the ingenious chapter called "The Case of the Contemporary Disciple." The first is a concealed polemic against Strauss and Feuerbach as left-wing Hegelians, and the second is an overt polemic against Hegel himself. Against left-wing Hegelianism, Kierkegaard contrasts Socrates as a teacher with the Christ. Socrates and his student have nothing to teach one another, no *davhar* or word to bring forward, yet each provides the other with a means towards self-understanding. But the Christ understands himself without the aid of students, and his students are there only to receive his incommensurable love. Against Hegel, Kierkegaard separates history from Necessity, for Christian truth is not a human possession, as Hegelian Idealism would believe. The contemporary disciple of the God as teacher and savior "was not contemporary with the splendor, neither hearing nor seeing anything of it." There is no immediacy by which one can be a contemporary of a divinity; the paradox of the peculiarly Kierkegaardian variety of "repetition" is at work here, and by an exploration of such repetition we can displace Kierkegaard's polemical wit into a speculation upon the Scene of Instruction, and simultaneously expose again an inadequacy in Freud's account of the compulsion to repeat, and that compulsion's relations to origins.

Repetition, in Kierkegaard, goes back at least to theses XII and XIII of his Master of Arts dissertation, *The Concept of Irony* (1841). Thesis XII smacks at Hegel for defining irony while considering only the modern but not so much the ancient Socratic form. Thesis XIII, also directed against Hegel, is one of the founding apothegms for any study of poetic misprision:

> Irony is not so much apathy, divested of all tender emotions of the soul; instead, it is more like vexation over the fact that others also enjoy what it desires for itself.

True repetition, for Kierkegaard, is eternity, and so only true repetition can save one from the vexation of irony. But this is an eternity in time, "the daily bread which satisfies with benediction." Indeed, this is the center of Kierkegaard's vision, and necessarily also of *his* anxiety of influence in regard to his reviled precursor, Hegel, for Kierkegaard's "repetition" is a substitute trope for Hegel's trope of "mediation," the process of dialectic itself. Kierkegaard's dialectic, by being more internalized, is doomed to even more subjectivity, a limitation that Kierkegaard characteristically sought to represent as a philosophical advance. If repetition is primarily a dialectical reaffirmation of the continued possibility of becoming a Christian, then its aesthetic displacement would reaffirm dialectically the continued possibility of becoming a poet. No contemporary disciple of a great poet then could be truly his precursor's contemporary, for the splendor is necessarily *deferred*. It can be reached through the mediation of repetition, by a return to origins and the incommensurable Election-love that the Primal Scene of Instruction can bestow, there at the point of origin. Poetic repetition repeats a Primal repression, a repression that is itself a fixation upon the precursor as teacher and savior, or on the poetic father as mortal god. The compulsion to repeat the precursor's patterns is not a movement beyond the pleasure principle to an inertia of poetic pre-incarnation, to a Blakean Beulah where no dispute can come, but rather is an attempt to recover the prestige of origins, the oral authority of a prior Instruction. Poetic repetition quests, despite itself, for the mediated vision of the fathers, since such mediation holds open the perpetual possibility of one's own sublimity, one's election to the realm of true Instructors.

But was there a mediated vision of the fathers for Kierkegaard himself? The answer, alas, can only be Hegel, the inventor of mediation. Kierkegaard was not Schopenhauer or Emerson or Nietzsche, who were what they would have been had Hegel never written a sentence or delivered a lecture. Rather, Kierkegaard was post-Hegelian as we are post-Freudian; there is no other option for us. Freud is there, making us belated, writing commentaries upon him, whether we wish it or not. Hegel would have made Kierkegaard belated, but like Emerson and Nietzsche the Danish speculator refused to be a secondary man. The modes of creative misinterpretation are numerous, and most of them reduce to ironies. "Repetition" ironically was Kierkegaard's path out of irony, lest he fall into the irony of irony, and so lose all invention. Kierkegaard's most inventive moment nevertheless is necessarily an irony, in which "the moment" is destroyed, and the idea of contemporaneity dies forever. That is the authentic literary achievement of "The Case of the Contemporary Disciple," since it demonstrates that true passion is always for the past, that only the past can be a poet's or a Christian's lover. The future belongs to repetition, to a marriage with what one has made, to a constructed joy. The past was a spontaneous joy, and spontaneity is not the taking up again of possibility one has taken up before, and always must take up again. Authentic passion, delirium of the senses, excludes the future, in Kierkegaard and in Kafka, his legitimate son.

Kierkegaard became one of the strongest modern poets at a very high price, again like Kafka, or like Nietzsche. Creative misreading needs to sacrifice the present moment, because the Scene of Instruction depends upon placing all love in the past. Kierkegaard puts this slyly: "Love is presupposing love; to have love is to presuppose love in others; to be loving is to presuppose that others are loving." And yet: "If there were no repetition, what then would life be? Who would wish to be a tablet upon which time writes every instant a new inscription? or be a mere memorial of the past?"

Kierkegaard's Nebuchadnezzar, recollecting when he was a beast and ate grass, mused upon the God of the Hebrews, and understood that only this Mighty One was free of the Scene of Instruction. Speaking for Kierkegaard, Nebuchadnezzar teaches us where creative misreading has touched its limit, and where the difficulty of becoming a Christian at last is resolved: "And no one knoweth anything of Him, who was His father, and how He acquired His power, and who taught Him the secret of His might."

Henry David Thoreau

(1817–1862)

ALL OF US, HOWEVER IDIOSYNCRATIC, BEGIN BY LIVING IN A GENERATION that overdetermines more of our stances and judgments than we can hope to know, until we are far along in the revisionary processes that can bring us to a Second Birth. I myself read *Walden* while I was very young, and "Civil Disobedience" and "Life without Principle" soon afterwards. But I read little or no Emerson until I was an undergraduate, and achieved only a limited awareness of him then. I began to read Emerson obsessively just before the middle of the journey, when in crisis, and have never stopped reading him since. More even than Freud, Emerson helped change my mind about most things, in life and in literature, myself included. Going back to Thoreau, when one has been steeped in Emerson for more than twenty years, is a curious experience. A distinguished American philosopher, my contemporary, has written that he underwent the reverse process, coming to Emerson only after a profound knowing of Thoreau, and has confessed that Emerson seemed to him at first a "second-rate Thoreau." I am not tempted to call Thoreau a second-rate Emerson, because Thoreau, at his rare best, was a strong writer, and revised Emerson with passion and with cunning. But Emerson was for Thoreau even more massively what he was for Walt Whitman and all Americans of sensibility ever since: the metaphor of "the father," the pragmatic image of the ego ideal, the inescapable precursor, the literary hero, the mind of the United States of America.

My own literary generation had to recover Emerson, because we came after the critics formed by the example and ideology of T.S. Eliot, who had proclaimed that "the essays of Emerson are already an encumbrance." I can recall conversations about Emerson with R.P. Blackmur, who informed me that Emerson was of no relevance, except insofar as he represented an extreme example for America of the unsupported and cata-strophic Protestant sensibility, which had ruined the Latin culture of Europe. Allen Tate more succinctly told me that Emerson simply was the devil, a judgment amplified in my single conversation with the vigorous Yvor Winters. In many years of friendship with Robert Penn Warren, my only disputes with that great poet have concerned Emerson, upon whom Warren remains superbly obdurate. As these were the critical minds that dominated American letters from 1945 to 1965 (except for Lionel Trilling, who was silent on Emerson), it is no surprise that Emerson vanished in that era. From 1965 through the present, Emerson has returned, as he always must and will, because he is the pragmatic origin of our literary culture. Walt Whitman and Emily Dickinson, Robert Frost and Wallace Stevens, Hart Crane, Elizabeth Bishop and John Ashbery have written the poems of our climate, but Emerson was and is that climate.

How does Thoreau now read in our recovered sense of the Emersonian climate? Is the question itself unfair? Rereading *Walden* and the major essays, I confess to an experience different in degree, but not in kind, from a fresh encounter with Thoreau's verse. As a poet, Thoreau is in the shadow of Wordsworth, towards whom his apotropaic gestures are sadly weak. In prose, conceptually and rhetorically, Thoreau strongly seeks to evade Emerson, wherever he cannot revise him directly. But this endless agon, unlike Whitman's, or the subtler subversion of Emerson by Dickinson and by Henry James, is won by the image of the father. Rereading Thoreau, either I hear Emerson overtly, or more darkly I detect him in what Stevens called "the hum of thoughts evaded in the mind."

II

During that 1945–1965 heyday of what then was called "the New Criticism," only *Walden*, among all of Thoreau's works, was exempt from censure. I have never understood the New Critical tolerance for *Walden*, except as a grudging bit of cultural patriotism, or perhaps as a kind of ulti-mate act of revenge against Emerson, the prophet who organized support for John Brown, cast out Daniel Webster because of the Fugitive Slave Act, and burned himself into a premature senility by his fierce contempt for the South and its culture throughout the Civil War. Thoreau, no less an enthusiast for John Brown, and equally apocalyptic against the South, somehow escaped the wrath of Tate, Warren, and their cohorts. This may have something to do with the myth of Thoreau as a kind of American Mahatma Gandhi, a Tolstoyan hermit practicing native arts and crafts out in the woods. Homespun and reputedly naive, such a fellow may have seemed harmless enough, unlike the slyly wicked Sage of Concord, Ralph Waldo Lucifer, impediment to the United States somehow acquiring a Southern and Latin culture.

The merely actual Thoreau has been so prettified that one does best to begin a consideration of the man with the opening paragraphs of Leon Edel's pungent pamphlet, in which an amiable disenchantment with our American Narcissus is memorably expressed:

> Of the creative spirits that flourished in Concord, Massachusetts, during the middle of the nineteenth century, it might be said that Hawthorne loved men but felt estranged from them, Emerson loved ideas more than men, and Thoreau loved himself. Less of an artist than Hawthorne, less of a thinker than Emerson, Thoreau made of his life a sylvan legend, that of man alone, in communion with nature. He was a strange presence in American letters—we have so few of them—an eccentric. The English tend to tolerate their eccentrics to the enrichment of their national life. In America, where democracy and conformity are often confused, the non-conforming Thoreau was frowned upon, and for good reason. He had a disagreeable and often bellicose nature. He lacked geniality. And then he had once set fire to the Concord woods—a curious episode, too lightly dismissed in the Thoreau biographies. He was, in the fullest sense of the word, a "curmudgeon," and literary history has never sufficiently studied the difficulties his neighbors had in adjusting themselves to certain of his childish ways. But in other ways he was a man of genius—even if it was a "crooked genius" as he himself acknowledged.
>
> A memorable picture has been left by Hawthorne's daughter of the three famous men of Concord skating one winter's afternoon on the river. Hawthorne, wrapped in his cloak, "moved like a self-impelled Greek statue, stately and grave," as one might expect of the future author of *The Marble Faun*. Emerson, stoop-shouldered, "evidently too weary to hold himself erect," pitched forward, "half lying on the air." Thoreau, genuinely skillful on his skates, performed "dithyrambic dances and Bacchic leaps," enchanted with himself. Their manner, of skating was in accord with their personalities and temperaments.
>
> Behind a mask of self-exaltation Thoreau performed as

before a mirror—and first of all for his own edification. He was a fragile Narcissus embodied in a homely New Englander. His life was brief. He was born in 1817, in Concord; he lived in Concord, and he died in Concord in 1862 shortly after the guns had spoken at Fort Sumter. A child of the romantic era, he tried a number of times to venture forth into the world. He went to Maine, to Staten Island, to Cape Cod, and ultimately to Minnesota, in search of health, but he always circled back to the Thoreau family house in Concord and to the presence of a domineering and loquacious mother. No other man with such wide-ranging thoughts and a soaring mind—it reached to ancient Greece, to the Ganges, to the deepest roots of England and the Continent—bound himself to so small a strip of ground. "He was worse than provincial," the cosmopolitan Henry James remarked, "he was parochial."

Edel's Jamesian slight can be dismissed, since Edel is James's devoted biographer, but the rest of this seems charmingly accurate. The great conservationist who set fire to the Concord woods; the epitome of Emersonian Self-Reliance who sneaked back from Walden in the evening to be fed dinner by Lidian Emerson; the man in whom Walt Whitman (whom Thoreau admired greatly, as man and as poet) found "a morbid dislike of humanity"—that, alas, was the empirical Thoreau, as contrasted to the ontological self of Thoreau. Since, to this day, Thoreau's self-mystifications continue to mystify nearly all of Thoreau's scholars, I find myself agreeing with Edel's judgment that the best discussions of Thoreau continue to be those of Emerson, James Russell Lowell, and Robert Louis Stevenson. Magnificent (and subtly balanced) as Emerson's funeral eulogy is, and brilliant as Lowell's much-derided essay continues to be, the best single remark on Thoreau remains Stevenson's: "It was not inappropriate, surely, that he had such close relations with the fish."

Lowell, sympathetic enough to Emerson, had little imagination to countenance the even more extreme disciple, Thoreau:

This notion of an absolute originality, as if one could have a patent-right in it, is an absurdity. A man cannot escape in thought, any more than he can in language, from the past and the present. As no one ever invents a word, and yet language somehow grows by general contribution and necessity, so it is with thought. Mr. Thoreau seems to me to insist in public on going back to flint and steel, when there is a match-box in his pocket which he knows very well how to use at a pinch. Originality consists in power of digesting and assimilating thoughts, so that they become part of our life and substance. Montaigne, for example, is one of the most original of authors, though he helped himself to ideas in every direction. But they turn to blood and coloring in his style, and give a freshness of complexion that is forever charming. In Thoreau much seems yet to be foreign and unassimilated, showing itself in symptoms of indigestion. A preacher-up of Nature, we now and then detect under the surly and stoic garb something of the sophist and the sentimentalizer. I am far from implying that this was conscious on his part. But it is much easier for a man to impose on himself when he measures only with himself. A greater familiarity with ordinary men would have done Thoreau good, by showing him how many fine qualities are common to the race. The radical vice of his theory of life was that he confounded physical with spiritual remoteness from men. A man is far enough withdrawn from his fellows if he keep himself clear of their weaknesses. He is not so truly withdrawn as exiled, if he refuse to share their strength. "Solitude," says Cowley, "can be well fitted and set right but upon a very few persons. They must have enough knowledge of the world to see the vanity of it, and enough virtue to despise all vanity." It is a morbid self-consciousness that pronounces the world of men empty and worthless before trying it, the instinctive evasion of one who is sensible of some innate weakness, and retorts the accusation of it before any has made it but himself. To a healthy mind, the world is a constant challenge of opportunity. Mr. Thoreau had not a healthy mind, or he would not have been so fond of prescribing. His whole life was a search for the doctor. The old mystics had a wiser sense of what the world was worth. They ordained a severe apprenticeship to law, and even ceremonial, in order to the gaining of freedom and mastery over these. Seven years of service for Rachel were to be rewarded at last with Leah. Seven other years of faithfulness with her were to win them at last the true bride of their souls. Active Life was with them the only path to the Contemplative.

It is curious that Lowell should have directed this attack upon Emersonian Self-Reliance at the disciple, not the master, yet Lowell, as he shows abundantly in his fine essay "Emerson the Lecturer," was overcome by the great lecturer's charisma, his mysterious but nearly universally acknowledged personal charm. Even Lowell's argument against Transcendentalist "solitude" would have been better directed against the author of *Society and Solitude* than the recalcitrant author of *Walden*. Lowell's essay survives, despite its unfairness, because of its accuracy, and even because of its ultimate judgment of Thoreau.

> We have said that his range was narrow, but to be a master is to be a master. He had caught his English at its living source, among the poets and prose-writers of its best days; his literature was extensive and recondite; his quotations are always nuggets of the purest ore: there are sentences of his as perfect as anything in the language, and thoughts as clearly crystallized; his metaphors and images are always fresh from the soil; he had watched Nature like a detective who is to go upon the stand; as we read him, it seems as if all-out-of-doors had kept a diary and become its own Montaigne.

To be the Montaigne of all-out-of-doors ought to have been distinction enough for anyone, yet Emerson confessed that he had hoped for more from this rugged and difficult disciple:

> His virtues, of course, sometimes ran into extremes. It was easy to trace to the inexorable demand on all for exact truth that austerity which made this willing hermit more solitary even than he wished. Himself of a perfect probity, he required not less of others. He had a disgust at crime, and no worldly success would cover it. He detected paltering as readily in dignified and prosperous persons as in beggars, and with equal scorn. Such dangerous frankness was in his dealing that his admirers called him "that terrible Thoreau," as if he spoke when silent, and was still present when he had departed. I think the severity of his ideal interfered to deprive him of a healthy sufficiency of human society.
>   The habit of a realist to find things the reverse of their appearance inclined him to put every statement in a paradox. A certain habit of antagonism defaced his earlier writings,—a trick of rhetoric not quite outgrown in his later, of substituting for the obvious word and thought its diametrical opposite. He praised wild mountains and winter forests for their domestic air, in snow and ice he would find sultriness, and commended

the wilderness for resembling Rome and Paris. "It was so dry, that you might call it wet."

The tendency to magnify the moment, to read all the laws of Nature in the one object or one combination under your eye, is of course comic to those who do not share the philosopher's perception of identity. To him there was no such thing as size. The pond was a small ocean; the Atlantic, a large Walden Pond. He referred every minute fact to cosmical laws. Though he meant to be just, he seemed haunted by a certain chronic assumption that the science of the day pretended completeness, and he had just found out that the *savans* had neglected to discriminate a particular botanical variety, had failed to describe the seeds or count the sepals. "That is to say," we replied, "the blockheads were not born in Concord; but who said they were? It was their unspeakable misfortune to be born in London, or Paris, or Rome; but, poor fellows, they did what they could, considering that they never saw Bateman's Pond, or Nine-Acre Corner, or Becky Stow's Swamp; besides, what were you sent into the world for, but to add this observation?"

Had his genius been only contemplative, he had been fitted to his life, but with his energy and practical ability he seemed born for great enterprise and for command; and I so much regret the loss of his rare powers of action, that I cannot help counting it a fault in him that he had no ambition. Wanting this, instead of engineering for all America, he was the captain of a huckleberry-party. Pounding beans is good to the end of pounding empires one of these days; but if, at the end of years, it is still only beans!

Emerson's ironies are as beautiful here as anywhere, and their dialectical undersong is wholly in Thoreau's favor. Henry Ford, a fervent and overt Emersonian, engineered for all America; and clearly Emerson himself, like many among us, would have preferred Thoreau to Ford, and a huckleberry-party to a car factory.

III

Thoreau's crucial swerve away from Emerson was to treat natural objects as books, and books as chunks of nature, thus evading all literary tradition, Emerson's writings not excepted. Unfortunately, Thoreau was not really an oppositional or dialectical thinker, like Emerson, though certain an oppositional personality, as the sane and sacred Emerson was not. Being also something of a prig and an elitist, again unlike Emerson, Thoreau could not always manage Emerson's insouciant praxis of building up a kind of Longinian discourse by quoting amply without citation. Self-consciousness kept breaking in, as it rarely does with Emerson, unless Emerson wills it thus. But, if you cannot achieve freedom in quotation, if you cannot convert the riches of others to your own use without a darkening of consciousness, then what can it mean to demand that books and natural objects interchange their attributes? *Walden*, for all its incessant power, is frequently uneasy because of an unspoken presence, or a perpetual absence that might as well be a presence, and that emerges in Thoreau's Journal:

> Emerson does not consider things in respect to their essential utility, but an important partial and relative one, as works of art perhaps. His probes pass one side of their center of gravity. His exaggeration is of a part, not of the whole.

This is, of course, to find the fault that is not there, and qualifies only as a weak misreading of Emerson. Indeed, it is to attribute to Emerson what is actually Thoreau's revision of Emerson, since it is Thoreau who considers things as books, not Emerson, for whom a fact was an epiphany of God, God being merely what was oldest in oneself, that which went back before the Creation-Fall. Emerson, like the considerably less genial Carlyle, was a kind of Gnostic, but the rebel Thoreau remained a Wordsworthian, reading nature for evidences of a continuity in the ontological self that nature simply could not provide.

Thoreau on "Reading" in *Walden* is therefore chargeable with a certain bad faith, as here in a meditation where Emerson, the Plato of Concord, is not less than everywhere, present by absence, and perhaps even more absent by repressed presence:

> I aspire to be acquainted with wiser men than this our Concord soil has produced, whose names are hardly known here. Or shall I hear the name of Plato and never read his book? As if Plato were my townsman and I never saw him,—my next neighbor and I never heard him speak or attended to the wisdom of his words. But how actually is it? His Dialogues, which contain what was immortal in him, lie on the next shelf, and yet I never read them. We are under-bred and low-lived and illiterate; and in this respect I confess I do not make any very broad

distinction between the illiterateness of my townsman who cannot read at all, and the illiterateness of him who has learned to read only what is for children and feeble intellects. We should be as good as the worthies of antiquity, but partly by first knowing how good they were. We are a race of tit-men, and soar but little higher in our intellectual flights than the columns of the daily paper.

It is not all books that are as dull as their readers. There are probably words addressed to our condition exactly, which, if we could really hear and understand, would be more salutary than the morning or the spring to our lives, and possibly put a new aspect on the face of things for us. How many a man has dated a new era in his life from the reading of a book. The book exists for us perchance which will explain our miracles and reveal new ones. The at present unutterable things we may find somewhere uttered. These same questions that disturb and puzzle and confound us have in their turn occurred to all the wise men; not one has been omitted; and each has answered them, according to his ability, by his words and his life. Moreover, with wisdom we shall learn liberality. The solitary hired man on a farm in the outskirts of Concord, who has had his second birth and peculiar religious experience, and is driven as he believes into silent gravity and exclusiveness by his faith, may think it is not true; but Zoroaster, thousands of years ago, travelled the same road and had the same experience; but he, being wise, knew it to be universal, and treated his neighbors accordingly, and is even said to have invented and established worship among men. Let him humbly commune with Zoroaster then, and, through the liberalizing influence of all the worthies, with Jesus Christ himself, and let "our church" go by the board.

The wisest man our Concord soil has produced need not be named, particularly since he vied only with Thoreau as a devoted reader of Plato. The second paragraph I have quoted rewrites the "Divinity School Address," but with the characteristic Thoreauvian swerve towards the authority of books, rather than away from them in the Emersonian manner. The reader or student, according to Emerson, is to consider herself or himself the text, and all received texts only as commentaries upon the scholar of one candle, as the title-essay of *Society and Solitude* prophesies Wallace Stevens in naming that single one for whom all books are written. It may be the greatest literary sorrow of Thoreau that he could assert his independence from Emerson only by falling back upon the authority of texts, however recondite or far from the normative the text might be.

One can read Thoreau's continued bondage in *Walden*'s greatest triumph, its preternaturally eloquent "Conclusion":

> The life in us is like the water in the river. It may rise this year higher than man has ever known it, and flood the parched uplands; even this may be the eventful year, which will drown out all our muskrats. It was not always dry land where we dwell. I see far inland the banks which the stream anciently washed, before science began to record its freshets. Every one has heard the story which has gone the rounds of New England, of a strong and beautiful bug which came out of the dry leaf of an old table of apple-tree wood, which had stood in a farmer's kitchen for sixty years, first in Connecticut, and afterwards in Massachusetts,—from an egg deposited in the living tree many years earlier still, as appeared by counting the annual layers beyond it; which was heard gnawing out for several weeks, hatched perchance by the heat of an urn. Who does not feel his faith in a resurrection and immortality strengthened by hearing of this? Who knows what beautiful and winged life, whose egg has been buried for ages under many concentric layers of woodenness in the dead dry life of society, deposited at first in the alburnum of the green and living tree, which has been gradually converted into the semblance of its well-seasoned tomb,—heard perchance gnawing out now for years by the astonished family of man, as they sat round the festive board,—may unexpectedly come forth from amidst society's most trivial and handselled furniture, to enjoy its perfect summer life at last!
>
> I do not say that John or Jonathan will realize all this; but such is the character of that morrow which mere lapse of time can never make to dawn. The light which puts out our eyes is darkness to us. Only that day dawns to which we are awake. There is more day to dawn. The sun is but a morning star.

The first of these paragraphs echoes, perhaps unknowingly, several crucial metaphors in the opening pages of Emerson's strongest single essay, "Experience," but more emphatically Thoreau subverts Emerson's emphasis upon a Transcendental impulse that cannot be repressed, even if one sets out deliberately to perform the experiment of "Experience," which is to follow empirical principles until they land one in an intolerable, more than skeptical, even nihilistic entrapment. Emerson, already more-than-Nietzschean in "Experience," is repudiated in and by the desperately energetic, indeed apocalyptic Transcendentalism of the end of *Walden*, an end that refuses Emersonian (and Nietzschean) dialectical irony. But the beautiful, brief final paragraph of *Walden* brings back Emerson anyway, with an unmistakable if doubtless involuntary allusion to the rhapsodic conclusion of *Nature*, where however the attentive reader always will hear (or over-hear) some acute Emersonian ironies. "Try to live as though it were morning" was Nietzsche's great admonition to us, if we were to become Overmen, free of the superego. Nietzsche was never more Emersonian than in this, as he well knew. But when Thoreau eloquently cries out: "The sun is but a morning star," he is not echoing but trying to controvert Emerson's sardonic observation that you don't get a candle in order to see the sun rise. There may indeed be a sun beyond the sun, as Blake, D.H. Lawrence, and other heroic vitalists have insisted, but Thoreau was too canny, perhaps too New England, to be a vitalist. *Walden* rings out mightily as it ends, but it peals another man's music, a man whom Thoreau could neither accept nor forget.

John Ruskin

(1819-1900)

—But there's a Tree, of many, one,
A single Field which I have looked upon,
Both of them speak of something that it gone:
The Pansy at my feet
Doth the same tale repeat:
Whither is fled the visionary gleam?
Where is it now, the glory and the dream?

RUSKIN WAS BORN IN LONDON, ON 8 FEBRUARY 1819, IN THE SAME YEAR
that Queen Victoria was born. His father, John James Ruskin, the son of a
bankrupt, self-slain Edinburgh wine merchant, had prospered in partner-
ship with the Domecq sherry vineyards, and aspired to raise himself out of
his lower middle class position, though he was forced to put aside artistic
and literary interests while he made his fortune. Ruskin's mother, Margaret
Cox, was John James Ruskin's cousin, and had waited nine years to marry
him, while he made his way in London. Energetic and shrewd as John
James Ruskin was, he appears to have been a weaker character than his
fiercely Evangelical wife, whose rigid nature dominated the formative years
of her only child's life, and who clearly was responsible for the psychic mal-
forming that made John Ruskin's emotional life a succession of disasters.
Margaret Ruskin, before her son's birth, dedicated him to the service of
God, intending him for the ministry. Nature intended otherwise, and made
even of the infant Ruskin an aesthetic visionary, fascinated by the world of
form and color. The world of language was revealed to the child, between
the ages of four and fourteen, by daily Bible readings with his mother. That
ten-year march and countermarch through the Book made Ruskin as Bible-
soaked a writer as Milton or Blake, and formed the ultimate basis for the

characteristic Ruskinian prose style, with its ornate and opulent diction, prophetic rhythm, and extraordinary emotional range.

Ruskin had the misfortune to be a child prodigy, as forced a one as John Stuart Mill. A poet at seven, educated largely at home, scarcely allowed friends, brooded over by a sternly loving mother and a totally indulgent and admiring father, Ruskin was ruined before his thirteenth birthday. He was ruined, one qualifies, in terms of his fully human potential, but not at all in regard to the unique gift that was his, and that his peculiar upbringing did much to nourish.

On his thirteenth birthday, Ruskin received the present of a copy of Samuel Rogers's long poem Italy, richly illustrated with steel engravings, including twenty-five plates from drawings by J.M.W. Turner. Immediately captured by Turner, Ruskin was to become an artist under this influence, but his painting like his poetry finally proved marginal, and the lasting effect of Turner was to confirm a critical gift of genius. As a critic of all the arts and of society, Ruskin became, and still remains, a unique figure in the European cultural tradition. This uniqueness was finally a uniqueness of sensibility, and cannot be understood apart from the history of sensibility.

The natural world Ruskin saw was half-created by his Romantic vision, a vision for which his personal sensibility provided the beginnings, but in which his great and essential teachers were Wordsworth and Turner, the dominant figures in the poetry and painting of their generation. Like Shelley before him, Ruskin was haunted throughout his life by Wordsworth's great "Ode: Intimations of Immortality from Recollections of Earliest Childhood." The fundamental experience of the Ode, and of "Tintern Abbey," is at one with the central and decisive experiences of Ruskin's life. Attempting to describe the unifying element in Ruskin's complex religious development, Derrick Leon, perhaps unintentionally, paraphrased "Tintern Abbey":

> Ruskin's real communion, throughout his life, was the communion of the artist and poet: his *panis supersubstantialis* those rare moments of fully awakened consciousness when the mind is detached and deliberately at rest; when the usual egotism of being is deliberately suppressed, and the emotional faculties, cleansed of all human desire and sorrow, respond in serenity and joy to the mystery and beauty of the external world.

In his old age, Ruskin looked back at his essential character as a child, and recognized again his affinity to Turner, Wordsworth, and Shelley, though he did not hesitate to give the preference to himself, the failed poet, over those who had succeeded:

> I was different, be it once more said, from other children even of my own type, not so much in the actual nature of the feeling, but in the mixture of it. I had, in my little clay pitcher, vialfuls, as it were, of Wordsworth's reverence, Shelley's sensitiveness, Turner's accuracy, all in one. A snowdrop was to me, as to Wordsworth, part of the Sermon on the mount; but I never should have written sonnets to the celandine, because it is of a coarse, yellow and imperfect form. With Shelley, I loved blue sky and blue eyes, but never in the least confused the heavens with my own poor little Psychidion. And the reverence and passion were alike kept in their places by the constructive Turnerian element; and I did not weary myself in wishing that a daisy could see the beauty of its shadow, but in trying to draw the shadow rightly, myself.

This self-congratulatory paragraph tells us why Wordsworth and Shelley were poets, and Ruskin only a critic, albeit a great one. Reverence, sensitiveness, and accuracy, taken together, are the theological virtues for criticism, but the combination can thwart creation. Ruskin, at the age of nine, was a better poet than Ruskin at twenty, when he won the Newdigate Prize at Oxford. At nine, Ruskin wrote good Wordsworthian verse, better perhaps than Wordsworth was writing in 1828:

> Skiddaw, upon thy heights the sun shines bright,
> But only for a moment; then gives place
> Unto a playful cloud which on thy brow
> Sports wantonly,—then floats away in air,—
> Throwing its shadow on thy towering height;
> And, darkening for a moment thy green side,
> But adds unto its beauty, as it makes
> The sun more bright when it again appears.

But, by 1839, Ruskin's imagination had not the patience to wait upon the restraints of verse. He knew the truth, or many divisions of it, and he sought the prophet's style in which to deliver it. Fortunately, the truth always remained a poet's truth, and relied on the sources of visionary experience, known to Ruskin from his childhood on, and confirmed in him by his discovery of the visual equivalent in Turner's work.

Ruskin's life, from the revelation of Turner on to his disastrous marriage, was a continuous process of self-discovery, assured and "organic" in its development. Foreign tours, with his parents, encouraged his passion for close observation of nature, for the study of geology and botany, and for incessant sketching and versifying. Even his unreciprocated first love, for Adele Domecq, daughter of his father's business partner, created no more disturbance than could be quieted by an outpouring of much pseudo-Byronic verse. The closeness of the family-circle was not affected by his studies at Christ Church, Oxford, from January 1837 on, as Mrs. Ruskin imperturbably settled in that city and required her son to appear for tea every evening, with Ruskin's father hastening to join them from London every weekend. Despite the family presence, Ruskin had a successful career at Oxford, composing his first book, *The Poetry of Architecture*, while still an undergraduate. But an attack of tuberculosis delayed his taking a degree, and sent him abroad instead, creating the circumstances that altered his career. His return to the Vale of Chamounix, his confronting again the sight of the sublimity of Mont Blanc, renewed the sense of exaltation he had first encountered at the same spot when he was fifteen. The visionary dialectic of Wordsworth's "Tintern Abbey" was renewed in Ruskin, and prepared him for a climactic return to Chamounix in August 1842. In *that* moment of renewal, as Wordsworthian a "spot of time" as any in *The Prelude*, the first volume of *Modern Painters* had its genesis. Ruskin returned to England, gave up all plans of taking orders, and devoted himself to vindicating the genius of Turner's Romantic landscape art, on principles grounded in the critic's own visionary experience.

By the time Ruskin had to seek healing consolation through another return to Chamounix, in 1854, his critical reputation was established, and his personal life was fairly well set toward destruction. He had published the second volume of *Modern Painters*, *The Seven Lamps of Architecture*, and *The Stones of Venice*, and he had married Euphemia Gray in 1848 with motives that have puzzled the best of his biographers. The marriage was not consummated, and was annulled in 1854, after the lady fled back to her parents. She married the Pre-Raphaelite painter Millais, whom Ruskin had befriended and patronized, and the entire affair soon passed out of the realm of scandal. Ruskin himself remained reticent on the matter (his marriage is not mentioned in his autobiography, *Praeterita*) and devoted himself more passionately to his work, which increasingly moved from art criticism to social prophecy. As the friend of Rossetti, Carlyle, and the Brownings, as the foremost expositor of the visual arts ever to appear in Great Britain, and as a prose poet of extraordinary power who took the whole concern of man as his subject, Ruskin appeared to have realized himself during the years from 1854 to 1860. Volumes three and four of *Modern Painters* came out in 1856, eliciting from George Eliot the definitive comment: "He is strongly akin to the sublimest part of Wordsworth." By 1860, Ruskin ought to have been at the supreme point of his development, and in a sense he was, but not in terms of continuity, for by 1860 he was at the turning, and entered into what was at once his great decade and his tragedy.

In 1860, Ruskin stood forth as a prophet fully armed in *Unto This Last*, his most eloquent and vital book. The central experiences of his life had led him beyond Wordsworth's quietism, and returned him to the biblical origins of his vision. The "theoretic faculty" of man, our ability to enter into the state of aesthetic contemplation depicted in "Tintern Abbey," had now to issue in the Hebraic and Protestant impulse to free all men toward finding the way to individual vision, to an enjoyment of the sense of something more divinely interfused. Eloquent as he always was, Ruskin rose to the heights of his rhetorical power in *Unto This Last*. If there is a kernel passage in his work, it is the one that climaxes:

> *There is no wealth but Life*—Life, including all its powers of love, of joy, and of admiration. That country is the richest which nourishes the greatest number of noble and happy human beings.

This is the moral force behind the apocalyptic yearnings of the fifth and final volume of *Modern Painters*, also published in 1860. A fully perceptive reader in that year might have seen Ruskin as being poised on the threshold of a creative period akin to the great years granted to a whole tradition of English poetic visionaries before him. The expectation would not have been altogether disappointed by Ruskin's works in the sixties, particularly by the sequence of *Munera Pulveris* (1863), *Sesame and Lilies* (1865), and *The Queen of the Air* (1869), but the decade essentially was one of brilliant decline, and two decades of writing after it showed the decline more consistently, until there came the final, intermittent brilliance of *Praeterita*, after which Ruskin had to be silent.

Part of the cause of this downward movement is found clearly enough by an examination of Ruskin's life from 1860 on. In that year Ruskin, already forty, met Rose La Touche, not yet ten, and their extraordinary love began. By 1860 Ruskin had no religious belief in any orthodox sense, having become intellectually agnostic, though his temperament remained a deeply Evangelical one. Rose was, at ten, something of a religious fanatic, and she evidenced already the tortured sensibility that was to result in the illness (at least partly mental) that killed her when she was twenty-five. Despite all the obvious barriers—of differences in age and belief, of the strong opposition of Rose's mother (who, perhaps unconsciously, seems to have desired Ruskin for herself)—Ruskin proposed marriage to Rose on her seventeenth birthday. Ambiguously, Rose delayed her answer for over a year, until correspondence between Ruskin's former wife and Mrs. La Touche revealed the supposed fact of his impotence. There followed a complex cycle of estrangements and reconciliations, concluding with a final reconciliation in 1874, by which time Rose's mental illness had become extreme. With her death, in 1875, Ruskin's long decline commenced. He became involved in spiritualism, and began to identify the memory of Rose with Dante's Beatrice and with Saint Ursula. One sympathetic biographer called the Ruskin of the late 1870s a morbid prig, and he was not far wrong. By 1878, Ruskin believed himself to have failed, in love and work alike, and with this sour belief came the onset of his own mental illness. He had been Slade Professor of Fine Art at Oxford since 1868, but the controversy with Whistler and subsequent trial, in 1877, caused him to resign that influential forum. He resumed the chair in 1883, but resigned again when it became clear he could no longer lecture coherently. Thenceforward he lived under what he termed the Storm Cloud, and his whole existence took on the beauty and terror of nightmare, haunted by the Evil One, who had intercepted all his desires, and who plagued him now in the shapes of peacock and cat. From this terror Ruskin partly rescued himself by a Wordsworthian return to childhood, celebrated by the writing of *Praeterita*. He returned also to a kind of religious belief, though he continued to hate the notion of justification by faith, and seems in his last days to have been more Catholic than Protestant in his outlook. In a final twilight period of deep peace alternating with total alienation from reality, Ruskin lived out his last days, dying on 20 January 1900.

There are three major areas of Ruskin's achievement: art, social, and literary criticism, and this essay is wholly devoted to only one of the three. I have allowed myself a broad interpretation of "literary criticism," since Ruskin is very much an anticipatory critic in regard to some schools of literary criticism in our own time. Ruskin is one of the first, if not indeed the first, "myth" or "archetypal" critic, or more properly he is the linking and transitional figure between allegorical critics of the elder, Renaissance kind, and those of the newer variety, like Northrop Frye, or like W.B. Yeats in his criticism. Even if he did not have this unique historical position, Ruskin would stand as one of the handful of major literary critics in nineteenth-century England, though his importance has been obscured by misapprehensions about his work. Most histories of literary criticism tag

Ruskin as a "moral" critic which is true only in Ruskin's own terms, but not at all in conventional ones. An Oxford lecture delivered by him in 1870 makes clear the special sense in which Ruskin insists upon the morality of art:

> You must first have the right moral state, or you cannot have art. But when the art is once obtained, its reflected action enhances and completes the moral state out of which it arose, and, above all, communicates the exultation to other minds which are already morally capable of the like. For instance take the art of singing, and the simplest perfect master of it—the skylark. From him you may learn what it is to sing for joy. You must get the moral state first, the pure gladness, then give it finished expression, and it is perfected in itself, and made communicable to others capable of such joy. Accuracy in proportion to the rightness of the cause, and purity of the emotion, is the possibility of fine art. You cannot paint or sing yourself into being good men; you must be good men before you can either paint or sing, and then the colour and sound will complete in you all that is best.

In this passage the "right moral state" and "being good men" are phrases that suggest conventional moral attitudes, yet the only moral state mentioned is that of the skylark, "the pure gladness." Behind Ruskin's passage are Wordsworth and Shelley, both in their skylark poems, and in their insistence upon the poet's joy and on poems as necessarily recording the best and happiest moments of the happiest and best minds. Ruskin's literary theory is primarily a Wordsworthian one, and as such it shows a family resemblance to all such theories down to Wallace Stevens, with his eloquent, Paterian insistence that "the morality of the poet's radiant and productive atmosphere is the morality of the right sensation." Ruskin's morality, as a critical theorist, is a morality of aesthetic contemplation, like the morality of "Tintern Abbey." It is not, in content, an Evangelical morality, though its fervor stamps it as a displaced version of Evangelicism. Ruskin's literary criticism has an explicit moral purpose, as Wordsworth's poetry does also, yet the purpose no more disfigures the criticism than it does the poetry. To understand Ruskin's criticism we need to study not only the pattern of Ruskin's life and career, but also the radical version of Romanticism his entire sensibility incarnated. Literary criticism rarely communicates the critic's own *experience* of literature, but in Ruskin's hands it very nearly always does, and in doing so touches upon the incommunicable. Ruskin did not believe that the imagination could create truth, but he did believe that it was the crucial faculty for the communication and interpretation of truth. Though Ruskin's judgment as a critic was fairly unsteady (he once declared Mrs. Browning's *Aurora Leigh* to be the greatest poem in the language), his central aesthetic experience was so powerful as to make him an almost miraculous medium for the truth of imagination to work through in order to reach sensibilities less uniquely organized than his own. In this respect, as in so many others, he resembles Wordsworth. Thus, speaking of Gothic as being representative of our universal childhood, Ruskin observes that all men:

> look back to the days of childhood as of greatest happiness, because those were the days of greatest wonder, greatest simplicity, and most vigorous imagination. And the whole difference between a man of genius and other men ... is that the first remains in great part a child, seeing with the large eyes of children, in perpetual wonder, not conscious of much knowledge,—conscious, rather, of infinite ignorance, and yet infinite power; a fountain of eternal admiration, delight, and creative force within him, meeting the ocean of visible and governable things around him.

If this is the source of creative imagination, it follows tragically but pragmatically that the workings of the mature imagination must be compensatory, for the story of art must be one in which gain can come only through loss, and the subsequent memory of the glorious time preceding loss. This pattern is familiar to every reader of Wordsworth, and is nowhere more eloquently expressed than it is by Ruskin. In a letter (28 September 1847) written to Walter Brown, once his tutor at Christ Church, Ruskin states the central experience of his life in phrases directly borrowed from the *Intimations* Ode:

> there was a time when the sight of a steep hill covered with pines cutting against blue sky, would have touched me with an emotion inexpressible, which, in the endeavour to communicate in its truth and intensity, I must have sought for all kinds of far-off, wild, and dreamy images. Now I can look at such a slope with coolness, and observation of *fact*. I see that it slopes at twenty or twenty-five degrees; I know the pines are spruce fir—"Pinus nigra"—of such and such a formation; the soil, thus, and thus; the day fine and the sky blue. All this I can at

once communicate in so many words, and this is all which is necessarily seen. But it is not all the truth: there is something else to be seen there, which I cannot see but in a certain condition of mind, nor can I make anyone else see it, but by putting him into that condition, and my endeavour in description would be, not to detail the facts of the scene, but by any means whatsoever to put my hearers mind into the same ferment as my mind.

Ruskin's activity as a critic of all the arts, of society, and of nature, is a quest to fulfill that "endeavour in description." What makes him a tragic critic (if so odd a phrase may be allowed) is his post-Wordsworthian and post-Turnerian sense of reality. In reply to Walter Brown's Wordsworthian statement of recompense for a loss of primal delight in nature, Ruskin wrote a letter (27 November 1847) which is an epilogue to the *Intimations* Ode:

> You say, in losing the delight I once had in nature I am coming down more to fellowship with others. Yes, but I feel it a fellowship of blindness. I may be able to get hold of people's hands better in the dark, but of what use is that, when I have no where to lead them but into the ditch? Surely, devoid of these imaginations and impressions, the world becomes a mere board-and-lodging house. The sea by whose side I am writing was once to me a friend, companion, master, teacher; now it is *salt water*, and salt water only. Is this an increase or a withdrawal of *truth*? I did not before lose hold or sight of the fact of its being salt water; I could consider it so, if I chose; my perceiving and feeling it to be more than this was a possession of higher truth, which did not interfere with my hold of the physical one.

This sense of loss haunts Ruskin's criticism, until at last it becomes the apocalyptic desire of his later works, from *Modern Painters V* (1860) on to *Praeterita* (1885–89). Kenneth Clark has said, very accurately, that Ruskin was by nature an impressionist, to which one can add that an apocalyptic impressionist is a very strange being; it is difficult to conceive of Revelation as Proust would have written it, yet that is what the prophetic Ruskin gives us. Ruskin remained true to Wordsworth and Turner in being interested primarily in *appearances*, and in taking those appearances as final realities. Yet Wordsworth learned how to evade the apocalyptic element even in the sublime modes of poetry, and Turner, like Keats, thought the earth and the sun to be enough. If there is a central meaning to Ruskin's great change about 1860, it is that his movement from description to prophecy refused to abandon the external world or the arts that he had learned to scrutinize so accurately. Instead Ruskin demanded more from both nature and art than even he had asked earlier, and so made more terrible the process of loss his sensibility had made inevitable. The Ruskin of the Storm Cloud is what Wordsworth would have been, had he allowed his characteristic dialectic of love between man and nature to survive, unchanged, the crisis of 1805, out of which "Peele Castle" was written as palinode.

This is the terrible pathos of Ruskin's art as a critic, that no one else has had so intense an intimation of loss within the imaginative experience itself. Remembering the vision that was his as a child, Ruskin could say that "for me, the Alps and their people were alike beautiful in their snow, and their humanity; and I wanted, neither for them nor myself, sight of any thrones in heaven but the rocks, or of any spirits in heaven but the clouds." This primary humanism never left Ruskin, as it did finally leave the older Wordsworth. What preserved it in Ruskin was the greater purity of his own Wordsworthianism; like the poet John Clare, he excelled Wordsworth as a visionary, and saw constantly what the greater poet could see only by glimpses:

> My entire delight was in observing without being myself noticed,—if I could have been invisible, all the better. I was absolutely interested in men and their ways, as I was interested in marmots and chamois, in tomtits and trout. If only they would stay still and let me look at them, and not get into their holes and up their heights! The living inhabitation of the world—the grazing and nesting in it,—the spiritual power of the air, the rocks, the waters, to be in the midst of it, and rejoice and wonder at it, and help it if I could,—happier if it needed no help of mine,—this was the essential love of Nature in me, this the root of all that I have usefully become, and the light of all that I have rightly learned.

If we call Ruskin's view of nature or of the self a mythical one, we need to qualify the classification, as Ruskin scarcely believed his view of either to be the product of his own creative powers. Wordsworth, and most of the Romantics after him, sought continuity between the earlier and the future self even at the expense of present time; Wordsworth indeed is mute in the face of nature at the living moment. Ruskin, like Blake, celebrated the pulsation of an artery, the flash of apprehension in which the poet's work is done. And, again like Blake, Ruskin placed his emphasis on *seeing* as the special mark of imagination. For Ruskin, unlike Wordsworth, the deepest imaginative effects are connected with the finite phenomena of nature, and the minute particulars of artistic detail. Wordsworth valued most highly in poetry "those passages where things are lost in each other, and limits vanish," but Ruskin, regarding art or nature, never ceased to see firm, determinate outlines, and every subtlety of detail. Ruskin, unlike Wordsworth, would not sacrifice either the landscape or the moment to the quest for continuity. Wordsworth's rewards for such sacrifices were immense, as Ruskin well knew, for no other writer has felt or made others feel so great a sense of the renewal of the past in the present, through the renovating influence of nature. Ruskin was an extraordinary psychologist, though a largely involuntary one, and did not believe that the therapy for an individual consciousness could come largely through a pursuit of after-images. Yet he wished to believe this, frequently wrote in the Wordsworthian mode, and achieved his final, autobiographical vision and last broken intervals of lucidity primarily through following Wordsworth's example, by tracing the growth of his own imagination. If Ruskin became one of the ruins of Romanticism, and even one of its victims, he became also one of its unique masters, who could justify asserting that "the greatest thing a human soul ever does in this world is to see something, and tell what it saw in a plain way. Hundreds of people can talk for one who can think, but thousands can think for one who can see. To see clearly is poetry, prophecy and religion all in one." Yet to see clearly was finally no salvation for Ruskin, but only gave him a maddening sense of loss, in the self and in nature alike.

Ruskin never gave up insisting that all art, literature included, was worship, but this insistence does not make him either a "religious" or a "moral" critic of literature. Though he moved in outward religion from Evangelical Protestantism to agnostic naturalism and on finally to a private version of primitive Catholicism, Ruskin's pragmatic religion always remained a Wordsworthian "natural piety," in which aesthetic and spiritual experience were not to be distinguished from one another. Ruskin's literary taste was formed by the King James Bible, more than any other reading, and therefore from the start he associated expressive and devotional values. In this also he stands with the great Romantics, whose theories of the Imagination are all displaced, radical Protestant accounts of the nakedness of the soul before God.

Ruskin's own theory of the Imagination is clearly derived from Coleridge's and it has been argued that all Ruskin adds to his master's account is a multiplication of unnecessary entities. Yet Ruskin does add to Coleridge's theory a confidence in the autonomy of the imagination that Coleridge himself never possessed. Indeed it is Coleridge whose criticism is distorted by the claims of conventional morality and institutional religion, and not Ruskin. Ruskin could not have written "that it has pleased Providence, that the divine truths of religion should have been revealed to us *in the form of* poetry" (italics mine) or that "an undevout poet is mad: in the strict sense of the word, an undevout poet is an impossibility." Because he lacked Coleridge's doubts, Ruskin allowed himself to elaborate upon Coleridge's categories, there being no point at which he felt the imagination had to yield to a higher or more assured faculty. If these elaborations have failed to be influential, they yet remain interesting in themselves and indicate where a less inhibited Romantic theory of Imagination may still quarry for its materials.

Fundamentally Ruskin favored two groups of poets, those like Dante, Spenser, Milton, and Wordsworth who dealt in detail with the whole destiny of man, from creation to apocalypse, and those he had loved in his own youth, like Scott and Byron. It is in the first that Ruskin's great strength as a critic lies, since he is given to special pleading for his childhood favorites. But there is an honorable place for special pleading in criticism, if it is done with the eloquent passion and exquisite discrimination of a Ruskin.

It is in his examination of the larger outlines of the structure of literature that Ruskin appears today to have been a major critical innovator. Because of his intimate knowledge of biblical and classical iconology, and of Dante, Spenser, and Milton as the heirs of such iconology, Ruskin arrived at a comprehensive theory of literature, which he never made fully explicit but which is evident throughout his criticism. One major assumption of this theory is that all great poetry whatsoever is allegorical; and that what it allegorizes is a fundamental myth of universal man, his fall from Paradise and his quest for a revelation that would restore him to Paradise. This myth is clearest in the Ruskin of the 1860s, of *The Queen of the Air*, and of *Sesame and Lilies*.

Though it is an obsession in the later Ruskin, a consciousness of this myth was always present in his criticism, since he relied from the start on a Wordsworthian experience of paradisal intimations within a wholly natural context. The Wordsworthian principle of continuity and dialectic of love between man and nature were generalized by the older Ruskin into the universal figures he had encountered in his early journeys from Genesis to Revelation. The symbols of *Modern Painters V*, *Munera Pulveris*, *Sesame and Lilies*, and *The Queen of the Air* are primarily biblical ones, even when Ruskin investigates the many guises of Athena in the elaborate mythologizings of *The Queen of the Air*. The Garden of Eden, the Serpent or Dragon, the unfallen maiden who replaces Mother Eve and becomes the prime hope of salvation; these are for Ruskin the principal figures in a mythopoeic fantasia of his own, which is almost too available for psychoanalytical reduction, of the kind to which Ruskin is generally subjected in our time. When, in *The Queen of the Air*, this fantasia is mixed with extraordinary excursions into botany, political economy, and primordial folklore, the result demands a reader more exuberant than most Ruskin scholars have been.

The Queen of the Air, in one of its aspects, resembles some works of Elizabethan mythography like Henry Reynolds's *Mythomystes*, but an even closer parallel can be found in Blake's poetry and prose. Like Ruskin, Blake counter points both classical and biblical myth against an imaginative story of his own, which in itself is a deliberate modification of Milton's accounts of Fall and Redemption. Ruskin does not seem to invent "Giant Forms" or titanic personages, as Blake does, but he invents and explores states-of-being in a manner very similar to Blake's, though he does not give them Blake's kind of categorical names. Ruskin's Athena is finally a goddess of his own creation, and as such she is one of the major myth-makings of the Victorian age.

Ruskin's earlier, and more Wordsworthian literary criticism, is dominated by the problem of landscape, in the same way that his later criticism centers on typological figures of redemption. *Modern Painters III* (1856) contains Ruskin's principal achievement as a literary critic before he entered upon his own mythical phase, but it is an achievement that has been misunderstood, partly because Ruskin's famous formulation of the Pathetic Fallacy has been misinterpreted. The theory of the Pathetic Fallacy is a searching criticism of Romanticism from within, for the sake of saving the Romantic program of humanizing nature from extinction through excessive self-indulgence. Ruskin is the first writer within the Romantic tradition to have realized the high spiritual price that had to be paid for Wordsworthianism, the human loss that accompanied the "abundant recompense" celebrated in "Tintern Abbey."

Ruskin was, more so even than most artists and critics, a kind of natural phenomenologist, to use a term now in fashion, or simply, a man to whom things spoke, and who spent his life describing "the ordinary, proper, and true appearances of things to us." Ruskin knew that, as man and artist, his debts and affinities were to what he called the second order of poets, the "Reflective or Perceptive" group (Wordsworth, Keats, Tennyson) and not to the first order, the "Creative" group (Shakespeare, Homer, Dante). Ruskin's purpose in expounding the Pathetic Fallacy, which characterizes the second order, is not to discredit the Wordsworthian kind of poetry, but to indicate its crucial limitation, which he knew himself to share.

Wordsworth and his followers present states of mind that "produce in us a falseness in all our impressions of external things." A.H.R. Ball, the most sympathetic student of Ruskin's literary criticism, was convinced that the theory of the Pathetic Fallacy contradicted Ruskin's own imaginative theory, which may be true, but the contradiction, if it exists, is only a seeming one. Ruskin understood that Romantic poetry, and its imaginative theory, were grounded upon the Pathetic Fallacy, the imputation of life to the object-world. To believe that there is the one life only, within us and abroad, was to heal the Enlightenment's split in consciousness between adverting mind and the universe of things, but at the price that the intuitive phenomenologist in Ruskin understood and resented. The myth of continuity, in Wordsworth and in his followers, Ruskin included, is the result of a homogeneity of sense-experience, which can result only from reduction. The psychiatrist J.H. Van den Berg, in his fascinating study *Metabletica*, traces this reduction to Descartes, who saw objects as localized space, extensiveness. Wordsworth's quest was to find a way out of all dualisms, Cartesian included, but ironically Wordsworth and his school followed Descartes, unknowingly, in reducing the present to an elaborated past, and making the future also only a consequence of the past. Ruskin's formulation of the Pathetic Fallacy is a profound protest against nineteenth-century homogeneities, particularly landscape homogeneities. It is perhaps sour wit, but it seems true to remark that Wordsworth could see only landscapes that he had seen before, and that no landscape became visible to him that he had not first estranged from himself.

Ruskin's protest is against this estrangement of things, and against the Romantic delight in seeing a reduction, and then elevating that reduction to the ecstasy of enforced humanization. Van den Berg remarks somberly that the Romantic inner self became necessary when contacts between man and the external world became less valued. Ruskin's rejection of Romantic mythopoeia as the Pathetic Fallacy shows a similar distrust of Wordsworthian self-consciousness, but the later Ruskin put such distrust aside, and became the major Romantic myth-maker of the Victorian era. The aesthetic tragedy of Ruskin is that works like *Sesame and Lilies* and *The Queen of the Air* are giant Pathetic Fallacies, but the mingled grandeur and ruin of those books only make them still more representative of post-Romantic art, and its central dilemma. Ruskin may yet seem the major and most original critic that Romanticism has produced, as well as one of its most celebrated avatars.

Walter Pater

(1839-1894)

... What is this song or picture, this engaging personality presented in life or in a book, to me? What effect does it really produce on me? Does it give me pleasure? and if so, what sort of degree of pleasure? How is my nature modified by its presence, and under its influence?

—PATER, Preface to *The Renaissance*

... Why should a poem not change in sense when there is a fluctuation of the whole of appearance? Or why should it not change when we realize that the indifferent experience of life is the unique experience, the item of ecstasy which we have been isolating and reserving for another time and place, loftier and more secluded.

—STEVENS, "Two or Three Ideas"

"AESTHETIC" CRITICISM

PATER IS A GREAT CRITIC OF A KIND COMMON ENOUGH IN THE NINETEENTH century—Coleridge, Lamb, Hazlitt, De Quincey, above all Ruskin—but scarcely to be found in the twentieth. Difficult to define, this sort of critic possesses one salient characteristic. His value inheres neither in his accuracy at the direct interpretation of meaning in texts nor in his judgments of relative eminence of works and authors. Rather, he gives us a vision of art through his own unique sensibility, and so his own writings obscure the supposed distinction between criticism and creation. "Supposed," because who can convince us of that distinction? To adapt Shelley's idea of the relation between poetry and the universe, let us say that criticism creates the poem anew, after the poem has been annihilated in our minds by the recurrence of impressions blunted by reiteration. Ruskin's or Pater's criticism tends to create anew not so much a particular work of art but rather the precisely appropriate consciousness of the perceptive reader or viewer. This does not mean that these great critics are monuments to the Affective Fallacy, or that literary historians with Formalist tendencies are justified in naming Ruskin and Pater as critical Impressionists. Oscar Wilde, who brilliantly vulgarized both his prime precursors, insisted that their work treated "the work of art simply as a starting-point for a new creation." Matthew Arnold had asserted that the "aim of criticism is to see the object as in itself it really is." A few years later, implicitly invoking Ruskin against Arnold, Pater slyly added that "the first step towards seeing one's object as it really is, is to know one's impression as it really is, to discriminate it, to realise it distinctly." Wilde, attempting to complete his master, charmingly amended this to the grand statement that "the primary aim of the critic is to see the object as in itself it really is not." Between Arnold's self-deception and Wilde's wit comes Pater's hesitant and skeptical emphasis upon a peculiar kind of vision, with which he identifies all aesthetic experience.

We owe to Pater our characteristic modern use of "aesthetic," for he emancipated the word from its bondage to philosophy, both when he spoke of the "aesthetic critic" in his "Preface" to *The Renaissance*, and when he named the work of Morris and Rossetti as the "aesthetic poetry" in *Appreciations*. Vulgarized again by his ebullient disciple Wilde, and by the parodies of Wilde as Bunthorne in Gilbert and Sullivan's *Patience*, and of Pater himself as Mr. Rose in W.H. Mallock's *The New Republic*, Pater had to endure the debasement of "aesthete" as a term, and we endure it still. Pater meant us always to remember what mostly we have forgotten, that "aesthete" is from the Greek *aisthetes*, "one who perceives." So the "aesthetic critic" is simply the perceptive critic, or literary critic proper, and "aesthetic poetry" is precisely the contemporary poetry that is most perceptive, that is, in one's judgment most truly poetry.

Pater's key terms as a critic are "perception" and "sensation," which is response to perception. "Vision" for Pater, as for Blake, is a synonym for Coleridge's or Wordsworth's "Imagination," and Pater further emulated Blake by questing after the "spiritual form" of phenomena as against "corporeal form." This is the "form" that: "Every moment ... grows perfect in hand or face," according to the almost preternaturally eloquent "Conclusion" to *The Renaissance*. In the marvelous "Postscript" (on "Romanticism") to *Appreciations*, Pater traces the genesis of form:

... there are the born romanticists, who start with an original, untried matter, still in fusion; who conceive this vividly, and hold by it as the essence of their work; who, by the very vividness and heat of their conception, purge away, sooner or later, all that is not organically appropriate to it, till the whole effect adjusts itself in clear, orderly, proportionate form; which form, after a very little time, becomes classical in its turn.

Vividness and *heat* purge away from the Romantic idea all that is not form, and form is the reward of the aesthete or perceptive man, if he has the strength to persist in his purgation. "In the end, the aesthetic is completely crushed and destroyed by the inability of the observer who has himself been crushed to have any feeling for it left." That dark observation is by Wallace Stevens, an heir (unwilling) of Pater's aestheticism. A more accurate observation of the aesthete's defeat comes from as great an heir, more conscious and willing, who attributed to Pater's influence his poetic generation's doomed attempt "to walk upon a rope, tightly stretched through serene air." Yeats nevertheless got across to the other side of the Nineties, and carried Pater alive into our century in *Per Amica Silentia Lunae* (1917) and *A Vision* (1925, 1937). Pater's vision of form culminates in Yeats's Phase 15: "Now contemplation and desire, united into one, inhabit a world where every beloved image has bodily form, and every bodily form is loved." Pater, for whom the attained form demanded purgation, an *askesis* (to which I shall return), hesitantly held back from this Yeatsian version of a High Romantic Absolute.

To know Pater, and to apprehend his influence not only on Stevens and Yeats, but on Joyce, Eliot, Pound, and many other writers of our century, we need to place Pater in his Oedipal context in the cultural situation of his own time. The pleasures of reading Pater are intense, to me, but the importance of Pater transcends those pleasures, and finally is quite out of proportion to Pater's literary achievement, fairly large as that was. Pater is the heir of a tradition already too wealthy to have required much extension or variation when it reached him. He revised that tradition, turning the Victorian continuation of High Romanticism into the Late Romanticism or "Decadence" that prolonged itself as what variously might be called Modernism, Post-Romanticism or, self-deceivingly, Anti-Romanticism, the art of Pound's Vortex. Though Pater compares oddly, perhaps not wholly adequately, with the great Victorian prose prophets, he did what Carlyle, Ruskin, Newman, Arnold could not do: he fathered the future. Himself wistful and elaborately reserved, renouncing even his own strength, he became the most widely diffused (though more and more hidden) literary influence of the later nineteenth upon the twentieth century.

In its diffusion, particularly in America, the Paterian influence was assimilated to strikingly similar elements in Nietzsche and Emerson, a process as indubitable as it is still largely unstudied. When Yeats proclaimed the "profane perfection of mankind" or Pound or Stevens their images of the poet as a crystal man, they combined Pater with Nietzsche and Emerson (both of whom he seems to have neglected). "Just take one step farther," Nietzsche urged, and "love yourself through Grace; then you are no longer in need of your God, and the whole drama of fall and redemption is acted out in yourself." "In the highest moments, we are a vision," is the antinomian counsel of Emerson. Pater's first essay, "Diaphaneite," read to an Oxford literary group in 1864, presented the artist as a transparent or crystal image of more-than-human perfection, an Apollonian hero. How often, in Modern poetry, we have heard these strains mingled, until by now our latest poets alternately intoxicate and eradicate themselves in the inhuman effort that might sustain a vision so exalted. Pater, though a theorist of the Dionysian, evaded the heroic vitalism of a Nietzsche or the quasi-divine self-reliance of an Emerson, declining to present himself either as prophet or as orator. Yet his baroque meditations upon art, hieratic and subdued, touch as firmly upon the ruinous strength of our major Modern poets as any other precursor of our sensibility does.

PRIVILEGED MOMENTS

Pater's context begins with his only begetter, Ruskin, whose effect can be read, frequently through negation, throughout Pater's work. Believing, as he says in "Style," that imaginative prose largely took the place of poetry in the modern world, Pater necessarily assumed, consciously I think, the characteristic malady of Post-Enlightenment poetry, the new creator's anxiety-of-influence in regard to his precursor's priority, which becomes a menacing spiritual authority, in a direct transference from the natural to the imaginative world. Ruskin, despite his irrelevant mania for ferocious moralizing, is the major "aesthetic critic," in Pater's sense, of the nineteenth century. Stylistically, Pater owed more to Swinburne, but stance rather than style is the crucial indebtedness of a poet or imaginative prose writer. This is Swinburne, sounds like Pater, yet menaces him not at all:

> All mysteries of good and evil, all wonders of life and death, lie in their hands or at their feet. They have known the causes of things, and are not too happy. The fatal labour of the world, the clamour and hunger of the open-mouthed all-summoning

grave, all fears and hopes of ephemeral men, are indeed made subject to them, and trodden by them underfoot; but the sorrow and strangeness of things are not lessened because to one or two their secret springs have been laid bare and the courses of their tides made known; refluent evil and good, alternate grief and joy, life inextricable from death, change inevitable and insuperable fate.

Swinburne is speaking of Michelangelo, Aeschylus, Shakespeare; masters of the Sublime, whose mastery does not lessen "sorrow and strangeness." The accent here becomes Pater's (Cecil Lang surmises that Gautier's prose is behind Swinburne's, and Gautier also affected the early Pater), but the attitude, superficially akin to Pater's, is profoundly alien to the Epicurean visionary. Swinburne broods on knowledge and powerlessness, but Pater cared only about perception, about seeing again what Michelangelo, Aeschylus, Shakespeare *saw*. Ruskin's Biblical style was no burden to the Hellenizing Pater, but Ruskin's critical stance was at once initial release yet ultimate burden to his disciple. For this is Pater's Gospel, but it is Ruskin's manifesto: "... the greatest thing a human soul ever does in this world is to see something, and tell what it saw in a plain way. Hundreds of people can talk for one who can think, but thousands can think for one who can see. To see clearly is poetry, prophecy and religion all in one." Pater was not concerned to tell what he saw in a plain way, but he was kindled by this exaltation of seeing.

Ruskin himself, though uniquely intense as a prophet of the eye, belonged to the Spirit of the Age in his emphasis, as Pater well knew. The primal source of later Romantic seeing in England was Wordsworth, who feared the tyranny of the eye, yet who handed on to his disciples not his fear of the visual, nor (until much later) his Sublime visionary sense, but his program for renovation through renewed encounters with visible nature. Carlyle, a necessary link between Wordsworth and Ruskin, equated the heroism of the poet with "the seeing eye." But a trouble, already always present in Wordsworth and Coleridge, developed fully in Ruskin's broodings upon vision. *Modern Painters III* (1856) distinguishes: "the difference between the ordinary, proper, and true appearances of things to us; and the extraordinary, or false appearances, when we are under the influence of emotion, or contemplative fancy; false appearances, I say, as being entirely unconnected with any real power or character in the object, and only imputed to it by us." This imputation of life to the object-world Ruskin called the "pathetic fallacy" and judged as "a falseness in all our impressions of external things." The greatest order of poets, the

"Creative" (Shakespeare, Homer, Dante), Ruskin declared free of the pathetic fallacy, finding it endemic in the second order of poets, the "Reflective or Perceptive" (Wordsworth, Keats, Tennyson). Himself a thorough Wordsworthian, Ruskin did not mean to deprecate his Reflective (or Romantic) grouping, but rather to indicate its necessary limitation. Like Pater after him, Ruskin was haunted throughout his life and writings by Wordsworth's "Intimations" Ode, which objectified for both critics their terrible sense of bereavement, of estrangement from the imaginative powers they possessed (or believed themselves to have possessed) as children. Both Ruskin and Pater began as Wordsworthian poets, and turned to imaginative prose partly because of the anxiety-of-influence induced in them by Wordsworth.

Ruskin's formulation of the pathetic fallacy protests the human loss involved in Wordsworth's compensatory imagination. As such, Ruskin's critique prophesies the winter vision of Wallace Stevens, from "The Snow Man" through to "The Course of a Particular." When Stevens reduces to what he calls the First Idea, he returns to "the ordinary, proper, and true appearances of things to us," but then finds it dehumanizing to live only with these appearances. So the later Ruskin found also, in his own elaborate mythicizings in *Sesame and Lilies* and related books, and in the Wordsworthian autobiography, *Praeterita*, that closed his work. What Wordsworth called "spots of time," periods of particular splendor or privileged moments testifying to the mind's power over the eye, Ruskin had turned from earlier, as being dubious triumphs of the pathetic fallacy. Pater, who subverted Ruskin by going back to their common ancestor, Wordsworth, may be said to have founded his criticism upon privileged moments of vision, or "epiphanies" as Joyce's Stephen, another Paterian disciple, was to term them.

The "epiphany," for us, has been much reduced, yet still prevails as our poets' starting-point for moving from sensation to mastery, or at least to self-acceptance:

Perhaps there are times of inherent excellence,

Perhaps there are moments of awakening,
Extreme, fortuitous, personal, in which

We more than awaken....

But Stevens's good moments, as here in *Notes Toward a Supreme Fiction*, have receded even from the modified Wordsworthianism that

Pater offered as privileged moments, or pathetic fallacies raised to triumphs of perception. For Ruskin's "Perceptive" poets are Pater's "Aesthetic" poets, not a second order but the only poets possible in the universe of death, the Romantic world we have come to inhabit. Joyce's Stephen, recording epiphanies as "the most delicate and evanescent of moments," is recollecting Pater's difficult ecstasy that flares forth "for that moment only." The neo-orthodox, from Hopkins through Eliot to Auden, vainly attempted to restore Pater's "moments" to the religious sphere, yet gave us only what Eliot insisted his poetry would not give, instances of "the intense moment / Isolated, with no before and after," the actual art (such as it is) of *Four Quartets* even as it was of *The Waste Land*. Pater remains the most honest recorder of epiphanies, by asking so little of them, as here in the essay on the poet Joachim Du Bellay in *The Renaissance*:

> A sudden light transfigures a trivial thing, a weathervane, a windmill, a winnowing flail, the dust in the barn door; a moment—and the thing has vanished, because it was pure effect; but it leaves a relish behind it, a longing that the accident may happen again.

"He had studied the nostalgias," like his descendant in Stevens's more qualified vision, and he did not pretend we could be renovated by happy accidents. Yet he offered a program more genuinely purgative than High Romanticism had ventured:

> ... painting and poetry ... can accomplish their function in the choice and development of some special situation, which lifts or glorifies a character, in itself not poetical. To realise this situation, to define, in a chill and empty atmosphere, the focus where rays, in themselves pale and impotent, unite and begin to burn ...

This, from the early essay on "Winckelmann," presents the embryo of a Paterian epiphany. Here is such an epiphany at its most central, in the crucial chapter, "The Will as Vision," of *Marius the Epicurean*:

> Through some accident to the trappings of his horse at the inn where he rested, Marius had an unexpected delay. He sat down in an olive garden, and, all around him and within still turning to reverie.... A bird came and sang among the wattled hedgeroses: an animal feeding crept nearer: the child who kept

it was gazing quietly: and the scene and the hours still conspiring, he passed from that mere fantasy of a self not himself, beside him in his coming and going, to those divinations of a living and companionable spirit at work in all things....

In this peculiar and privileged hour, his bodily frame, as he could recognize, although just then, in the whole sum of its capacities, so entirely possessed by him—Nay! actually his very self—was yet deter mined by a far-reaching system of material forces external to it.... And might not the intellectual frame also, still more intimately himself as in truth it was, after the analogy of the bodily life, be a moment only, an impulse or series of impulses, a single process ...? How often had the thought of their brevity spoiled for him the most natural pleasures of life.... —To-day at least, in the peculiar clearness of one privileged hour, he seemed to have apprehended ... an abiding place....

Himself—his sensations and ideas—never fell again precisely into focus as on that day, yet he was the richer by its experience.... It gave him a definitely ascertained measure of his moral or intellectual need, of the demand his soul must make upon the powers, whatsoever they might be, which had brought him, as he was, into the world at all....

All of Pater is in this passage. Wordsworth lamented the loss of an earlier glory, ultimately because such glory was equal to an actual sense of immortality. He celebrated "spots of time," not because they restored that saving sense, but in the hope they testified to his spirit's strength over a phenomenal world of decay, and so modestly hinted at some mode of survival. Ruskin, until he weakened (on his own terms), insisted on the Homeric strength of gazing upon ocean, and seeing no emblem of continuity but only pure physical nature: "Black or clear, monstrous or violet-coloured, cold salt water it is always, and nothing but that." Pater's Marius has been found by a skeptical but comforting compromise between the natural visions of Wordsworth and Ruskin. "Peculiar and privileged," or "extreme, fortuitous, personal" as Stevens was to call it, the tame of reverie abides in Ruskin's "pure physical nature," yet holds together in continuity not only past and present but what was only potential in the past to a sublimity still possible in the future. The self still knows that it reduces to "sensations and ideas" (the subtitle of *Marius the Epicurean*), still knows the brevity of its expectation, knows even more strongly it is joined to no immortal soul, yet now believes also that its own integrity can be at one with the system of forces outside it. Pater's strange achievement is to have assimilated Wordsworth to Lucretius, to have compounded an idealistic naturalism with a corrective materialism. By de-idealizing the epiphany, he makes it available to the coming age, when the mind will know neither itself nor the object but only the dumbfoundering abyss that comes between.

HISTORICISMS: RENAISSANCE AND ROMANTICISM

Pater began to read Ruskin in 1858, when he was just nineteen, eight years before he wrote his first important essay, "Winckelmann." From then until the posthumously published writings, Pater suffered under Ruskin's influence, though from the start he maintained a revisionary stance in regard to his precursor. In place of Ruskin's full, prophetic, even overwhelming rhetoric, Pater evolved a partial, hesitant, insinuating rhetoric, yet the result is a style quite as elaborate as his master's. The overt influence, Pater buried deep. He mentioned Ruskin just once in his letters, and then to claim priority over Ruskin by two years as the English discoverer of Botticelli (as late as 1883, Ruskin still insisted otherwise, but wrongly). Ruskin is ignored, by name, in the books and essays, yet he hovers everywhere in them, and nowhere more strongly than in *The Renaissance* (1873), for Pater's first book is primarily an answer to *The Stones of Venice* (1851, 1853) and to the five volumes of *Modern Painters* (1843–1860). Where Ruskin had deplored the Renaissance (and located it in Italy, between the fourteenth and sixteenth centuries), elevating instead the High Middle Ages, Pater emulated the main movement of English Romanticism by exalting the Renaissance (and then anticipated later studies by locating its origins in twelfth-century France). Yet the polemic against Ruskin, here as elsewhere, remains implicit. One of Pater's friends reported that once, when talking of Ruskin's strength of perception, Pater burst out: "I cannot believe that Ruskin saw more in the church of St. Mark than I do." Pater's ultimate bitterness, in this area, came in 1885, when Ruskin resigned as Slade Professor of Fine Art at Oxford. Pater offered himself for the professorship, but it went to one Hubert Von Herkomer, and not to the author of the notorious book on the Renaissance, whose largest departure from Ruskin was in opposing a darker and hedonistic humanism to the overtly moral humanism of his aesthetic precursor.

The vision of Pater's Renaissance centers upon the hope of what Yeats was to call Unity of Being. Drawing his epigraph from the Book of Psalms, Pater hints at the aesthetic man's salvation from the potsherds of English Christianity in the 1860's: "Though ye have lain among the pots, yet shall ye be as the wings of a dove covered with silver, and her feathers with yellow gold" (Psalms 68:13). The aesthetic man, surrounded by the decaying absolutes inherited from Coleridge-as-theologian, accepts the truths of solipsism and isolation, of mortality and the flux of sensations, and glories in the singularity of his own peculiar kind of contemplative temperament. Pater would teach this man self-reconcilement and self-acceptance, and so Unity of Being. In the great figures of the Renaissance—particularly Botticelli, Michelangelo, Leonardo—Pater presents images of this Unity of aesthetic contemplation. Ruskin, a greater critic than Pater, did not over-idealize the possibilities of aesthetic contemplation, not even in books as phantasmagoric as *The Queen of the Air*. Pater's desperation, both to go beyond Ruskin and to receive more from art, is at once his defining weakness in comparison to Ruskin, and his greater importance for what was to come, not just in the 1880s and 1890s, but throughout our century.

In his vision of the Renaissance, Pater inherits the particular historicism of English Romanticism, which had found its own origins in the English Renaissance, and believed itself a renaissance of that Renaissance. Between the High Romantics and Pater many losses were felt, and of these Darwin compelled the largest. The Renaissance is already a Darwinian book, rather in the same way that *The Stones of Venice* was still a Coleridgean book. Pater's moral tentativeness necessarily reflected his own profound repressions, including his aversion to heterosexuality, and the very clear strain of sadomasochism in his psyche. But the intellectual sanction of Pater's skeptical Epicureanism was provided by the prevalent skepticism even of religious apologias in the age of Newman and the Oxford Movement. Evolution, whether as presented by Christian historicisms or by Darwin himself, gave the self-divided Pater a justification for projecting his temperament into a general vision of his age's dilemmas. His later work, considered further on in this Introduction, found a governing dialectic for his skepticism in the Pre-Socratics and Plato, but in *The Renaissance* the personal projection is more direct, and proved more immediately influential.

The "Preface" to *The Renaissance* outlines a cycle in the concept of renaissance, which goes from an early freshness with "the charm of *askesis*, of the austere and serious girding of the loins in youth" to "that subtle and delicate sweetness which belongs to a refined and comely decadence." The Greek word *askêsis* (or *askesis*) originally referred to athleticism, but easily transferred itself, even in ancient time, to an exercise in spiritualizing purgation. Paterian *askesis* is less a sublimation (as it seems when first used in the "Preface") than it is an aesthetic self-curtailment, a giving-up of certain powers so as to help achieve more originality in one's self-mastery. An Epicurean or hedonistic *askesis* is only superficially a paradox, since it is central in the Lucretian vision that Pater labored to attain. For Lucretius, truth is always in appearances, the mind is a flow of sensory patterns, and moral good is always related directly to pleasurable sensations. But intense pleasure, as Epicurus taught, is grossly inferior to possessing a tranquil temperament. Pater's Epicureanism, in *The Renaissance*, was more radical, and hesitates subtly at exalting a quasi-homosexual and hedonistic humanism, particularly in the essays on Leonardo and on Winckelmann.

In the essay on "Two Early French Stories," Pater identifies his "medieval Renaissance" with "its antinomianism, its spirit of rebellion and revolt against the moral and religious ideas of the time." Pater's own antinomianism is the unifying element in his great first book, as he elaborately intimates "a strange idolatry, a strange rival religion" in opposition to the Evangelical faith of Ruskin and the revived orthodoxies of the Oxford Movement. The extraordinary essay on Botticelli, a triumphant prose poem, sees in his Madonna "one of those who are neither for Jehovah nor for His enemies," and hints at a sadomasochistic sadness with which Botticelli conceives the universe of pleasure he has chosen. In the essay on Leonardo, which may be Pater's finest poem, the visionary center is reached in the notorious (and wholly magnificent) passage on *La Gioconda*, which Yeats brilliantly judged to be the first Modern poem, but which he proceeded to butcher by printing in verse form as the first poem in *The Oxford Book of Modern Verse* (1936). Yeats, in his "Introduction," asked an insightful and largely rhetorical question: "Did Pater foreshadow a poetry, a philosophy, where the individual is nothing, the flux of *The Cantos* of Ezra Pound, objects without contour ..., human experience no longer shut into brief lines, ... the flux ... that within our minds enriches itself, re-dreams itself ...?"

Freud, in his study of Leonardo, found in the Mona Lisa the child's defense against excessive love for his mother, by means of identifying with her and so proceeding to love boys in his own image, even as he had been loved. In one of his most troubling insights, Freud went on to a theory of the sexual origins of all thought, a theory offering only two ways out for the gifted; a compulsive, endless brooding in which all intellectual curiosity remains sexual, or a successful sublimation, in which thought, to some extent, is liberated from its sexual past. Is Pater, throughout *The Renaissance*, and particularly in the "Leonardo" and the "Conclusion," merely a fascinating, compulsive brooder, or has he freed his thought from his own over-determined sexual nature? Some recent studies reduce Pater only to the former possibility, but this is to underestimate an immensely subtle mind. Here is the crucial passage, not a purple patch but a paean to the mind's mastery over its own compulsiveness:

> The presence that rose thus so strangely beside the waters, is expressive of what in the ways of a thousand years men had come to desire. Hers is the head upon which all "the ends of the world are come," and the eyelids are a little weary. It is a beauty wrought out from within upon the flesh, the deposit, little cell by cell, of strange thoughts and fantastic reveries and exquisite passions. Set it for a moment beside one of those white Greek goddesses or beautiful women of antiquity, and how would they be troubled by this beauty, into which the soul with all its maladies has passed! All the thoughts and experience of the world have etched and moulded there, in that which they have of power to refine and make expressive the outward form, the animalism of Greece, the lust of Rome, the mysticism of the middle age with its spiritual ambition and imaginative loves, the return of the Pagan world, the sins of the Borgias. She is older than the rocks among which she sits; like the vampire, she has been dead many times, and learned the secrets of the grave; and has been a diver in deep seas, and keeps their fallen day about her; and trafficked for strange webs with Eastern merchants, and, as Leda, was the mother of Helen of Troy, and, as Saint Anne, the mother of Mary; and all this has been to her but as the sound of lyres and flutes, and lives only in the delicacy with which it has moulded the changing lineaments, and tinged the eyelids and the hands. The fancy of a perpetual life, sweeping together ten thousand experiences, is an old one; and modern philosophy has conceived the idea of humanity as wrought upon by, and summing up in itself, all modes of thought and life. Certainly Lady Lisa might stand as the embodiment of the old fancy, the symbol of the modern idea.

Most broadly, this is Pater's comprehensive vision of an equivocal goddess whom Blake called "the Female Will" and the ancient Orphics named *Ananke*, meaning "Necessity." Pater dreads and desires her, or perhaps desires her precisely through his dread. Desire dominates here, for the sight of her is a privileged moment, an epiphany of the only divinity Pater truly worshipped. In the essay following, on "The School of Giorgione," Pater speaks of "profoundly significant and animated instants, a mere gesture, a look, a smile, perhaps—some brief and wholly concrete moment—into which, however, all the motives, all the interests and effects of a long history, have condensed themselves, and which seem to absorb past and future in an intense consciousness of the present." The Lady Lisa, as an inevitable object of the quest for all which we have lost, is herself a process moving toward a final entropy, summing up all the estrangements we have suffered from the object-world we once held close, whether as children, or in history. She incarnates too much, both for her own good and for ours. The cycles of civilization, the burden our consciousness bears, render us latecomers but the Lady Lisa perpetually carries the seal of a terrible priority. Unity of Being she certainly possesses, yet she seems to mock the rewards Pater hoped for in such Unity. A powerful juxtaposition, of the ancient dream of a literal immortality, of living all lives, and of Darwinianism ("modern philosophy"), ends the passage with an astonishing conceptual image. The Lady Lisa, as no human could hope to do, stands forth as a body risen from death, and also as symbol of modern acceptance of Necessity, the non-divine evolution of our species. She exposes, as Pater is well aware, the hopelessness of the vision sought by *The Renaissance*, and by all Romantic and Post-Romantic art.

Yet, with that hopelessness comes the curious reward of the supreme Paterian epiphany. Rilke remarked of the landscape behind the Madonna Lisa that "it is Nature which came into existence ... something distant and foreign, something remote and without allure, something entirely self-contained...." Following Rilke, the psychologist J.H. Van den Berg associates this estrangement of an outer landscape with the growth of a more inward, alienated self than mankind had known before:

> The inner life was like a haunted house. But what else could it be? It contained everything. Everything extraneous had been put into it. The entire history of the individual. Everything that had previously belonged to everybody, everything that had been collective property and had existed in the world in which everyone lived, had to be contained by the individual. It could not be expected that things would be quiet in the inner self.

In his way, Van den Berg, like Rilke, sides with Ruskin and not with Pater, for the implicit argument here is that the Romantic inner self cost too much in solipsistic estrangement. But Pater was a divided man, humanly wiser than he could let himself show as a Late Romantic moralist-critic. His vision of the Mona Lisa is as much a warning as it is an ideal. This, he says, is our Muse, mistress of Unity-of-Being. The poets of the

Nineties, including the young Yeats, chose to see the ideal and not to heed the warning. The further work of Pater, after *The Renaissance*, shows the Aesthetic Critic accepting his own hint, and turning away from self-destruction.

One cannot leave the "Conclusion" to *The Renaissance* without acknowledging the power which that handful of pages seems to possess even today, a hundred years after their composition. In their own generation, their pungency was overwhelming; not only did Pater withdraw them in the second edition, because he too was alarmed at their effect, but he toned them down when they were restored in the third edition (I have given the changes in this volume's Notes). The skeptical eloquence of the "Conclusion" cost Pater considerable preferment at Oxford. There is a splendidly instructive letter from John Wordsworth (clerical grandnephew of the poet) to Pater, written in 1873, indignantly summing up the "Conclusion" as asserting: "that no fixed principles either of religion or morality can be regarded as certain, that the only thing worth living for is momentary enjoyment and that probably or certainly the soul dissolves at death into elements which are destined never to reunite." One can oppose to this very minor Wordsworth a reported murmur of Pater's: "I wish they would not call me a hedonist. It gives such a wrong impression to those who do not know Greek."

Early Pater, in all high seriousness, attains a climax in those wonderful pages on the flux-of-sensations, and the necessity of dying with a faith in art, that conclude *The Renaissance*. Written in 1868, they came initially out of a review of William Morris's poetry that became the suppressed essay on "Aesthetic Poetry." They gave Pater himself the problem of how he was to write up to so fierce a demand-of-self: "To burn always with this hard, gemlike flame, to maintain this ecstasy, is success in life."

FICTIVE SELVES

Pater's own life, by his early standards, was only ambiguously a success. His work, after *The Renaissance*, is of three kinds, all of them already present in his first book. One is "imaginary portraits," a curious mixed genre, of which the novel *Marius the Epicurean* is the most important, and of which four excellent shorter examples are given [elsewhere]: the semi-autobiographical "The Child in the House," two stories from the book called *Imaginary Portraits*, and a classical example from *Greek Studies*. Another grouping of Pater's work, critical essays, were mostly gathered in *Appreciations*, from which I have selected liberally. The last group, classical studies proper, stand a little apart from the rest of his work, are more lightly represented in this book, and will be considered at the close of this Introduction.

"Imaginary portraits," in Pater's sense, are an almost indescribable genre. Behind them stand the monologues of Browning and of Rossetti, the *Imaginary Conversations* of Landor, perhaps Sainte-Beuve's *Portraits contemporains*. Like *The Renaissance* and *Appreciations*, they are essays or quasi-essays; like "The Child in the House" they are semi-autobiographical; yet it hardly helps to see "Sebastian Van Storck," or "Denys l'Auxerrois" or "Hippolytus Veiled" as being essays or veiled confessions. Nor are they romance-fragments, though closer to that than to short stories. It may be best to call them what Yeats called his Paterian stories, "Mythologies," or "Romantic Mythologies." Or, more commonly, they could be called simply "reveries," for even at their most marmoreal and baroque they are highly disciplined reveries, and even the lengthy *Marius the Epicurean* is more a historicizing reverie than it is a historical novel. "Reverie" comes from the French *rêver*, "to dream," and is already used in music to describe an instrumental composition of a dreamlike character. The power and precariousness alike of Pater's reveries are related to their hovering near the thresholds of wish-fulfillment. I suspect that Pater's nearest ancestor here is Browning, even as Ruskin looms always behind Pater's aesthetic criticism. Just as Browning made fictive selves, to escape his earlier strain of Shelleyan subjectivity in the verse-romances *Pauline*, *Paracelsus*, and *Sordello*, so Pater turned to "imaginary portraits" to escape the subjective confession that wells up in his "Leonardo da Vinci" and "Conclusion" to *The Renaissance*. On this view, The Renaissance is Pater's version of Shelley's *Alastor* or Keats's *Endymion*; it is a prose-poem of highly personal Romantic quest after the image of desire, visualized by Pater in the Mona Lisa. Turning from so deep a self-exposure, Pater arrives at his kind of less personal reverie, a consciously fictive kind.

Pater had no gifts for narrative, or drama, or psychological portrayal, and he knew this well enough. Unlike Browning, he could not make a half-world, let alone the full world of a mythopoeic master like Blake. Pater, who intensely admired both poets, oriented his portraits with more specific reference to the most inescapable of Romantic poets, Wordsworth, concerning whom he wrote the best of his essays in strictly literary criticism. In the nearly-as-distinguished essay on "Coleridge," Pater justly praises Wordsworth as a more instinctual poet than Coleridge. Wordsworth is praised for "that flawless temperament ... which keeps his conviction of a latent intelligence in nature within the limits of sentiment or instinct, and confines it to those delicate and subdued shades of expression which perfect art allows." Pater, too consciously, seeks in his portraits to be instinctual rather than intellectual, hoping that thus he can avoid drama and self-consciousness. Unfortunately, he cannot sustain the Wordsworthian comparison, as again he knew, for though he shared Wordsworth's early naturalism, he lacked the primordial, Tolstoyan power that sustains poems like "The Ruined Cottage," "Michael," "The Old Cumberland Beggar." Yet he yearned for such power, and would have been a Wordsworthian novelist, like George Eliot and Hardy, if he had found the requisite strength. But this yearning, poignantly felt all through the beautiful Wordsworth essay, was a desperate desire for his opposite. Wordsworth lived in nature, Pater in a dream. Longing for the sanctities of earth, Pater found his true brothers in Rossetti and Morris, poets of phantasmagoria, and his true children in Yeats and the Tragic Generation. The "imaginary portraits" are crucial to our understanding of Pater, but as art they are equivocal achievements, noble but divided against themselves.

SORROWS OF INFLUENCE

Pater is not the greatest critic English Romanticism produced—Coleridge and Ruskin vie for that eminence—but he is certainly the most underrated major nineteenth-century critic, in our own time. He is superior to his older rival, Arnold, and to his disciple, Wilde, both of whom receive more approval at this moment. Yet even as a literary critic, he is evasive, and remains more a master of reverie than of description, let alone analysis, which is alien to him. This becomes a curious critical strength in him, which requires both description and analysis to be apprehended.

Appreciations begins with the extraordinary essay on "Style," which is Pater's *credo* as a literary critic. As the essay urges awareness of the root-meanings of words, we need to remember that "style" originally meant an ancient instrument for writing on a waxed tablet, and having one pointed end for incising words, and one blunt end for rubbing out writing, and smoothing the tablet down. We might also remember that "appreciations" originally meant "appraisals." Before appraising Wordsworth, Coleridge, Rossetti, Morris, Lamb, and others, Pater offers us a vision of his stylistic attitude, incisive but also ascetic. Ian Fletcher, Pater's best scholar, reminds us that Pater's idea of style is "as a mode of perception, a total responsive gesture of the whole personality." Since Pater's own style is the most highly colored and self-conscious of all critics who have written in English, there is a puzzle here. Pater attempted to write criticism as though he were style's martyr, another Flaubert, and his insistence upon *askesis*, the exercise of self-curtailment, hardly seems compatible with a whole personality's total response. We do not believe that the style is the man when we read Pater, and a glance at his letters, which are incredibly dull and non-revelatory, confirms our disbelief. Pater's style, as befits the master of Wilde and Yeats, is a mask, and so Pater's idea of style and his actual style are irreconcilable. As always, Pater anticipates us in knowing this, and the essay "Style" centers upon this division.

Prose, according to Pater, is both music's opposite and capable of transformation into the condition of music, where form and matter seem to dissolve into one another. Pater's subject is always the mystery of utter individuality in the artistic personality; his style strives extravagantly to award himself such individuality. Whether in matter or style, Pater has therefore a necessary horror of literary influence, for to so desperate a quester after individuality *all* influence is over-influence. Pater's subject-matter is also Ruskin's and Arnold's; his style is also Swinburne's, or rather one of Swinburne's styles. Unlike Emerson and Nietzsche, who refused to see themselves as latecomers, Pater's entire vision is that of a latecomer longing for a renaissance, a rebirth into imaginative earliness. The hidden subject of *Appreciations* is the anxiety of influence, for which Pater's remedy is primarily his idea of *askesis*. "Style" urges self-restraint and renunciation, which it calls an economy of means but which in Pater's actual style seems more an economy of ends. Ruskin, threatening precursor, was profuse in means and ends, master of emphasis and of a daemonic, Sublime style, which in his case *was* the man. Swerving from Ruskin, Pater turns to Flaubert in "Style," seeking to invent a father to replace a dominant and dangerous aesthetic parent. But guilt prevails, and Pater's anxiety emerges in the essay's long concluding paragraph, which astonishingly seems to repeal the special emphasis of everything that has come before. "Good art, but not necessarily great art," Pater sadly murmurs, suddenly assuring us that greatness depends not upon style but on the matter, and then listing Dante, Milton, the King James Bible, and Hugo's *Les Misérables*, which seems rather exposed in this sublime company, and hardly rivals Flaubert in its concern with form. By the test of finding a place in the structure of human life, Hugo will receive the palm before Flaubert, Ruskin before Pater, Tennyson (secretly despised by Pater) before Rossetti and Morris. The final *askesis* of the champion of style is to abnegate himself before the burden of the common life he himself cannot bear.

In the essay, "Wordsworth," Pater has the happiness of being able to touch the commonal through the greatest mediating presence of nineteenth-century poetry. The essays on Wordsworth of Arnold and, *contra* Arnold, of A.C. Bradley, have been profoundly influential on rival schools of modern Wordsworthian interpretation, and Pater has not, but a reading of the three essays side by side will show Pater's superiority. His

Wordsworth is neither Arnold's poet of Nature nor Bradley's poet of the Sublime, but rather a poet of instinctual pagan religion. Wordsworth would have been outraged by Pater's essay, and most modern scholars agree that Pater's Wordsworth is too much Pater's Marius and too little Wordsworth. Against which, here is Pater's account of Wordsworth's actual religion, *as a poet*:

> Religious sentiment, consecrating the affections and natural regrets of the human heart, above all, that pitiful awe and care for the perishing human clay, of which relic-worship is but the corruption, has always had much to do with localities, with the thoughts which attach themselves to actual scenes and places. Now what is true of it everywhere, is truest of it in those secluded valleys where one generation after another maintains the same abiding place; and it was on this side, that Wordsworth apprehended religion most strongly. Consisting, as it did so much, in the recognition of local sanctities, in the habit of connecting the stones and trees of a particular spot of earth with the great events of life, till the low walls, the green mounds, the half-obliterated epitaphs seemed full of voices, and a sort of natural oracle, the very religion of those people of the dales, appeared but as another link between them and the earth, and was literally a religion of nature.

What is most meaningful for Pater are those voices coming from low walls, green mounds, tombstones. These things remain *things* in Wordsworth, wholly other than ourselves, yet we are deeply affected by what emanates from them. Pater was converted by them to the only religion he ever sincerely held, "literally a religion of nature." Just as the spots of time gave Wordsworth not a sense of the Divine, but precise knowledge to what point and how his own mind displayed a mastery over outward sense, so for Pater the spots of time he located in works of art gave a precise knowledge of the limited efficacy of the great Romantic program for renovation. The Romantics, as Pater understood and Arnold did not, were not nature-poets, but rather exemplars of the power of the mind, a power exerted against the object-world, or mere universe of death. Like Ruskin, and like Yeats and Stevens, Pater is a Romantic critic of Romanticism. Whether Pater writes on Giorgione or Winckelmann, the myth of Dionysus or Plato and the Doctrine of Change, Rossetti or Wilde, he writes as a conscious post-Wordsworthian, and his true subject is the partial and therefore tragic (because momentary) victory that art wins over the flux of sensations. The step beyond Pater is the one taken by his disciple, Yeats, who insists on the tragic joy of art's defeat, and who in his savage last phase celebrates the flux, exulting in his own doctrine of change.

Pater, withdrawing in *Appreciations* as in *Marius* from hailing the Heraclitean flux, is most moved by Wordsworth's quiet and primordial strength, the instinctual power of "impassioned contemplation." The eloquent and compassionate essay on "Coleridge" begins from Pater's recognition that Coleridge lacked this strength, and goes on to reject Coleridge's theological reliance upon outworn Absolutes. More strikingly, Pater pioneers in rejecting the Organic Analogue that Coleridge popularized. The motto of Pater's essay on Coleridge might well come from Nietzsche: "But do I bid thee be either plant or phantom?" Coleridge, Pater suggests, bid us be both, and so "obscured the true interest of art," which is to celebrate and lament our intolerably glorious condition of being mortal gods.

Beyond his steady defense of art's dignity against metaphysical and religious absolutes, Pater's nobility and uniqueness as a nineteenth-century literary critic stem from his insistence that the later nineteenth-century poet "make it new," even as that poet (like Pater himself) remains fully conscious of the inescapable sorrows of influence. Such a poet wanders in the half-lights of being a latecomer, trailing after the massive, fresh legacy of Goethe, Wordsworth, Blake, Hugo, Keats, Shelley, Baudelaire, Browning, even as Pater trailed after De Quincey, Lamb, Hazlitt, Coleridge, Arnold and the inescapable Ruskin, quite aside from Swinburne and the unmentioned Emerson and Nietzsche. Pater is still the best critic Pre-Raphaelite poetry has had, largely because he understood so well the anxiety of influence consciously present in Rossetti and unconsciously at work in Morris. The great essay on Morris, "Aesthetic Poetry," properly close to the "Conclusion" to *The Renaissance* which was quarried from it, presents Pater's most unguarded vision of poetic experience, so that Pater inevitably suppressed it:

> ... exotic flowers of sentiment expand, among people of a remote and unaccustomed beauty, somnambulistic, frail, androgynous, the light almost shining through them.... The colouring is intricate and delirious, as of "scarlet lilies." The influence of summer is like a poison in one's blood, with a sudden bewildered sickening of life and all things.... A passion of which the outlets are sealed, begets a tension of nerve, in which the sensible world comes to one with a reinforced brilliancy

and relief—all redness is turned into blood, all water into tears.... One characteristic, of the pagan spirit the aesthetic poetry has ... —the sense of death and the desire of beauty: the desire of beauty quickened by the sense of death....

Remarkably hinting that sadomasochistic yearnings and the anxiety of being a late representative of a tradition are closely related, Pater implies also that the heightened intensity of Morris and Rossetti (and of Pater) compensates for a destructively excessive sexual self-consciousness. The sensible world becomes phantasmagoria because one's own nature is baffled. A critic who understands the dialectic of style, as Pater magnificently did, is in no need of psychoanalytic reduction, as these essays on Morris and Rossetti show. *Appreciations*, which influenced Wilde and Yeats, Joyce and Pound, and more covertly Santayana and Stevens, has had little influence upon modern academic criticism, but one can prophesy that such influence will yet come. In a letter (January 8, 1888) to the young poet Arthur Symons, Pater recalled the marvelous dictum of Rossetti: "Conception, my boy, FUNDAMENTAL BRAINWORK, that is what makes the difference in all art." Pater's apt purpose in this recall was to urge Symons, and the other poets of his generation—Yeats, Dowson, Lionel Johnson—to make it new again through the fundamental brainwork necessary to overcome anxieties-of-influence. Here is the prophecy, addressed to the Paterian poets of the Tragic Generation, which Pound and his Modernists attempted to fulfill:

> I think the present age an unfavourable one to poets, at least in England. The young poet comes into a generation which has produced a large amount of first-rate poetry, and an enormous amount of good secondary poetry. You know I give a high place to the literature of prose as a fine art, and therefore hope you won't think me brutal in saying that the admirable qualities of your verse are those also of imaginative prose; as I think is the case also with much of Browning's finest verse....

The Poundian dictum, that verse was to be as well written as prose, initially meant Browningesque verse and Paterian prose, as Pound's early verse and prose show. That literary Modernism ever journeyed too far from its Paterian origins we may doubt increasingly, and we may wonder also whether modern criticism as yet has caught up with Pater.

CENTRIFUGAL AND CENTRIPETAL

In the important essay on Romanticism that he made the "Postscript" to *Appreciations*, Pater insisted that: "Material for the artist, motives of inspiration, are not yet exhausted ...," yet he wondered how "to induce order upon the contorted, proportionless accumulation of our knowledge and experience, our science and history, our hopes and disillusion ..." To help induce such an order seems to be the motive for *Plato and Platonism* (1893) and the posthumously published *Greek Studies* (1895). The Plato of Walter Pater is Montaigne's Plato (and probably Shelley's), a skeptical evader of systems, including his supposed own, whose idea of order is the dialectic: "Just there, lies the validity of the method—in a dialogue, an endless dialogue, with one's self." Clearly this is Pater more than Plato, and we need not wonder why Pater favored this above his other books. In the chapter, "The Genius of Plato," which I have included, Pater gives us another reverie, an idealized imaginary portrait of what he would have liked the mind of Pater to be. A comparison with Emerson's Plato (also influenced by Montaigne) is instructive, for the Plato of *Representative Men* is criticized for lacking "contact," an Emersonian quality not far removed from "freedom" or wildness. Unlike Plato, the author of the *Dialogues*, Walter Pater's visionary indeed lacks "contact," even as Pater severely made certain he himself lacked it.

Pater gives us the author of *The Republic* as "a seer who has a sort of sensuous love of the unseen," and whose mythological power brings the unseen closer to the seen. This Plato is possible and possibly even more than marginal, yet he does seem more Ficino or Pico della Mirandola than he was Plato, for he is more a poet of ideas than a metaphysician, and more of a solipsistic Realist than an Idealist. Above all, he is Pater's "crystal man," a model for Yeats's vision of an *antithetical* savior, a greater-than-Oedipus who would replace Christ, and herald a greater Renaissance than European man had known.

From reading both Hegel and Darwin, Pater had evolved a curious dialectic of history, expounded more thoroughly in *Greek Studies*, using the terms "centripetal" and "centrifugal" as the thesis and antithesis of a process always stopping short of synthesis:

> All through Greek history we may trace, in every sphere of the activity of the Greek mind, the action of these two opposing tendencies,—the centrifugal and centripetal.... There is the centrifugal, the Ionian, the Asiatic tendency, flying from the centre ... throwing itself forth in endless play of undirected

imagination; delighting in brightness and colour, in beautiful material, in changeful form everywhere, in poetry, in philosophy ... its restless versatility drives it towards ... the development of the individual in that which is most peculiar and individual in him.... It is this centrifugal tendency which Plato is desirous to cure, by maintaining, over against it, the Dorian influence of a severe simplification everywhere, in society, in culture....

The centrifugal is the vision of Heraclitus, the centripetal of Parmenides, or in Pater's more traditional terms from the "Postscript" to *Appreciations*, the centrifugal is the Romantic, and the centripetal the Classic. Pater rather nervously praises his Plato for Classic correctiveness, for a conservative centripetal impulse against his own Heraclitean Romanticism. Reductively, this is still Pater reacting against the excesses of *The Renaissance*, and we do not believe him when he presents himself as a centripetal man, though Yeats was partially persuaded, and relied upon Pater's dialectic when he created his own version of an aesthetic historicism in *A Vision*.

Pater, in his last phase, continued to rationalize his semi-withdrawal from his own earlier vision, but we can doubt that even he trusted his own hesitant rationalizations. We remember him, and read him, as the maker of critical reveries who yielded up the great societal and religious hopes of the major Victorian prose-prophets, and urged us to abide in the mortal truths of perception and sensation. His great achievement, in conjunction with Swinburne and the Pre-Raphaelites, was to empty Ruskin's aestheticism of its moral bias, and so to purify a critical stance appropriate for the apprehension of Romantic art. More than Swinburne, Morris, Rossetti, he became the father of Anglo-American Aestheticism, and subsequently the direct precursor of a Modernism that vainly attempted to be Post-Romantic. I venture the prophecy that he will prove also to be the valued precursor of a Post-Modernism still fated to be another Last Romanticism. We can judge, finally, this ancestor of our own sensibility as he himself judged Plato:

> His aptitude for things visible, with the gift of words, empowers him to express, as if for the eyes, what except to the eye of the mind is strictly invisible, what an acquired asceticism induces him to rank above, and sometimes, in terms of harshest dualism, oppose to, the sensible world. Plato is to be interpreted not merely by his antecedents, by the influence upon

him of those who preceded him, but by his successors, by the temper, the intellectual alliances, of those who directly or indirectly have been sympathetic with him.

Friedrich Nietzsche

(1844-1900)

ORIGIN AND PURPOSE, FOR THE SAKE OF LIFE, MUST BE KEPT APART; THAT fierce admonition is central to Nietzsche. Can they be kept apart, for very long, in an individual psychology? Nietzsche's true strength was as a psychologist, but he finally asked of us what no psychologist rightfully can expect, since the cyclic return of aim or purpose to origin is not to be evaded, a dark lesson taught by poets and speculators throughout recorded time. Beginnings have more than prestige; they foster the perpetual illusion of freedom, even though to invade that illusion generally results in dying.

Nietzsche's deepest teaching, as I read it, is that authentic meaning is painful, and that the pain itself is the meaning. Between pain and meaning comes memory, a memory of pain that then becomes a memorable meaning:

> "How can one create a memory for the human animal? How can one impress something upon this partly obtuse, partly flighty mind, attuned only to the passing moment, in such a way that it will stay there?"

One can well believe that the answers and methods for solving this primeval problem were not precisely gentle; perhaps indeed there was nothing more fearful and uncanny in the whole prehistory of man than his *mnemotechnics*. "If something is to stay in the memory it must be burned in; only that which never ceases to *hurt* stays in the memory"—this is a main clause of the oldest (unhappily also the most enduring) psychology on earth. One might even say that wherever on earth solemnity, seriousness, mystery, and gloomy coloring still distinguish the life of man and a people, something of the terror that formerly attended all promises, pledges, and vows on earth is *still effec-tive*: the past, the longest, deepest and sternest past, breathes upon us and rises up in us whenever we become "serious." Man could never do without blood, torture, and sacrifices when he felt the need to create a memory for himself; the most dreadful sacrifices and pledges (sacrifices of the first-born among them), the most repulsive mutilations (castration, for example), the cruelest rites of all the religious cults (and all religions are at the deepest level systems of cruelties)—all this has its origin in the instinct that realized that pain is the most powerful aid to mnemonics.

I hesitate to name this as Nietzsche's most fundamental insight, but I myself always remember it first when I think of Nietzsche. That the hurt itself should be the *logos*, the link of meaning that connects character and feeling, is the implicit teaching of all religions, which indeed are "systems of cruelties" as Nietzsche calls them, and I am certain he would have placed Marxism and psychoanalysis among them. But I fear that Nietzsche's insight is darker and more comprehensive than that. It embraces all literature as well, since what *On the Genealogy of Morals* goes on to call "the ascetic spirit" might as well be called "the aesthetic spirit" also, or the ascetic/aesthetic ideal:

That this idea acquired such power and ruled over men as imperiously as we find it in history, especially wherever the civilization and taming of man has been carried through, expresses a great fact: the *sickliness* of the type of man we have had hitherto, or at least of the tamed man, and the physiolog-ical struggle of man against death (more precisely: against dis-gust with life, against exhaustion, against the desire for the "end"). The ascetic priest is the incarnate desire to be differ-ent, to be in a different place, and indeed this desire at its greatest extreme, its distinctive fervor and passion; but pre-cisely this power of his desire is the chain that holds him cap-tive so that he becomes a tool for the creation of more favor-able conditions for being here and being man—it is precisely this *power* that enables him to persuade to existence the whole herd of the ill-constituted, disgruntled, underprivileged, unfortunate, and all who suffer of themselves, by instinctively going before them as their shepherd. You will see my point: this ascetic priest, this apparent enemy of life, this *denier*—

precisely he is among the greatest *conserving* and yes—creating forces of life.

With singular contempt, Nietzsche keeps repeating that, in the case of an artist, ascetic ideals mean nothing whatever, or so many things as to amount to nothing whatever. This is part of his polemic against his once-idealized Wagner, but it is also the defense of a failed poet who could not acknowledge his failure, as Zarathustra dreadfully demonstrates. The desire to be different, to be elsewhere, is the one motive for metaphor in Nietzsche, and perhaps in everyone else as well. If it leads to a Moses, then it leads to a Goethe also. The antithetical spirit in Nietzsche, his own version of the ascetic and the aesthetic, drives him towards what I venture to call a poetics of pain, which has to be read antithetically, as meaning nearly the reverse of what it appears to say:

> *Art*—to say it in advance, for I shall some day return to this subject at greater length—art, in which precisely the *lie* is sanctified and the will to *deception* has a good conscience, is much more fundamentally opposed to the ascetic ideal than is science: this was instinctively sensed by Plato, the greatest enemy of art Europe has yet produced. Plato versus Homer: that is the complete, the genuine antagonism—there the sincerest advocate of the "beyond," the great slanderer of life; here the instinctive deifier, the golden nature. To place himself in the service of the ascetic ideal is therefore the most distinctive corruption of an artist that is at all possible; unhappily, also one of the most common forms of corruption, for nothing is more easily corrupted than an artist.

The agon between Plato and Homer here is misread, creatively or strongly, as a struggle between the ascetic and the aesthetic, rather than as the struggle for aesthetic supremacy Nietzsche elsewhere declared it to be. But Nietzsche's superb irony makes my attempt to "correct" him a redundancy; what artists have not shown such corruption in which they place themselves in the service of the ascetic ideal? Indeed, what other option have they, or we, according to Nietzsche? Which is to say: how are we to read the final section of the *Genealogy*?

> Apart from the ascetic ideal, man, the human *animal*, had no meaning so far. His existence on earth contained no goal; "why man at all?"—was a question without an answer; the will for man

and earth was lacking; behind every great human destiny there sounded as a refrain a yet greater "in vain!" This is precisely what the ascetic ideal means: that something was *lacking*, that man was surrounded by a fearful *void*—he did not know how to justify, to account for, to affirm himself; he *suffered* from the problem of his meaning. He also suffered otherwise, he was in the main a sickly animal: but his problem was not suffering itself, but that there was no answer to the crying question, "*why* do I suffer?"

Man, the bravest of animals and the one most accustomed to suffering, does *not* repudiate suffering as such; he *desires* it, he even seeks it out, provided he is shown a *meaning* for it, a *purpose* of suffering. The meaninglessness of suffering, *not* suffering itself, was the curse that lay over mankind so far—*and the ascetic ideal offered man meaning*! It was the only meaning offered so far; any meaning is better than none at all; the ascetic ideal was in every sense the *"faute de mieux" par excellence* so far. In it, suffering was *interpreted*; the tremendous void seemed to have been filled; the door was closed to any kind of suicidal nihilism. This interpretation—there is no doubt of it—brought fresh suffering with it, deeper, more inward, more poisonous, more life-destructive suffering: it placed all suffering under the perspective of *guilt*.

But all this notwithstanding—man was *saved* thereby, he possessed a meaning, he was henceforth no longer like a leaf in the wind, a plaything of nonsense—the "sense-less"—he could now will something; no matter at first to what end, why, with what he willed: *the will itself was saved.*

We can no longer conceal from ourselves *what* is expressed by all that willing which has taken its direction from the ascetic ideal; this hatred of the human, and even more of the animal, and more still of the material, this horror of the senses, of reason itself, this fear of happiness and beauty, this longing to get away from all appearance, change, becoming, death, wishing, from longing itself—all this means—let us dare to grasp it—*a will to nothingness*, an aversion to life, a rebellion against the most fundamental presuppositions of life; but it is and remains a will! ... And, to repeat in conclusion what I said at the beginning: man would rather will *nothingness* than *not* will.

To give suffering a meaning is not so much to relieve suffering as it is to enable meaning to get started, rather than merely repeated. What

Nietzsche shares most deeply with the Hebrew Bible and with Freud is the drive to find sense in everything, to interpret everything, but here Nietzsche is at his most dialectical, since he knows (and cannot accept) the consequences of everything having a meaning. There could never be anything new, since everything would have happened already. That is the Hebrew Bible's loyalty to Yahweh, its trust in the Covenant, and finally that is Freud's faith in the efficacy of interpretation. And that is also Nietzsche's most profound argument with the Hebrew Bible.

"Man ... suffered from the problem of his meaning" and then yielded to the ascetic ideal, which made the suffering itself into the meaning, and so opened the perspective of guilt. Rather than be void of meaning, man took the void *as* meaning, a taking that saved the will, at a fearful cost. Nietzsche has no alternative but to accuse the poets of nihilism, an accusation in which he himself did not altogether believe. But his association of memory, pain, and meaning is unforgettable and productive, suggesting as it does an antithetical poetics not yet fully formulated, yet lurking in his forebodings of an uncannier nihilism than any yet known.

II

"We possess art lest we should perish of the truth." If a single apothegm could sum up Nietzsche on the aesthetic, it would be that. Poetry tells lies, but the truth, being the reality principle, reduces to death, our death. To love truth would be to love death. This hardly seems to me, as it does to Gilles Deleuze, a tragic conception of art. The world is rich in meaning because it is rich in error, strong in suffering, when seen from an aesthetic perspective. Sanctifying a lie, and deceiving with a good conscience, is the necessary labor of art, because error about life is necessary for life, since the truth about life merely hastens death. The will to deceive is not a tragic will, and indeed is the only source for an imaginative drive that can counter the ascetic drive against life. But these antithetical drives, as in Freud's *Beyond the Pleasure Principle*, form the figure of a chiasmus. Nietzsche is scarcely distinguishable from the Pater of *Marius the Epicurean*, who also so mingles the ascetic and the aesthetic that we cannot undo their mutual contaminations, at least in the strong poet.

Richard Rorty makes the crucial observation that only the strong poet, in Nietzsche, is able to appreciate his own contingency, and thus to appropriate it:

> The line between weakness and strength is thus the line
> between using language which is familiar and universal and

producing language which, though initially unfamiliar and idiosyncratic, somehow makes tangible the blind impress all one's behavings bear.

Rorty goes on to say that Nietzsche does not avoid an "inverted Platonism—his suggestion that a life of self-creation can be as complete and as autonomous as Plato thought a life of contemplation might be." In some terrible sense, Nietzsche did live his life as though it were a poem, and found a value in the idea of his own suffering, a value not unrelated to his adversary, the ascetic ideal. In his own terms, Nietzsche was one of the corrupted strong poets, but such corruption is indistinguishable from strength, even as the ascetic and the aesthetic spirits do blend together. More even than Pater, Nietzsche is an aesthete, giving everything to perception, and finding valid perception only in the arts. Yet Nietzsche, unlike Pater, has his own kind of uneasy conscience at his own aestheticism.

Does Nietzsche offer any mode of understanding reality that does not depend upon literary culture? Clearly not, and that seems to me his difference from all previous psychologists and philosophers. Though he insisted that he was wiser than the poets, he never presented us with that wisdom. If you are going to be the poet of your own life, then you are going to share, at best, the wisdom of the strong poets, and not of the philosophers, theologians, psychologists, or politicians. I think that Nietzsche's true strength, his originality, was that he did realize the cognitive implications of poetic wisdom. To call our cosmos the primordial poem of mankind, something that we have composed ourselves, sounds like Shelley, but is Nietzsche:

1046 (1884)

1. We want to hold fast to our senses and to our faith in them—and think their consequences through to the end! The nonsensuality of philosophy hitherto as the greatest nonsensicality of man.

2. The existing world, upon which all earthly living things have worked so that it appears as it does (durable and changing *slowly*), we want to go on building—and not criticize it away as false!

3. Our valuations are a part of this building; they emphasize and underline. Of what significance is it if entire religions say: "all is bad and false and evil"! This condemnation of the entire process can only be a judgment of the ill-constituted!

4. To be sure, the ill-constituted can be the greatest suffer-
ers and the most subtle? The contented could be of little value?

5. One must understand the artistic basic phenomenon that
is called "life"—the building spirit that builds under the most
unfavorable conditions: in the slowest manner——A demon-
stration of all its combinations must first be produced afresh: it
preserves itself.

Walter Pater would have had no difficulty in endorsing this; his own
emphasis upon sensation and perception as constitutive of his kind of reality would be wholly consonant with Nietzsche, except that Pater is overtly and candidly solipsistic. Nietzsche, rebellious student of Schopenhauer,
might not have agreed with his mentor (or with Wittgenstein) that what
the solipsist means is right.

What the poet means is hurtful, Nietzsche tells us, nor can we tell
the hurt from the meaning. What are the pragmatic consequences for criticism of Nietzsche's poetics of pain? To ask that is to ask also what I am
convinced is the determining question of the canonical: what makes one
poem more memorable than another? The Nietzschean answer must be
that the memorable poem, the poem that has more meaning, or starts
more meaning going, is the poem that gives (or commemorates) more
pain. Like Freud's ghastly Primal History Scene (in *Totem and Taboo*), the
strong poem repeats and commemorates a primordial pain. Or to be more
Nietzschean (and more Paterian), the strong poem constitutes pain, brings
pain into being, and so creates meaning.

The pain is the meaning. I find this formulation peculiarly and per-
sonally disturbing because, ever since I was a small boy, I have judged
poems on the basis of just how memorable they immediately seemed. It is
distressing to reflect that what seemed inevitable phrasing to me (and still
does), was the result of inescapable pain, rather than of what it seemed to
be, bewildering pleasure. But then the Nietzschean Sublime, like the
Longinian and the Shelleyan, depends upon our surrendering easier pleasures in order to experience more difficult pleasures. Strong poetry is difficult, and its memorability is the consequence of a difficult pleasure, and a
difficult enough pleasure is a kind of pain.

Rorty is right, I think, in associating Nietzsche's poetics with the
acceptance of contingency, to which I would add only that it is very painful
to accept contingency, to be the contained rather than the container. The
uneasy fusion of the aesthetic and ascetic spirits (I would prefer to call
them stances) figures again in Nietzsche's ability to compound with factic-
ity. Stevens's Nietzschean "The Poems of Our Climate" ends with a return

to the primordial poem of mankind, to what had been so long composed, and so ends with the Nietzschean exaltation of the aesthetic lie, lest we perish of the truth:

> Note that, in this bitterness, delight,
> Since the imperfect is so hot in us,
> Lies in flawed words and stubborn sounds.

Sigmund Freud

(1856-1939)

C{HARLES} R{YCROFT} EXPLAINS HIS USE OF THE WORD "INNOCENCE" IN THE title of his *The Innocence of Dreams* as a reference to "the idea that dreams back knowingness, display an indifference to received categories, and have a core which cannot but be sincere and is uncontaminated by the self-conscious will." Such an explanation is itself innocent and hardly accounts for the polemical force of the title, since the book is largely written against Freud where Freud is strongest, in the interpretation of dreams. The actual rhetorical force of Rycroft's title is that it contains an implicit interpretation of Freudian theory, in effect making the title of what Freud called the "Dream Book" into *The Guilt of Dreams*. So many years after the publication of *Die Traumdeutung* (1900), it is an admirable act of audacity for an experienced psychoanalyst like Rycroft to dissent so completely from the Freudian theory of dream interpretation. But whether Rycroft has much more than audacity to offer in this book is a question that thoughtful readers must decide by returning to the text of Freud. That impetus to return, like analytic audacity, has its own value, and also must be judged a service that Rycroft has helped perform.

These are still the days, in many critical circles, of "French Freud," meaning Jacques Lacan and his influence. Lacan and his admirers assert continuously that the principal virtue of Lacan is that he *has* gone back to the problematics of a serious reading of Freud's text as text. Whether one credits this assertion, or takes precisely the contrary view with Richard Wollheim, who insists that Lacan gives us psycholinguistics and not Freud's psychoanalysis, the issue is clearly one of accurately *reading* Freud. Rycroft takes no part in this debate, but I fear that his performance as a reader of Freud will encourage the disciples of Lacan. Unlike Wollheim, whose *Sigmund Freud* (1971) is a close and formidable reading, and unlike

Philip Rieff in this country, Rycroft gives us an account of Freud that I am compelled to judge as a weak misreading. My judgment, if correct, will not remove all value from Rycroft's book, since its constructive aspect stems not so much from his argument against what Freud truly never said as it does from his own experience as an analyst.

Rycroft starts out by setting himself against the analogical method that is always central to Freud's work. So Rycroft argues: "Freud maintained that dreams are neurotic symptoms or, to be more precise, are analogous to neurotic symptoms." This is to begin by missing a crucial point, precisely stated by Rieff in *Freud: The Mind of The Moralist*:

> The inclusiveness of Freud's idea of a symptom should be kept
> in mind: ultimately all action is symptomatic. There are "nor-
> mal" symptoms, like the dream, as well as somatic symptoms
> like a facial tic or a paralyzed leg.

Rycroft believes that for Freud "dreams and neurotic symptoms betoken failures of repression." Freud's largest actual statement about dreams has a different emphasis: "*a dream is a (disguised) fulfillment of a (suppressed or repressed) wish.*" Though Rycroft does not say so, I suspect that his reaction away from Freud on dreams begins with his distaste for the crisis-like aspect of *The Interpretation of Dreams*, which seems to me the book's most literary quality. The crisis for Freud was double, involving both the death of his father and the agonistic relationship with Fliess. Doubtless Freud's greatest work pays a price in darkened knowledge because of its origin in Freud's path-breaking self-analysis. Freud's own dreams became for him "normal" occurrences of what in others he would have judged to be the "psychopathological." It can be argued against Freud that the dream need not have been the inevitable paradigm of hallucination, but though the choice was arbitrary, it was analogically workable. Most powerful interpretive models tend to be arbitrary in their origins, but become inescapable in later interpretive traditions. It was *for Freud* that dream-interpretation proved the royal road to the Unconscious. Coming after Freud, we inherit his insight at the expense of his dominance over us.

Rycroft's fundamental dissent from this dominance comes in his account of the Primary and Secondary Processes, an account which is again not Freud's own. But rather than contrast each of Rycroft's summaries with the actual Freudian text, a wearisome process, I advance to Rycroft's list of the four defects he finds in the Freudian relation of Primary Process to dreaming. These are:

(1)   Since everyone dreams, Freud implicitly argues that everyone is neurotic.

(2)   To assume that acquiring the capacity for rational or Secondary Process thinking depends on repression of the Primary Process "implies that human beings enter the world totally unadapted to meet it, an inherently improbable assumption."

(3)   By supposedly relating imagination and creative activity to the Primary Process, Freud had to characterize them as "in principle neurotic, regressive and symptom-like."

(4)   Freud's formulations belong to his "mechanistic assumption that the mind is a mental apparatus within which energy circulates.... Unfortunately, however, we really have no idea what mental energy is or what the concept means."

Of Rycroft's four objections, the first has been met already by Rieff's accurate account of Freud's idea of a symptom. The second is indeed Freud's tragic premise, and ultimately explains why there is a civil war in the human psyche, so that the Unconscious and not nature or the state is what most inescapably threatens each of us. The third, to which I will return later, is wholly inadequate to Freud's quite troubled and finally evasive view of art. The fourth begins by accusing Freud of a reductionism that he proudly espoused and then goes on to a complaint that Freud met quite cheerfully by acknowledging that his theory of drives was the necessary mythology that psychoanalysis had to exploit. To sum up Rycroft's objections, their common element is an inability to accept what is most basic in Freud's theories of the mind, which means that Rycroft has become another "humanistic" revisionist of Freud, or most simply, if Rycroft is still a psychoanalyst, then Freud was something else.

If I myself were to criticize Freud's theories of dream-interpretation, I would start with what seems to me his most striking notion about dream-thought, which is that such thought is truly marked by clarity, although its clarity has been repressed. For Freud, the manifest "text" of the dream, its telling by the patient to the analyst, carries the stigma of being the work of the Unconscious, but the "latent" content or true significance of the dream is itself not Primary but Secondary Process labor. Something Secondary and rational has been repressed, and the work of analytical interpretation undoes the repression and yields a clear account of a "normal" thought.

Jung scorned the Freudian idea here in both respects. For Jung, the true thought at the origin of the dream and its true interpretation must both come up out of the Primal or Gnostic Abyss of a truly creative Unconscious. Though I accept Freud and not Jung on dreams, there is little doubt but that Jung shows more affection for dreams than for their interpretations, whereas what delights Freud is what he can make out of dreams. It is in this rather ironic sense that Rycroft actually teaches "the innocence of dreams."

Wollheim, who seems to me as faithful an expositor as Freud could find, usefully emphasizes that the element of wish *in* dreams is not expressed *by* dreams, and so Freud was able to posit what he called the dream-work as something that disguised wish. This must mean that wish is repressed *before* it gets into the dream. Such a conclusion also serves to devalue dreams and reminds us again that the Freudian Unconscious is a deliberate reduction of the rich, dark Abyss of the ancient (and now Jungian) Unconscious.

What gives Freud the interpretive self-confidence to so reduce dreams, and to insist so mercilessly that dream-thought, as opposed to dream-work, is at one with his own rationalizing interpretations? Part of the answer, and another vulnerable aspect of Freudian procedure, is that Freud's dream-text for interpretation is partly written by Freud himself, since it is a version of dream that emerges from the analytic session. This means that it is subject to the dynamics of the transference, and so is a telling that takes place within the context of the analyst's authority.

Rieff gallantly attempts to rescue the dream from the full consequences of Freud's authority by seeing every dreamer as a natural poet and intellectual precisely in the effort to outwit his interpreter, the force of culture as personified in Freud: "The chief quality of the dream as *interpreted* is not so much its meaning as the elaborateness of its meaningful disguises." Upon this, two observations: first, that Freud would have disagreed with Rieff here, though my own sympathies are with Rieff, and second, it is exactly this aspect of Freudian interpretation that partly justifies Lacan. If there is so large a gap between the elaborations of manifest content and the simplicity of latent content, then dreams (in their Freudian context of the transference) provoke the Lacanian strong misreading of the priority of signifier over signified or the contrast between rich figuration and poverty-stricken meaning. It is worth recalling that Rieff anticipated many of the major insights of the Lacanian school and indeed set their pattern when he remarked: "In radical opposition to constitutional psychology, Freud puts language before body."

Rycroft would have profited by pondering Rieff again before he too easily dismissed the cunning intensities of Freudian dream-interpretation. Freud characteristically condemns the dream as an unfaithful translation of the dream-thoughts, and so "a highly incomplete and fragmentary version of them." Rieff invokes Hazlitt, with his dictum that "poetry represents forms chiefly as they suggest other forms, feelings as they suggest other feelings." Commenting upon this as analogue to Freud, Rieff catches the essential agonistic relationship between Freud and the dream:

> Assuming a dream never means what it says, that it is always a substitute for something else which cannot be said and leads to further associations which are in themselves substitutes, Freud may compliment a dream so far as to call it an "exceptionally clever dream production." But this is the compliment paid by a gracious antagonist; Freud treated a dream as an opponent in the work of interpretation, trying by its cleverness to outwit the interpreter.

This means that a dream, however elaborate, is only a substitute for a truer text, indeed an interpretive substitute and so particularly suspect. A dream, in the Freudian view, is thus a belated text, an inadequate commentary upon a missing poem. Its plot is probably irrelevant; what matters is some protruding element, some image that seems hardly to belong to the text. In this sense, Freud is a legitimate father to Lacan and Derrida, with their deconstructions of the drive, except that he would have urged them to the abysses of the dream and not of his own texts.

Rycroft, once he has moved on from Freud to various types of dreams, their relations to sleep, and to cultural patterns, transcends the drubbing I have been administering. This makes me wish he had not taken on Freud, but that is the burden of the writing psychoanalyst, who is tempted to a battle he is doomed to lose. Rycroft is drily persuasive when he writes that neither he nor anyone he has known seems to have had what Ernest Jones would classify as a true nightmare, the criteria of Jones's *On the Nightmare* (1910) being too severe for mere reality to satisfy. Similarly, Rycroft is able to use the later Freud against the author of *The Interpretation of Dreams* on the difficult issue of anxious dreams. Anxiety is a subject by which Rycroft's intellect is kindled, and he makes an original contribution (at least to me) when he shows that it is possible to dream *about* anxiety without necessarily having a dream that itself causes anxiety. I wish he had done more, in this book, to demonstrate that Freud's later modifications of his theories of defense and anxiety render his ideas on dreams less valid or stimulating.

Freud is a weaker antagonist on the subject of sleep and the physiol-
ogy of dreams, which seems to the Rycroft's best chapter. Freud was not
much interested in sleep, and he assumed that the function of the dream
was just to keep the dreamer from waking. Here Rycroft has the universal
advantage of all latecomers: more facts. Freud did not know that there was
normal sleep, with several depths, and also paradoxical sleep, during which
the sleeper in some ways hovers near wakefulness. Evidently most dreams,
perhaps even all, take place during paradoxical sleep, which seems to be as
much a necessity as normal sleep. Rycroft will not go so far as to say we
sleep in order to dream, but he goes back to the great neurologist
Hughlings Jackson (died 1911), who thought that sleep both got rid of the
previous day's useless memories and consolidated the necessary ones,
probably during dreamless sleep. If Jackson yet proves to be correct, then
one function of dreams is quite unlike anything Freud conceived, since
without dreams we would be burdened by more data than we could bear.

In a witty, brief penultimate chapter, Rycroft offers a reprise, saying
that the manifest content of his book is his attempt to go back beyond
Freud (and Jung) to what he calls the traditional, literary view of dreams,
with the difference of holding on to certain Freudian ideas, particularly
body symbolism in dream imagery and the genetic inheritance of the family romance. The latent theme of the book then would have to be, as he
says, the question of the origin of creative or imaginative energy. This is
the subject of Rycroft's final chapter, but unfortunately there is little here
that is either new or important. Rycroft falls back upon unanalyzed
Coleridgean Imagination and undiscussed Keatsian negative capability,
while he largely dismisses Freud upon art and artists. Psychoesthetics is a
still inchoate field, but Rycroft seems to know nothing of it, whether
British, American, or French.

I conclude, in a coda, by suggesting what I wish Rycroft had discussed, if only he had felt more respect for the Freudian achievement in
dream-interpretation. Rieff's assertion that psychoanalysis parodies the
traditions of religious hermeneutics is still valid and provocative. But psychoanalysis is also a reductive parody of poetry, which may be another way
of saying that poetry has always been a transcendental kind of psychoanalysis, a mode marked by patterns of transference and counter-transfer-
ence, or of influence and its anxieties. Freud spoke truly (and also somewhat anxiously) in his repeated admissions that the poets had been there
before him. Certainly Lacan, at his rare best, gives us what the poets have
given more fully and freely. Dreams, like psychoanalysis, parody and
reduce poems, if we follow Freud by treating dreams in terms of their
latent content or "meaning." But dreams, in their manifest content, in plot

and imagery, share in the poetic elements that tend to defy reduction and reductiveness.

Freud wanted and needed his reductions, his quest being scientific and therapeutic. As a therapeutic diviner of dreams he is beyond all competition, ancient and modern, and this more because of than in spite of his interpretive overconfidence. But dreams are not poems, not even bad poems, and Freud was too wary to expend his formidable energies in reducing poems. Rycroft has an honorable nostalgia for treating dreams with a more literary respect than Freud accorded them. It would be more interesting to accept Freud's voluntary limitation and then to see just what kind of an enabling act was constituted by this pragmatic disrespect for dreams. Beyond this acceptance, and this seeing, might come a fresh awareness of the multiple ways in which poetry and psychoanalysis converge and yet differ as modes of interpretation. Freud found his peers in the poets because of their *power of interpretation*, but his aims were not compatible with the largest ambitions of poetry, as I think he came to understand.

W.E.B. Du Bois

(1868-1963)

NEARLY A CENTURY AGO, IN 1903, W.E.B. DU BOIS, IN HIS *THE SOULS OF Black Folk*, composed one of the central passages of African American literary consciousness:

> After the Egyptian and Indian, the Greek and Roman, the Teuton and Mongolian, the Negro is a sort of seventh son, born with a veil, and gifted with second sight in this American world,—a world which yields him no true self-consciousness, but only lets him see himself through the revelation of the other world. It is a peculiar sensation, this double consciousness, this sense of always looking at one's self through the eyes of others, of measuring one's soul by the tape of a world that looks on in amused contempt and pity. One ever feels his two-ness, an American, a Negro; two souls, two thoughts, two unreconciled strivings; two warring ideals in one dark body, whose dogged strength alone keeps it from being torn.

Whether Du Bois was aware that he was revising Emerson, I do not know, but there seems an ironic modification of Emerson embedded in Du Bois's double consciousness. For Emerson, the double consciousness was universal, and was also primarily a positive goad to self-trust:

> "Man is the dwarf of himself. Once he was permeated and dissolved by spirit. He filled nature with his overflowing currents. Out from him sprang the sun and moon; from man, the sun; from woman, the moon. The laws of his mind, the periods of his actions externized themselves into day and night, into the

year and the seasons. But, having made for himself this huge shell, his waters retired; he no longer fills the veins and veinlets; he is shrunk to a drop. He sees, that the structure still fits him, but fits him colossally. Say, rather, once it fitted him, now it corresponds to him from far and on high.

He adores timidly his work. Now is man the follower of the sun, and woman the follower of the moon. Yet sometimes he starts in his slumber, and wonders at himself and his house, and muses strangely at the resemblance betwixt him and it. He perceives that if his law is still paramount, if still he have elemental power, if his word is sterling yet in nature, it is not conscious power, it is not inferior but superior to his will. It is Instinct." Thus my Orphic poet sang.

At present, man applies to nature but half his force. He works on the world with his understanding alone. He lives in it, and masters it by a penny-wisdom; and he that works most in it, is but a half-man, and whilst his arms are strong and his digestion good, his mind is imbruted, and he is a selfish savage. His relation to nature, his power over it, is through the understanding; as by manure; the economic use of fire, wind, water, and the mariner's needle; steam, coal, chemical agriculture; the repairs of the human body by the dentist and the surgeon. This is such a resumption of power, as if a banished king should buy his territories inch by inch, instead of vaulting at once into his throne. Meantime, in the thick darkness, there are not wanting gleams of a better light,—occasional examples of the action of man upon nature with his entire force,—with reason as well as understanding. Such examples are; the traditions of miracles in the earliest antiquity of all nations; the history of Jesus Christ; the achievements of a principle, as in religious and political revolutions, and in the abolition of the Slave-trade; the miracles of enthusiasms, as those reported by Swedenborg, Hohenlohe, and the Shakers; many obscure and yet contested facts, now arranged under the name of Animal Magnetism; prayer; eloquence; self-healing; and the wisdom of children. These are examples of Reason's momentary grasp of the sceptre; the exertions of a power which exists not in time or space, but an instantaneous in-streaming causing power. The difference between the actual and the ideal force of man is happily figured by the schoolmen, in saying, that the knowledge of man is an evening knowledge, *vespertina cognitio*, but that of God is a morning knowledge, *matutina cognitio*.

Du Bois has his own version of the split between the mere Understanding and the illuminating Reason, but his terms are necessarily social, and not metaphysical. What Emerson measured as an asset, Du Bois shrewdly weighed as a dialectical burden, a challenge to African American intellectuals and artists, a challenge profoundly painful but pragmatically provocative. The legacy of Du Bois is endless, and all but constitutes a poetics of pain.

His long life (Du Bois died in Ghana, at the age of ninety-five, on August 27, 1963) allowed a seventy-year campaign in black activism, still unmatched in epic grandeur, and sometimes Quixotic in its later gestures. Quite aside from his enormous and ongoing influence upon later and current African American intellectuals, Du Bois remains perpetually readable. A bitter ironist, Du Bois ranks high in any hierarchy of American polemical writing. His anger, inevitable and incessant, is disciplined by his need to persuade as well as exhort. Granted his extraordinary endurance and persistence, he remains an exemplary figure, one who would not give up.

A way of assessing the continued relevance of Du Bois is to consider the relation of his "double consciousness" to Ralph Ellison's *Invisible Man* (1952), still the most eminent work of African American literature nearly a half-century after its initial publication. William Lyne, a scholar of Du Bois's effect upon black writers, tries to separate out the strands of *Invisible Man*'s fusion of literary High Modernism (Henry James, T.S. Eliot, James Joyce) and a "Blues consciousness," the jazz element in Ellison's work. Lynne's attempt is admirable, yet attempts to take apart what the novelist has accomplished: a permanent, dialectical interplay of James Joyce and Louis Armstrong.

Ellison fiercely scorned his mindless critics, black and white, who insisted that his adherence to the aesthetic criteria of High Modernism represented a betrayal of the folk ethos. Berndt Ostendorf, the distinguished German scholar of African American culture, is brilliantly exact in describing Ellison's highly deliberate revision of Emerson and of Du Bois:

> What Ralph Waldo Emerson and W.E.B. Du Bois called *double consciousness* Ellison prefers to call a *double vision*. This revision of Emerson's and Du Bois's concept provides a key example, in fact, of Ellison's turning an apparent liability into an asset.

Invisible man's "double vision" is compared by Ostendorf to the great critic Kenneth Burke's idea of "perspectives by incongruity." Burke saw *Invisible Man* as reconstituting its epoch, which from an African American perspective might well be termed "the epoch of W.E.B. Du Bois."

Aldous Huxley

(1894-1963)

ALDOUS HUXLEY CANNOT BE JUDGED TO HAVE ACHIEVED LASTING EMINENCE either as a novelist or as a spiritual guide. The best of his novels were *Antic Hay* and *Point Counter Point*, which I enjoyed in my youth, but now regard as very literate Period Pieces. His most famous fiction, *Brave New World*, scarcely sustains rereading: its basic metaphor, in which Henry Ford replaces Jesus Christ, now seems strained and even silly. Huxley's one great book is his *Collected Essays*, which includes such superb performances as "Wordsworth in the Tropics," "Tragedy and the Whole Truth," and "Music at Night." In this introduction, I turn mostly aside from Huxley-as-essayist in order to center upon his anthology-with-comments, *The Perennial Philosophy*, and two curious little books, *The Doors of Perception* and *Heaven and Hell*, both concerned with his visionary experiences induced by taking drugs.

Huxley defines the Perennial Philosophy as: "the metaphysic that recognizes a divine Reality substantial to the world of things and lives and minds; the psychology that finds in the soul something similar to, or even identical with, divine Reality; the ethic that places man's final end in the knowledge of the immanent and transcendent Ground of all being." The figures and texts testifying to this metaphysic, psychology, and ethic are very various: St. Augustine, St. Bernard, the Bhaghvad-Gita, the Buddha, St. Catherine of Siena, Chuang Tzu, *The Cloud of Unknowing*, Meister Eckhart, Fénelon, St. Francis de Sales, St. John of the Cross, Lao Tzu, Jalal-uddin Rumi, *Theologica Germanica*, Thomas Traherne. It will be noted that my list of these fifteen spiritual authorities is alphabetical, they being so diverse that no other ordering seems possible. But, to Aldous Huxley, they are all One Big Thing: The Perennial Philosophy. This Californian eclecticism helped to make Huxley one of the gurus of the New Age, but it renders me uneasy, despite my own spiritual convictions, which are not wholly antithetical to Huxley's.

Huxley's second wife, Laura, wrote a poignant memoir of her husband, *This Timeless Moment*, in which she reveals that she aided him in his dying moments with a substantial shot of LSD, as he desired. One hesitates to call the death of any distinguished author a Period Piece, but 1963 (the year of Huxley's death) cultivated very different fashions than 2003, when the dying are likelier to prefer morphine to mescalin or lysergic acid. I recall reading *The Doors of Perception*, and its sequel, *Heaven and Hell*, when they were published in the mid-Fifties, with a certain skepticism, as to whether aesthetic or spiritual experiences ought to be so palpably ascribed or reduced to a chemical base. Almost half a century later, rereading these treatises, my skepticism increases. Is there a difference, *in kind*, between the strawberry ice-cream *soma* of *Brave New World* and swallowing mescalin dissolved in water, as Huxley does at the onset of *The Doors of Perception*.

Huxley would have pointed out, with exquisite courtesy, that his mescalin-induced visions increased his awareness of Art and of God, while the Brave New Worlders, stuffed with *soma*, merely danced a sort of conga, spanking one another to the beat of:

> Orgy-porgy, Ford and fun
> Kiss the girls and make them One.
> Boys at one with girls at peace;
> Orgy-porgy gives release.

It is rather a distance from that to the Perennial Philosophy, but in each instance a chemical substance gives release. New Ages are always destined to become Old Ages, and Huxleyan spirituality alas now seems antique. Aldous Huxley was a superb essayist, but not quite either a novelist or a sage.

Gershom Scholem

(1897–1982)

"Kabbalah" has been, since about the year 1200, the popularly accepted word for Jewish esoteric teachings concerning God and everything God created. The word "Kabbalah" means "tradition," in the particular sense of "reception," and at first referred to the whole of Oral Law. But there existed among the Jews, both in their homeland and in Egypt, during the time of ferment when Christianity began, a considerable body of theosophical and mystical lore. These speculations and beliefs appear to have been influenced by Gnosticism and Neoplatonism, and it seems fair to characterize the history of subsequent Kabbalah as being a struggle between Gnostic and Neoplatonic tendencies, fought out on the quite alien ground of Judaism, which in its central development was to reject both modes of speculation. But Kabbalah went out and away from the main course of Jewish religious thought, and uncannily it has survived both Gnosticism and Neoplatonism, in that Kabbalah today retains a popular and apparently perpetual existence, while Gnosticism and Neoplatonism are the concern of only a few specialists. As I write, the desk in front of me has on it a series of paperback manuals, purchased in drugstores and at newsstands, with titles like *Tree of Life*, *Kabbalah: An Introduction*, *Kabbalah Today*, and *Understanding the Kabbalah*. There are no competing titles on Gnosticism today, or on understanding Neoplatonism, and it is important that the continued popularity of Kabbalah be considered in any estimate of the phenomenon of the current survival and even revival of ancient esotericisms.

Popular handbooks of Kabbalah are not always very exact in their learning, and tend to be dangerously eager to mix Kabbalah up with nearly everything else in current religious enthusiasms, from Sufism to Hinduism. But this too by now is a Western tradition, for Christian popularizations of Kabbalah starting with the Renaissance compounded Kabbalah with a variety of non-Jewish notions, ranging from Tarot cards to the Trinity. A singular prestige has attended Kabbalah throughout its history, and such prestige again is worth contemporary consideration. Accompanying this prestige, which is the prestige of supposedly ultimate origins, is an extraordinary eclecticism that contaminated Kabbalah with nearly every major occult or theosophical strain in the Renaissance and later in Enlightened Europe. A reader deeply versed in the interpenetrations of Kabbalah with these strains learns to be very tolerant of every popular version of Kabbalah he encounters. The five I have read recently were all terribly confused and confusing, but all were palpably sincere and even authentically enthusiastic in their obfuscations.

Yet educated readers need not rely upon such manuals. The lifework of Gershom Scholem of the Hebrew University, Jerusalem, was summed up by him, magnificently, in the various articles on Kabbalah in the *Encyclopaedia Judaica*, only a few years ago. These entries, revised by Scholem, are now available in one large volume of nearly five hundred pages, published under the title *Kabbalah*. Most of what follows in this essay is based upon either this book or on Scholem's other major studies of Kabbalah, several of which are easily available in American paperback reprints. Where I will depart from Scholem cannot be on any factual matters in kabbalistic scholarship, but will concern only some suggestions on the continued relevance of Kabbalah for contemporary modes of interpretation, and a few personal speculations on how Kabbalah itself might be interpreted from some contemporary perspectives.

Scholem's massive achievement can be judged as being unique in modern humanistic scholarship, for he has made himself indispensable to all rational students of his subject. Kabbalah is an extraordinary body of rhetoric or figurative language, and indeed is a theory of rhetoric, and Scholem's formidable achievement is as much rhetorical or figurative as it is historical. In this deep sense, Scholem has written a truly kabbalistic account of Kabbalah, and more than any other modern scholar, working on a comparable scale, he has been wholly adequate to his great subject. He has the same relation to the texts he has edited and written commentaries upon that a later poet like John Milton had to the earlier poems he absorbed and, in some ways, transcended. Scholem is a Miltonic figure in modern scholarship, and deserves to be honored as such.

II

Any brief account of Kabbalah has to begin with descriptions of

Gnosticism and of Neoplatonism, for these opposed visions are the starting points of the more comprehensive vision of Kabbalah. To most modern sensibilities, Gnosticism has a strong and even dangerous appeal, frequently under other names, but Neoplatonism scarcely moves anyone in our time. William James reacted to the Neoplatonic Absolute or God, the One and the Good, by saying that "the stagnant felicity of the Absolute's own perfection moves me as little as I move it." No one is going to argue with James now, but a thousand years and more of European cultural tradition would not have agreed with him.

Neoplatonism was essentially the philosophy of one man, the Hellenic Egyptian Plotinus (205–70 C.E.), whose seminars in Rome were subsequently written out as the *Enneads* ("sets of nine"). Seeing himself as the continuator of Plato, Plotinus sought vindication for the three mystic and transcendent realities that he called "hypostases": the One or the Good, Intelligence, the Soul. Beneath these hypostases was the world of nature, including human bodies. To bridge the abyss between the unified Good and a universe of division and evil, Plotinus elaborated an extraordinary trope or figure of speech, "emanation." The One's plenitude was so great that its love, light, glory brimmed over, and without the One itself in any way decreasing, its glory descended, first into the realm of Intelligence (the Platonic Ideas or Ideal Forms), next into a region of Soul (including each of our souls), and at last into the body and nature. On this bottom level, evil exists, but only by virtue of its distance from the Good, its division of an ultimate Oneness into so many separate selves, so many objects. The body and nature are not bad, in the vision of Plotinus, but merely have gone too far away from their beloved fatherland. By an intellectual discipline, Plotinus held, we can return to the One even in this life.

Plotinus had a strong dislike for the Gnostics, against whom he wrote an eloquent treatise, calling them "those who say that the Maker of the world and the world are evil." There is no great scholarly book of our time on Neoplatonism (for many of the same reasons that there are no drugstore manuals), but there is a superb work, *The Gnostic Religion*, by Hans Jonas, a worthy complement to Scholem's *Kabbalah*. Jonas usefully compares Gnosticism to nihilism and existentialism, citing many analogues between Valentinus, the greatest of the Gnostic speculators, and the philosopher Heidegger. Gnosticism, according to Jonas, is the extremist version of the syncretic, general religion that dominated the eastern Mediterranean world during the first two Christian centuries. Jonas refers to this general religion of the period as a "dualistic transcendent religion of salvation." "Dualistic" here means that reality is polarized into: God against the creation, spirit against matter, good against evil, soul against the body. "Transcendent" here means that God and salvation are alike: transmundane, beyond our world. Gnosticism takes its name from *gnosis*, a Greek word for "knowledge." Though the Church Fathers attacked Gnosticism as a Christian heresy, it appears to have preceded Christianity, both among the Jews and the Hellenes. Gnostic "knowledge" is supposed knowledge "of God," and so is radically different from all other knowledge, for the *gnosis* is the only form that salvation can take, according to its believers. This is therefore not rational knowledge, for it involves God's knowing the Gnostic adept, even as the Gnostic knows Him.

Gnosticism was always anti-Jewish, even when it arose among Jews or Jewish Christians, for its radical dualism of an alien God set against an evil universe is a total contradiction of the central Jewish tradition, in which a transcendent God allows Himself to be known by His people as an immediate presence, when He chooses, and in which His creation is good except as it has been marred or altered by man's disobedience or wickedness. Confronted by the Gnostic vision of a world evilly made by hostile demons, the talmudic rabbis rejected this religion of the alien God with a moral passion surpassing the parallel denunciations made by Plotinus. We can contrast here the most famous formula of Valentinian *gnosis* with an equally famous rabbinic pronouncement of anathema upon such speculations:

> What makes us free is the knowledge of who we were, what we have become; where we were, wherein we have been thrown; whereto we speed, wherefrom we are redeemed; what is birth and what rebirth.

> Whosoever speculated on these four things, it were better for him if he had not come into the world—what is above? what is beneath? what was beforetime? and what will be hereafter?

The rabbis believed such speculation to be morally unhealthy, a judgment amply vindicated by the sexual libertinism of many Gnostics. Since Kabbalah, in all of its earlier phases, remained a wholly orthodox Jewish phenomenon, in belief and in moral behavior, it seems a puzzle that Kabbalah had so large a Gnostic content. This puzzle can be clarified by even the briefest account of the origins of the Kabbalah. Kabbalah proper begins in twelfth-century Provence, but Scholem and others have traced its direct descent from the earliest Jewish esotericism, the apocalyptic writings of which the Book of Enoch is the most formidable. This earliest Jewish theosophy and mysticism centered about two biblical texts, the first chapter of the prophet Ezekiel and the first chapter of Genesis. These gave impetus to two modes of visionary speculation, *ma'aseh merkabah* ("the work of the Chariot") and *ma'aseh bereshit* ("the work of creation"). These esoteric meditations were orthodox parallels to Gnostic reveries on the *pleroma*, the unfallen divine realm, and can be considered a kind of rabbinical quasi-Gnosticism, but not yet Kabbalah.

III

Some eight centuries after the Gnostics subsided, a short book, the *Sefer Yetzirah* ("Book of Creation"), became widely circulated among learned Jews. There are at least half-a-dozen English translations of *Sefer Yetzirah* available, and the little book probably will always be popular among esotericists. In itself, it is of no literary or spiritual value, but historically it is the true origin of Kabbalah. The date of its composition is wholly uncertain, but it may go back to the third century. Later kabbalist gossip attributed it to the great Rabbi Akiba, whom the Romans had martyred, which accounts for much of the book's prestige. What matters about *Sefer Yetzirah* is that it introduced, in a very rudimentary form, the central structural notion of Kabbalah, the Sefirot, which in later works became the divine emanations by which all reality is structured. Since the next kabbalistic text of importance, the *Sefer ha-Bahir*, was not written until the thirteenth century, and since that work presents the Sefirot in fuller but not final development, all students of Kabbalah necessarily confront the problematic of a thousand years of oral tradition. All of Jewish medievalism becomes a vast labyrinth in which the distinctive ideas of Kabbalah were invented, revised, and transmitted in an area ranging from Babylonia to Poland. In these vast reaches of space and time, even Scholem becomes baffled, for the very essence of oral tradition is that it should defeat all historical and critical scholarship.

The *Sefer ha-Bahir* (*bahir* means "bright") has been translated into German by Scholem, another service, as this book is incoherent, and its mixture of learned Hebrew and vernacular Aramaic makes it difficult even for specialists. Though fragmentary, the *Bahir* is a book of some real literary value, and truly begins the kabbalistic style of parable and figurative language. Its major figuration is certainly the Sefirot, the attributes of God emanating out from an infinite center to every possible finite circumference. Where the Sefirot, in the *Sefer Yetzirah*, were only the ten primary numbers, a neo-Pythagorean notion, in the *Bahir* they are divine properties and powers, and supernal lights, aiding in the work of creation.

But this was still only a step toward the true emergence of Kabbalah, which took place in thirteenth-century southern France, and then spread across the border to find its home among the Jews of Spain, a process culminating in the masterpiece or Bible of Kabbalah, the *Sefer ha-Zohar*. The Zohar ("splendor") was written by Moses de Leon between 1280 and 1286 in Guadalajara, and with its circulation Kabbalah became a full-scale system of speculation. After seven hundred years the Zohar, with all its faults, remains the only indubitably great book in all of Western esotericism. Most of the Zohar is written in Aramaic, but as an artificial, highly literary language, rather than as a vernacular. There is an adequate five-volume English translation (published by the Soncino Press) still in print, and well worth reading, but it represents only a portion of the Zohar, which is, however, a unique book in that it is impossible to say what a complete version of it would be. The book (if it is a book) varies from manuscript to manuscript, and seems more a collection of books or a small library than what ordinarily we would describe as a self-centered work.

Rather than attempt a description of the Zohar here, I shall pass on immediately to a summary account, largely following Scholem, of the basic concepts and images of Kabbalah, and then return to glance at the Zohar before giving a sketch of the later Kabbalah, which was created after the Jews were exiled from Spain. For the Zohar is the central work of classical Kabbalah, centering on the doctrine of the Sefirot, but Kabbalah from the sixteenth century until today is a second or modern Kabbalah, largely the creation of Isaac Luria of Safed in Palestine (1534–72), and needs a rather different exposition.

Classical Kabbalah begins with a Neoplatonic vision of God. God is the *ein-sof* ("without end"), totally unknowable, and beyond representation, all images of Whom are merely hyperboles. As *ein-sof* has no attributes, His first manifestation is necessarily as *ayin* ("nothing"). Genesis had said that God created the world out of nothing. Kabbalah took this over as a literal statement, but interpreted it revisionistically as meaning just the opposite of what it said. God, being "*ayin*," created the world out of "*ayin*," and thus created the world out of *Himself*. The distinction between cause and effect was subverted by this initial kabbalistic formula, and indeed such rhetorical subversion became a distinctive feature of Kabbalah: "cause" and "effect" are always reversible, for the kabbalists regarded them as linguistic fictions, long before Nietzsche did.

Kabbalah, which thus from the start was revisionary in regard to Genesis (though asserting otherwise), was also revisionary of its pagan source in Neoplatonism. In Plotinus, emanation is a process out *from* God, but in Kabbalah the process must take place *within* God Himself. An even more crucial difference from Neoplatonism is that all kabbalistic theories of emanation are also theories of language. As Scholem says, "the God who manifests Himself is the God who expresses Himself," which means that the Sefirot are primarily *language*, attributes of God that need to be described by the various names of God when He is at work in creation. The Sefirot are complex figurations for God, tropes or turns of language that *substitute* for God. Indeed, one can say that the Sefirot are like poems, in that they are names implying complex commentaries that make them into texts. They are not allegorical personifications, which is what all popular manuals of Kabbalah reduce them to, and though they have extraordinary potency, this is a power of signification rather than what we customarily think of as magic.

Sefirah, the singular form, would seem to suggest the Greek "sphere," but its actual source was the Hebrew *sappir* (for "sapphire"), and so the term referred primarily to God's radiance. Scholem gives a very suggestive list of kabbalistic synonyms for the Sefirot: sayings, names, lights, powers, crowns, qualities, stages, garments, mirrors, shoots, sources, primal days, aspects, inner faces, and limbs of God. At first the kabbalists dared to identify the Sefirot with the actual substance of God, and the Zohar goes so far as to say of God and the Sefirot: "He is They, and They are He," which produces the rather dangerous formula that God and language are one and the same. But other kabbalists warily regarded the Sefirot only as God's tools, vessels that are instruments for Him, or as we might say, language is only God's tool or vessel. Moses Cordovero, the teacher of Luria and the greatest systematizer of Kabbalah, achieved the precarious balance of seeing the Sefirot as being at once somehow both God's vessels and His essence, but the conceptual difficulty remains right down to the present day, and has its exact analogues in certain current debates about the relationship between language and thought.

The Sefirot, then, are ten complex images for God in His process of creation, with an interplay between literal and figurative meaning going on within each Sefirah. There is a fairly fixed and definite and by now common ordering for the Sefirot:

1. *Keter Elyon* or *Keter* (the "supreme crown")
2. *Hokhmah* ("wisdom")
3. *Binah* ("intelligence")
4. *Gedullah* ("greatness") or *Hesed* ("love")
5. *Gevurah* ("power") or *Din* ("judgment" or "rigor")
6. *Tiferet* ("beauty") or *Rahamim* ("mercy")
7. *Nezah* ("victory" or "lasting endurance")
8. *Hod* ("majesty")

9. *Yesod* ("foundation")

10. *Malkhut* ("kingdom")

It is best to consider these allegorical images as carefully as possible, for the interplay of these images in some sense is the classical or zoharic Kabbalah, though *not* the later Kabbalah of Luria, out of which finally the Hasidic movement was to emerge. It is not a negative criticism of Scholem to say that the Sefirot have not interested him greatly. Scarcely a dozen pages out of the five hundred in *Kabbalah* are devoted to the details of Sefirot symbolism, just as only ten pages of the four hundred and fifty of Scholem's earlier *Major Trends in Jewish Mysticism* were concerned with expounding the Sefirot. Scholem is impatient with them, and prefers to examine larger mythological and historical aspects of Kabbalah. In contrast, popular expositions of Kabbalah for many centuries down to the drugstore present tend to talk about nothing but the Sefirot. What is their fascination for so many learned minds, as well as for the popular imagination? Contemporary readers encounter the Sefirot in curious places, such as Malcolm Lowry's *Under the Volcano* or Thomas Pynchon's *Gravity's Rainbow*, where these fundamental images of Kabbalah are used to suggest tragic patterns of overdetermination, by which our lives are somehow lived for us in spite of ourselves. Like the Tarot cards and astrology, with which popular tradition has confounded them, the Sefirot fascinate because they suggest an immutable knowledge of a final reality that stands behind our world of appearances. In some sense the Sefirot have become the staple of a popular Platonism or Hegelianism, a kind of magic idealism. Popular kabbalism has understood, somehow, that the Sefirot are neither *things* nor *acts*, but rather are *relational events*, and so are persuasive representations of what ordinary people encounter as the inner reality of their lives.

Keter, the "crown," is the primal will of the Creator, and is scarcely distinguishable from the *ein-sof*, except as being first effect to His first cause. But, though an effect, *keter* is no part of the Creation, which reflects *keter* but cannot absorb it. As it cannot be compared to any other image, it must be called *ayin*, a "nothingness," an object of quest that is also the subject of any search. As a name of God, *keter* is the *ehyeh* of the great declaration of God to Moses in Exodus 3:14; God says, *ehyeh asher ehyeh*, "I Am That I Am," but the kabbalists refused to interpret this as mere "being." To them, *keter* was at once *ehyeh* and *ayin*, being and nothingness, a cause of all causes and no cause at all, beyond action. If Kabbalah can be interpreted, as I think it can, as a theory of influence, then *keter* is the paradoxical idea of influence itself. The irony of all influence, initially, is that the source is emptied out into a state of absence, in order for the receiver to accommodate the influx of apparent being. This may be why we use the word "influence," originally an astral term referring to the occult effect of the stars upon men.

Below *keter* as crown, the Sefirot were generally depicted as a "tree of emanation." This tree grows downward, as any map of influence must. Another frequent depiction of the Sefirot is the "reversed tree," in which the emanations are arranged in the form of a man. In either image, the right-hand side begins with the first attribute proper, *hokhmah*, generally translated as "wisdom," but better understood as something like God's meditation or contemplation of Himself, and frequently called the "father of fathers" or the uncreated Tables of the Law. Freud's imago of the father is a close enough contemporary translation.

The matching imago of the mother, on the left side, is *binah*, usually rendered as "intelligence," but meaning something more like a passive understanding (Kabbalah is nothing if not sexist). *Binah* is sometimes imaged as a mirror (very much in a Gnostic tradition) in which God enjoys contemplating Himself. We can call *keter* the divine self-consciousness, *hokhmah* the active principle of knowing, and *binah* the known, or reflection upon knowledge, or the veil through which God's "wisdom" shines. In another kabbalistic image, certainly derived from Neoplatonism, *binah* as mirror acts as a prism, breaking open divine light into apprehensible colors.

The seven lesser Sefirot are the more immediate attributes of creation, moving out from *binah* in its role of supreme mother. Where the three upper Sefirot together form *arikh anpin* (Aramaic for "long face"), the great or transcendental "face" of God, the seven lower emanations form the "short face" or *ze'eir anpin*, the immanent countenance of God, and sometimes are called the Sefirot of "construction." Unlike the great face, the constructive principles are conceived by analogy, and so are nearly identical with the principles of figurative or poetic language. The first, on the father's or right-hand side, most often called *hesed*, is love in the particular sense of God's covenant-love, *caritas* or "grace" in Christian interpretation. Its matching component on the mother's or left-hand side is most often called *din*, "severity" or "rigorous judgment." God's covenant-love requires a limit or outward boundary, which is provided by *din*. This makes *din* the kabbalistic equivalent of the Orphic and Platonic *ananke* or necessity, the law of the cosmos. Creation, for the Kabbalah, depends upon the perpetual balance and oscillation of *hesed* and *din* as antithetical principles.

It is an unintentional irony of the Sefirot that they increase enormously in human and imaginative interest as they descend closer to our condition. Even the most exalted of kabbalist writers relax and are more inventive when they reach the lower half of the Sefirotic tree. With the sixth Sefirah, *tiferet*, the "mercy" or heart of God, we are in the aesthetic realm of God's "beauty," which for the Kabbalah is all the beauty there is. *Tiferet* is the principle of mediation, reconciling the "above" and the "below" on the tree, and also drawing together the right side and the left side, masculine and feminine. All kabbalistic references to centering are always to *tiferet*, and *tiferet* sometimes stands by itself for the "small face" or God's immanence, and is frequently spoken of as the dwelling-place of the *shekhinah* or "Divine Presence" (of which more later). In kabbalistic dialectic, *tiferet* completes the second triad of *hesed-din-tiferet*, and governs the third triad of *nezah-hod-yesod*.

Nezah or God's "victory" emanates from *hesed*, and represents the power of nature to increase itself, in a kind of apotheosis of male force. *Hod*, the female counterpart emanating from *din*, is a kind of equivalent to "mother nature" in the Western Romantic sense (a kabbalist would have called Wordsworth's or Emerson's Nature by the name of *hod*). *Hod* is "majesty" of the merely natural sort, but for the Kabbalah nothing of course is merely natural. Out of the creative strife of *nezah* and *hod* comes *yesod*, "foundation," which is at once human male sexuality and the ongoing balance of nature.

The tenth and last of the Sefirot is properly the most fascinating, *malkhut* or "kingdom," where "kingdom" refers to God's immanence in nature. From *tiferet*, *malkhut* inherits the *shekhinah*, and manifests that glory of God in His world. So *malkhut* is called the "descent," meaning the descent of the *shekhinah*. *Malkhut* is also called the "lower mother" as against the "higher mother" of *binah*. As the closest of the Sefirot to us, *malkhut* sums them up, and makes the world of emanation a pragmatic unity. The kabbalist encounters the Sefirot only through *malkhut*, which makes of kabbalism necessarily a sexual mysticism or erotic theosophy.

IV

In their total structure, the Sefirot are identified with the *merkabah* or "celestial chariot" in which the prophet Ezekiel saw the Divine manifest Himself. This identification led to a series of further symbolic analogies or correspondences—cosmological, philosophical, psychological, indeed every area in which overdetermined meanings could be plotted out. Popular kabbalism concerns itself with these overdeterminations, but they are not the prime spiritual significance of the Sefirot. That significance comes in the interrelationships of the Sefirot, their reflections of one another within themselves.

The great master of these reflections was Moses Cordovero (1522–70), the best example of a systematic thinker ever to appear among kabbalists. But the movement from the Zohar to Cordovero and on to Cordovero's pupil and surpasser, Luria, returns us from doctrine to history, for the later Kabbalah is the product of a second and intensified Exile, following the expulsion of the Jews from Spain in 1492. Perhaps Scholem's greatest achievement as a scholar has been his analysis of Lurianic Kabbalah as a myth of exile. The Sefirot, though they lend themselves to such a myth, are too close to the unfallen worlds fully to accommodate fresh onsets of historical suffering. I touch here upon what I take to be the deepest meaning of Kabbalah, and will digress upon it, before returning to problems of theosophical meaning.

Louis Ginzberg, one of the greatest of modern talmudists, introduced the Palestinian Talmud by remarking that post-biblical Jewish literature was "predominantly interpretative and commentative." This is true even of Kabbalah, which is curious for a body of work professedly mystical and speculative, even indeed mythopoeic. But this emphasis upon *interpretation* is finally what distinguishes Kabbalah from nearly every other variety of mysticism or theosophy, East or West. The kabbalists of medieval Spain, and their Palestinian successors after the expulsion from Spain, confronted a peculiar psychological problem, one that demanded a revisionist solution. How does one accommodate a fresh and vital new religious impulse, in a precarious and even catastrophic time of troubles, when one inherits a religious tradition already so rich and coherent that it allows very little room for fresh revelations or even speculations? The kabbalists were in no position to formulate or even reformulate much of anything in their religion. Given to them already was not only a massive and completed Scripture, but an even more massive and intellectually finished structure of every kind of commentary and interpretation. Their stance in relation to all this tradition became, I think, the classic paradigm upon which Western revisionism in all areas was to model itself ever since, usually in rather indirect emulation. For the kabbalists developed implicitly a psychology of belatedness, and with it an explicit, rhetorical series of techniques for opening Scripture and even received commentary to their own historical sufferings, and to their own, new theosophical insights. Their achievement was not just to restore *gnosis* and mythology to a Judaism which had purged itself of such elements, but more crucially to provide the masses of suffering Jewry with a more immediate and experiential personal faith than the strength of orthodox tradition might have allowed. Hasidism was the ultimate descendant of Kabbalah, and can be regarded as the more positive ultimate achievement of a movement that led, in its

darker aspects, to morasses of magic and superstition, and to false messiahs and even apostates.

The Zohar, astonishingly beautiful as it frequently is, is not in itself
greatly representative of what became, from the Spanish exile on, the true
voice of Kabbalah. Though Cordovero and Luria derived fundamentally
from the Zohar, their systems and visions actually have little in common
with it. The Zohar is organized as an apparent commentary upon
Scripture, just as much of the later Kabbalah is organized as an apparent
commentary upon the Zohar, but it is the genius of revisionism to swerve
so far from its canonical texts as to make the ancestral voices into even
their own opposites. A contemporary reader encountering the Zohar will
have trouble finding in it a clear statement about the structure and function of the Sefirot, let alone any of the more complex refinements of
Kabbalah. Such a reader will find himself confronted by hundreds of hom-
ilies and little stories, many of them haunting in their enigmas, but finally
compelling the reader to wish that the Zohar would obey its own injunction about how to interpret Scripture or the Torah:

> As wine in a jar, if it is to keep, so is the Torah, contained with-
> in its outer garment. Such a garment is made up of many sto-
> ries, but we, we are required to pierce the garment.

To pierce the garment of the Zohar is almost impossible, but in some
sense that was the achievement of Cordovero and of Luria.

V

Scholem makes the point that after 1492 and the fresh dispersal of
the Jews, the Kabbalah ceased to be esoteric and became "public property." From about 1530 on, Safed in Palestine became the center of the new
Kabbalah, and from Safed there emanated out to the Diaspora what
became a new popular religion, which captured much of Judaism, and has
left an influence (now much diminished) on it ever since. Isaac Luria was
much the largest source of this new religion, and will receive more analysis here, as he does in Scholem, but Cordovero was a clearer and more systematic theorist, and some account of his ideas remains the best introduction to the intricacies of the Lurianic Kabbalah.

As early as the 13th century, kabbalists spoke of the Sefirot reflecting
themselves within themselves, so that each "contained" all the others.
Complex systems of pathways of Sefirot within Sefirot were set up, and
meditation upon these pathways became the characteristic kabbalistic

exercise, whether in vision, prayer, or intellectual speculation. This theosophical pathbreaking becomes in Cordovero what Ginzberg and other scholars have described accurately as a theory of influence. Cordovero invented a new category, *behinot*, to convey the multiform aspects within each Sefirot, aspects that account for the links between Sefirot. These are the six *behinot* or phases of the ten Sefirot, as differentiated by Cordovero: (1) Concealed before manifestation within the preceding Sefirah; (2) Actual manifestation in the preceding Sefirah; (3) Appearance as Sefirah in its own name; (4) Aspect that gives power to the Sefirah above it, so as to enable that Sefirah to be strong enough to emanate yet further Sefirot; (5) Aspect that gives power to the Sefirah itself to emanate out the other Sefirot still concealed within it; (6) Aspect by which the following Sefirah is in turn emanated out to its own place, after which the cycle of the six *behinot* begins again.

This cycle may seem baffling at first, but is a remarkable theory of influence, as causal yet reversed relationships. To be understood today it needs translation into other terms, and these can be psychoanalytic, rhetorical, or imagistic, for the six *behinot* can be interpreted as psychological mechanisms of defense, rhetorical tropes, or areas of poetic imagery. Whereas the Sefirot, as attributes of God, are manifestly supernatural channels of influence (or, rhetorically speaking, divine poems, each a text in itself), the *behinot* work more like human agencies, whether psychic or linguistic. Scholem indicates that, in Cordovero, the Sefirot "actually become the structural elements of all things," but they do this only by their aspects, or *behinot*. One might indeed call Cordovero the first structuralist, an unacknowledged ancestor of many contemporary French theorists of the "human sciences."

In order to see precisely the great dialectical leap that Isaac Luria took away from his teacher, Cordovero, it is necessary to expound the true, dark heart of Kabbalah: its vision of the problem of evil. Scholem rightly remarks that Jewish philosophy was not very much interested in the problem of evil, and it seems just to observe that talmudic tradition was also too healthy to brood excessively on evil. But Kabbalah departed both from normative Judaism and from Neoplatonism in its obsessive concern with evil. For Neoplatonism, evil has no metaphysical reality, but Gnosticism engaged evil as the reality of this world, which presumably is why Gnosticism now lives, under a variety of disguises, while Neoplatonism is the province of scholars. Probably, this is why the Lurianic Kabbalah came to dominate popular Judaism for many centuries, giving birth first to a series of false messiahs, and finally to the lasting glory of the Baal Shem Tov and his Hasidism.

The book *Bahir* speaks of the Sefirah *gevurah* or *din* as the left hand of God, and so as a permitted evil. Out of this came the kabbalistic doctrine that located evil in what Freud called the superego, or in kabbalistic terms, the separation of *din* from *hesed*, stern judgment from love. The world of *din* brought forth the *sitra ahra* or "the other side," the sinister qualities that came out of a name of God, but then fell away.

The Zohar assigned to the *sitra ahra* ten Sefirot all its own, ten sinister crowns representing the remnants of worlds that God first made and then destroyed. In one of the great poetic images of esoteric tradition, Moses de Leon compared evil to the bark of the tree of the Sefirot, the *kelippah*. The creatures of this bark—Samael and his wife Lilith, or Satan and the chief of witches (of whom more later)—became in the Zohar almost worthy antagonists of God. *Kelippot*, conceived first as bark, became regarded also as husks or shells or broken vessels of evil. But even in the *kelippot*, according to the Zohar, there abides a saving spark of God. This notion, that there are sparks in the *kelippot* that can be redeemed, and redeemed by the acts of men alone and not of God, became the starting-point of Lurianic Kabbalah.

VI

The problem of original genius in every intellectual area, past a certain date (a date upon which no two people can agree), is always located in the apparently opposed principles of continuity and discontinuity. Yet the very word Kabbalah means tradition, and every master of Kabbalah has stressed his own continuity rather than his discontinuity with previous speculators. Luria is extraordinarily original, indeed he may have been the only visionary in the entire history of Kabbalah whose basic ideas were original, since the entire tradition from the *Sefer Yetzirah* through Cordovero is finally only an amalgam, however strangely shaped, of Neoplatonism and Gnosticism. But Luria had the originality of certain great poets—Dante, Milton, Blake—though since the important accounts of his visions are not written by him, but by rival and contrasting disciples, it is difficult to compare Luria's powers of invention with those of other creators.

Before Luria, all of Kabbalah saw creation as a progressive process, moving in one direction always, emanating out from God through the Sefirot to man, a movement in which each stage joined itself closely to the subsequent stage, without enormous leaps or backward recoilings. In Luria, creation is a startlingly regressive process, one in which an abyss can separate any one stage from another, and in which catastrophe is always a central event. Reality for Luria is always a triple rhythm of contraction, breaking apart, and mending, a rhythm continuously present in time even as it first punctuated eternity.

Luria named this triple process: *tzimtzum, shevirat ha-kelim, tikkun* (contraction, the breaking-of-the-vessels, restitution). *Tzimtzum* originally seems to have meant a holding-in-of-the-breath, but Luria transformed the word into an idea of limitation, of God's hiding of Himself, or rather entering into Himself. In this contraction, God clears a space for creation, a not-God. This cleared point the Zohar had called *tehiru*, or fundamental space. Luria saw the *tzimtzum* as God's concentration within Himself of the Sefirah of *din*, rigor, but part of this power of stern judgment remained behind in the cleared *tehiru*, where it mixed together with the remnants of God's self-withdrawn light, called by Luria the *reshimu*. Into the mixture (out of which our world is to be formed), God sends a single letter, the *yod*, the first letter of His great name, YHWH, the Tetragrammaton. This *yod* is the active principle in creation, even as the *reshimu* is the passive principle.

This creation, according to Luria, was of *kelim*, "vessels," of which the culminating vessel was *adam kadmon* or primal man. Two kinds of light had made these vessels, the new or incoming light that had accompanied the *yod* or word of God, and the light left behind in the *tehiru* after the *tzimtzum*. The collision of lights is an enormously complex process, for which this present essay lacks space, but the crucial element in the complexity is that *adam kadmon*, man as he should be, is a kind of perpetual war of light against light. This war emanates out from his head in patterns of *writing*, which become fresh vessels of creation, newly manifested structures of Sefirot. But though the three upper Sefirot held firm, and contained the pugnacious light, the six Sefirot from *hesed* to *yesod* broke apart. This breaking or scattering of the vessels was caused by the force of the light hitting all at once, in what can be interpreted as too strong a force of *writing*, stronger than the "texts" of the lower Sefirot could sustain. Paradoxically, God's name was too strong for His words, and the breaking of the vessels necessarily became a divine act of *substitution*, in which an original pattern yielded to a more chaotic one that nevertheless remained pattern, the guarantee of which was that the vessel of the tenth and last Sefirah, *malkhut* or the female world, broke also, but less sharply than the other vessels.

Though some of the light in the shattered vessels returned immediately to God, much of it fell down with the vessels, so as to form the *kelippot* or evil forces of the universe. But these *kelippot* still have pattern or design, as well as sparks of light imprisoned within them. Luria appears to have believed that all this catastrophe came about because of an original excess of *din*, a plethora of rigor in God Himself, and it is in the Sefirah of *din* that the smashing-apart begins. Scholem theorizes that Luria saw the whole function of creation as being God's catharsis of Himself, a vast sublimation in which His terrible rigor might find some peace. This is not unlike Freud's extraordinary explanation as to why people fall in love, which is to avoid an overfilled inner self. As man must love, in Freud's view, in order to avoid becoming sick, so Luria's God has to create, for His own health. But He could create only by catastrophe, in Luria's judgment, an opinion again very like that of Freud's disciple, Ferenczi, whose book *Thalassa* also ascribes every act of creation to a necessary catastrophe.

Remarkable as these first two stages of Luria's vision are, both *tzimtzum* and *shevirah* are less important in his doctrine than *tikkun*, the saving process of restoration and restitution, for this is the work of the human, taking place through a complex agency called the *partzufim* or "faces," the Lurianic equivalent of Cordovero's *behinot*. Scholem calls the *partzufim* "configurations" or *gestalten*, but like the *behinot* they seem to be at once psychic and linguistic, defense mechanisms and rhetorical tropes. As patterns of images, the *partzufim* organize the shattered world after the vessels have broken apart, and as principles of organization they substitute for or take the place of the Sefirot. *Keter* or the crown is substituted for by the *partzuf* of *arikh anpin*, or God as the "long-faced one," that is to say, the God who is indulgent or forbearing even in fallen history. *Hokhmah* and *binah* are replaced by what Freud called the Imagos, *abba* and *imma*, "father" and "mother," who together create the fourth and most important *partzuf* called *ze'eir anpin*, the "short-faced" or "impatient" or "unindulgent" God, who stands in judgment upon history. *Ze'eir anpin* substitutes for the six lower Sefirot, from *din* to *yesod*, the six that broke apart most dreadfully. *Ze'eir anpin* thus substitutes also quite directly for the *behinot* of Luria's teacher, Cordovero, and in some sense this *partzuf* can be considered as Luria's revisionist misprision or creative misunderstanding of his direct precursor's most original and important doctrine. Luria's last *partzuf* is called *nukba de-ze'eir*, the female of the impatient God, and substitutes for *malkhut* or the kingdom.

Together, the *partzufim* make up a new and second *adam kadmon*, for the *tikkun* or restoration of creation must be carried out by the religious acts of individual men, of all Jews struggling in the Exile, and indeed of all men and women struggling in the Exile that Luria saw as the universal human existence. The nature of such religious acts of *tikkun* is again too complex to define in a limited space, but essentially these are acts of meditation, acts that lift up and so liberate the fallen sparks of God from their imprisonment in the shards of the *kelippot*. Such acts of meditation are at once psychic and linguistic, but for Luria they are magical too, so that they enter the sphere of practical Kabbalah, a puzzling world that this essay must conclude by entering also.

VII

As a psychology of belatedness, Kabbalah manifests many prefigurations of Freudian doctrine. Yet most of these stem from the psychological notions of Neoplatonism, and are not original with Kabbalah. Thus, the kabbalistic division of the soul into three parts is Neoplatonic, where the lowest soul is the *nefesh* or vital being with which everyone is born. The *ru'ah* or *anima* comes about later through a spiritual awakening, but only with the highest awakening is the true soul born, the *neshamah* or *spiritus*. Lurianic Kabbalah added further souls, so as to achieve a psychic cartography. But a more truly original notion, and one more prophetic of Freud, is the *tzelem*, or divine image in every man, first set forth in the Zohar and then developed by Luria and his disciples. The *tzelem* is a modification of the later Neoplatonic idea of the Astral Body, a kind of quasi-material entity that holds together mind and physical body, and that survives the death of the body proper.

In Lurianic Kabbalah, the Astral Body also serves the function of determining an individual human personality, so that the difference between one of us and another is not necessarily in any part of the soul, but in the enigmatic joining of soul and body, that is, in the relationship between our consciousness and our body. What makes us individual, our *tzelem*, is the way our particular body feels about our psyche, or the way that psyche feels about the body to which it is linked. Scholem says that "without the *tzelem* the soul would burn the body up with its fierce radiance," and one can add conversely that the body's desires would consume the soul without the *tzelem*. It is as though Luria were saying, in our terms, that the body is the unconscious as far as the soul is concerned, or that the soul is the unconscious from the stance of the body.

It was only a step from the idea of the *tzelem* to the Lurianic version of the transmigration of souls, called gilgul. Luria seems to have taught that there were families of souls, united by the root of a common spark. Each person can take up in himself the spark of another soul, of one of the dead, provided that he and the dead share the same root. This leads to the larger idea of a kind of eternal recurrence, with the saving difference that *gilgul* can be the final form of *tikkun*, in which the fallen soul can have its flaws repaired. The legend of the *dibbuk* is a negative version of the same idea.

With the idea of gilgul, speculative Kabbalah passes into practical Kabbalah, a world of "white" magic, dependent, however, entirely upon the sacredness of a divine language. It is very difficult to distinguish practical Kabbalah from the whole body of Jewish magic and superstition, the vast accumulation of folklore that so long a tradition brings forth. Very late or popular Kabbalah also became mixed with the "occult sciences," particularly astrology and alchemy, but these have little to do with Kabbalah proper.

Two areas of practical Kabbalah seem most authentic: demonology and what was called *gematria*, the explanation of words according to their numerical values, by set rules. Kabbalistic demonology became absorbed by the wilder aspects of Hasidism, and is now familiar to a wide group of contemporary readers through the fiction of Isaac Bashevis Singer. Such demonology ultimately centers upon two figures, Lilith and Samael. One can wonder why Lilith has not become the patroness of some of the more extreme manifestations of the women's liberation movement, as her legendary career shows a strong counter-current of guilt toward women (and fear of them) moving in Kabbalah.

Kabbalah enshrined the *shekhinah* or Divine Presence in the shape of a woman, an image of splendor-in-exile, and the Sefirot are relatively fairly balanced between male and female sides. Yet kabbalistic texts awaken into a peculiar vividness whenever Lilith is invoked. Though she seems to have begun as a Babylonian wind-demoness, she became very thoroughly naturalized in Jewish contexts. A pre-kabbalistic legend held that she was Adam's first wife, and that she abandoned him on the issue of sexual equality, with the immediate cause of separation being that of positions in sexual intercourse, Adam favoring the missionary posture, while she insisted on the ascendancy. In Kabbalah, Lilith dwindled from a heroic self-asserter into a strangler of infants, and into the muse of masturbation, bearing endless imps to those guilty of self-gratification. Kabbalah also married her off to Samael, the principal later Jewish name for Satan as the Angel of Death. The obsessive emphasis upon Lilith's lustfulness throughout kabbalistic literature is an obvious indication of the large element of repression in all those Gnostic fantasies that inhabit the entire history of Kabbalah.

If Lilith is a Gnostic reversal of the *shekhinah*, a demonic parody of the kabbalistic pathos of attempting to exalt aspects of Exile, then it seems fair to say that the techniques of *gematria* were a kind of parody of the sometimes sublime kabbalistic exaltation of language, and of the arts of interpretation. For *gematria* is interpretative freedom gone mad, in which any text can be made to mean anything. But its prevalence was itself a mark of the desperation that underlay much of Kabbalah. To open an ancient text to the experiential sufferings of contemporary men and women was the not ignoble motive of much kabbalism. *Gematria*, with its descents into occult numerologies, is finally best viewed as an index to how tremendous the suffering was, for the pressure of the sorrow came close to destroying one of the greatest interpretative traditions in cultural history.

"Mysticism" is a word I have avoided in this essay, for Kabbalah seems to be more of an interpretative and mythical tradition than a mystical one. There were kabbalistic ecstatics, and subtraditions of meditative intensities, of prayer conducted in an esoteric manner. But Kabbalah differs finally from Christian or Eastern mysticism in being more a mode of intellectual speculation than a way of union with God. Like the Gnostics, the kabbalists sought *knowledge*, but unlike the Gnostics they sought knowledge in the Book. By centering upon the Bible, Kabbalah made of itself, at its best, a critical tradition, though distinguished by more invention than critical traditions generally display. In its degeneracy, Kabbalah has sought vainly for a magical power over nature, but in its glory it sought, and found, a power of the mind over the universe of death.

Jean-Paul Sartre

(1905-1980)

SARTRE'S ACHIEVEMENT BEGAN IN 1938, WITH HIS EARLY NOVEL *LA NAUSÉE*. Now, in 2000, what survives of Sartre? Fashions go by, and Existentialism is mostly a blurred memory. The novels of Sartre, with the possible exception of *La Nausée*, are no longer read. A better dramatist than he was a narrator, Sartre still has some life in the theater: *No Exit* continues to be revived, with some success. As political sage and as moralist, Sartre once had enormous currency, yet that eminence also has receded. Was he, after all, a grand period piece, triumphant in the 1950s and earlier 1960s, and then rendered largely irrelevant by the advent of the Counterculture in 1967–70?

Rather than relying only upon my own perspectives in regard to Sartre, I choose to invoke the late novelist-philosopher Iris Murdoch, who published a lucid short book, *Sartre: Romantic Rationalist*, in 1953, when Sartre's influence was most prevalent.

It could be argued that Sartre's largest achievements came after Murdoch's study: *Saint Genet, The Words, The Family Idiot: Gustave Flaubert*. But Murdoch, the author of such superb novels as *The Good Apprentice* and *Bruno's Dream*, can be judged to have anticipated Sartre's final phase as biographer and autobiographer, after she demonstrated so clearly his limits as philosopher, novelist, and moral psychologist:

> But Sartre's special talent is social diagnosis and psychoanalysis; he is at his most brilliant when he dissects some deformed life and lays it out for our inspection.

Sartre, analyzing Flaubert, Genet, and himself, indeed manifests brilliance, whereas his fiction generally reduces to "intellectually pleasing schemes and patterns" (Murdoch). Not much in Sartre's narratives can survive a comparison with Dostoevsky or Conrad or Faulkner. Sartre always knows too well what he thinks he is doing, and his characters never break away from him. In this he is like Camus, his friend and rival, who wrote moral essays and called them fiction. A few pages of Proust, read almost at random, suffice to obliterate the ideograms that Sartre and Camus vainly wish to establish as persons.

Murdoch, writing in the early 1950s, praised Sartre because "he has the style of the age." But when that age passes, what abides? Sartre's vision of Genet interests me rather more than Genet does, but that scarcely can be said of Sartre's Flaubert. Yet who could expect otherwise? The single book by Sartre I tend to reread is *The Words*, because it is a marvelous account of the gestation of a consciousness. Murdoch shrewdly sums up Sartre's obsession with consciousness:

> For him the psyche is coextensive with consciousness. Whereas for Freud the deepest human impulse is sexual, for Sartre it is the urge toward "self-coincidence" which is the key to our being.

One cannot make Sartre into Molière or Racine; he was not a great dramatist. Perhaps he should have turned earlier to literary biography and autobiography, but he wished too strongly to alter the lives of his readers. His will be a partial survival only, yet *The Words* alone would be enough for him to be remembered as we go on into another era.

Albert Camus

(1913-1960)

SARTRE REMAINS THE CLASSIC COMMENTATOR UPON CAMUS, WHOM HE assimilated to Pascal, to Rousseau, and to other French moralists, "the precursors of Nietzsche." To Sartre, Camus was "very much at peace within disorder," and so *The Stranger* was "a classical work, an orderly work, composed about the absurd and against the absurd." Shrewdly, Sartre finally assigned *The Stranger* not to the company of Heidegger or Hemingway, but to that of *Zadig* and *Candide*, the tales of Voltaire. Rereading Camus's short novel after forty years, I marvel at Sartre's keen judgment, and find it very difficult to connect my present impression of the book with my memory of how it seemed then. What Germaine Brie termed its heroic and humanistic hedonism seems, with the years, to have dwindled into an evasive hedonism, uncertain of its own gestures. The bleak narrative retains its Hemingwayesque aura, but the narrator, Meursault, seems even smaller now than he did four decades ago, when his dry disengagement had a certain novelty. Time, merciless critic, has worn *The Stranger* rather smooth, without however quite obliterating the tale.

René Girard, the most Jansenist of contemporary critics, "retried" *The Stranger*, and dissented from the verdict of "innocent" pronounced by Camus upon Meursault:

> If supernatural necessity is present in *L'Etranger*, why should Meursault alone come under its power? Why should the various characters in the same novel be judged by different yardsticks? If the murderer is not held responsible for his actions, why should the judges be held responsible for theirs?

Girard is reacting to an unfortunate comment by Camus himself: "A man who does not cry at the funeral of his mother is likely to be sentenced to death." In Girard's judgment, the quest of Camus was to convince us that judgment of guilt is always wrong. Girard calls this an "egotistical Manichaeism" and convicts Camus of "literary solipsism," particularly in one devastating sentence: "Camus betrays solipsism when he writes *L'Etranger* just as Meursault betrays it when he murders the Arab." On this reading, the "innocent murder" is a metaphor for the creative process. Meursault is a bad child and Camus becomes as a child again when he writes Meursault's novel. Girard considers the novel an aesthetic success, but a morally immature work, since Meursault himself is guilty of judgment, though Camus wishes his protagonist not to be judged. "The world in which we live is one of perpetual judgment," Girard reminds us, in Pascalian vein. For Girard, the figures comparable to Meursault are Dostoevsky's Raskolnikov and Dimitri Karamazov. For Camus, those figures presumably were Kafka's Joseph K, and K the land surveyor. Either comparison destroys *The Stranger*, which has trouble enough competing with Malraux and Hemingway. Against Girard, I enter my own dissent. *The Stranger* is barely able to sustain an aesthetic dignity and certainly is much slighter than we thought it to be. But it is not morally flawed or inconsistent. In its cosmos, guilt and innocence are indistinguishable, and Jewish or Christian judgments are hopelessly irrelevant. Meursault is not, as Girard says, a juvenile delinquent, but an inadequate consciousness dazed by the sun, overwhelmed by a context that is too strong for him:

> On seeing me, the Arab raised himself a little, and his hand went to his pocket. Naturally, I gripped Raymond's revolver in the pocket of my coat. Then the Arab let himself sink back again, but without taking his hand from his pocket. I was some distance off, at least ten yards, and most of the time I saw him as a blurred dark form wobbling in the heat haze. Sometimes, however, I had glimpses of his eyes glowing between the half-closed lids. The sound of the waves was even lazier, feebler, than at noon. But the light hadn't changed; it was pounding as fiercely as ever on the long stretch of sand that ended at the rock. For two hours the sun seemed to have made no progress; becalmed in a sea of molten steel. Far out on the horizon a steamer was passing; I could just make out from the corner of an eye the small black moving patch, while I kept my gaze fixed on the Arab.
>
> It struck me that all I had to do was to turn, walk away, and think no more about it. But the whole beach, pulsing with heat,

was pressing on my back. I took some steps toward the stream. The Arab didn't move. After all, there was still some distance between us. Perhaps because of the shadow on his face, he seemed to be grinning at me.

I waited. The heat was beginning to scorch my cheeks; beads of sweat were gathering in my eyebrows. It was just the same sort of heat as at my mother's funeral, and I had the same disagreeable sensations—especially in my forehead, where all the veins seemed to be bursting through the skin. I couldn't stand it any longer, and took another step forward. I knew it was a fool thing to do; I wouldn't get out of the sun by moving on a yard or so. But I took that step, just one step, forward. And then the Arab drew his knife and held it up toward me, athwart the sunlight.

A shaft of light shot upward from the steel, and I felt as if a long, thin blade transfixed my forehead. At the same moment all the sweat that had accumulated in my eyebrows splashed down on my eyelids, covering them with a warm film of moisture. Beneath a veil of brine and tears my eyes were blinded; I was conscious only of the cymbals of the sun clashing on my skull, and, less distinctly, of the keen blade of light flashing up from the knife, scarring my eyelashes, and gouging into my eyeballs.

Then everything began to reel before my eyes, a fiery gust came from the sea, while the sky cracked in two, from end to end, and a great sheet of flame poured down through the rift. Every nerve in my body was a steel spring, and my grip closed on the revolver. The trigger gave, and the smooth underbelly of the butt jogged my palm. And so, with that crisp, whipcrack sound, it all began. I shook off my sweat and the clinging veil of light. I knew I'd shattered the balance of the day, the spacious calm of this beach on which I had been happy. But I fired four shots more into the inert body, on which they left no visible trace. And each successive shot was another loud, fateful rap on the door of my undoing.

The "absurd" and the "gratuitous" seem wrong categories to apply here. We have a vision of possession by the sun, an inferno that fuses consciousness and will into a single negation, and burns through it to purposes that may exist, but are not human. Gide's Lafcadio, a true absurdist, said he was not curious about events but about himself, while Meursault is not curious about either. What Meursault at the end calls "the benign indifference of the universe" is belied by the pragmatic malevolence of the sun. The true influence upon *The Stranger* seems to me Melville's *Moby-Dick*, and for the whiteness of the whale Camus substitutes the whiteness of the sun. Meursault is no quester, no Ahab, and Ahab would not have allowed him aboard the *Pequod*. But the cosmos of *The Stranger* is essentially the cosmos of *Moby-Dick*; though in many of its visible aspects Meursault's world might seem to have been formed in love, its invisible spheres were formed in fright. The Jansenist Girard is accurate in finding Gnostic hints in the world of Camus, but not so accurate in judging Camus to possess only a bad child's sense of innocence. Judging Meursault is as wasteful as judging his judges; that blinding light of the sun burns away all judgment.

II

Forty years after its initial publication, Camus's *The Plague* (1947) has taken on a peculiar poignance in the era of our new plague, the ambiguously named AIDS. *The Plague* is a tendentious novel, more so even than *The Stranger*. A novelist requires enormous exuberance to sustain tendentiousness; Dostoevsky had such exuberance, Camus did not. Or a master of evasions, like Kafka, can evade his own compulsions, but Camus is all too interpretable. The darkest comparison would be to Beckett, whose trilogy of *Molloy*, *Malone Dies*, and *The Unnamable* conveys a sense of menace and anguish, metaphysical and psychological, that dwarfs *The Plague*.

Oran, spiritually rejecting the healthy air of the Mediterranean, in some sense brings the Plague upon itself; indeed Oran is the Plague, before the actual infection arrives. That may sound impressive, but constitutes a novelistic blunder, because Camus wants it both ways and cannot make it work either way. Either the relatively innocent suffer an affliction from outside, or the at least somewhat culpable are compelled to suffer the outward sign of their inward lack of grace. Truth doubtless lies in between, in our lives, but to *represent* so mixed a truth in your novel you must be an accomplished novelist, and not an essayist, or writer of quasi-philosophical tales. Dostoevsky dramatized the inwound textures of transcendence and material decay in nearly every event and every personage, while *The Plague* is curiously bland whenever it confronts the necessity of dramatizing anything.

I am unfair in comparing Camus to Beckett, Kafka, Dostoevsky, titanic authors, and it is even more unfair to contrast *The Plague* with Dickens's *A Tale of Two Cities*, since Dickens is very nearly the Shakespeare of novelists. Yet the two books are surprisingly close in vision, structure, theme, and in the relation of language to a reality of overwhelming menace. Camus's Plague is a version of Dickens's Terror, and Dr. Rieux, Rambert, Father Paneloux, Tarrou, and the volunteer sanitary workers all follow in the path of the noble Carton, since all could proclaim: "It is a far, far better thing that I do, than I have ever done." One can think of the Plague as AIDS, Revolutionary Terror, the Nazi occupation, or what one will, but one still requires persuasive representations of persons, whether in the aggregate or in single individuals.

"Indifference," properly cultivated, can be a stoic virtue, even a mode of heroism, but it is very difficult to represent. Here also Camus fails the contest with Melville or Dostoevsky. Consider a crucial dialogue between Tarrou and Dr. Rieux, both of them authentic heroes, by the standards of measurement of any morality, religion, or societal culture:

> "My question's this," said Tarrou. "Why do you yourself show such devotion, considering you don't believe in God? I suspect your answer may help me to mine."
>
> His face still in shadow, Rieux said that he'd already answered: that if he believed in an all-powerful God he would cease curing the sick and leave that to Him. But no one in the world believed in a God of that sort; no, not even Paneloux, who believed that he believed in such a God. And this was proved by the fact that no one ever threw himself on Providence completely. Anyhow, in this respect Rieux believed himself to be on the right road—in fighting against creation as he found it.
>
> "Ah," Tarrou remarked. "So that's the idea you have of your profession?"
>
> "More or less." The doctor came back into the light.
>
> Tarrou made a faint whistling noise with his lips, and the doctor gazed at him.
>
> "Yes, you're thinking it calls for pride to feel that way. But I assure you I've no more than the pride that's needed to keep me going. I have no idea what's awaiting me, or what will happen when all this ends. For the moment I know this; there are sick people and they need curing. Later on, perhaps, they'll think things over; and so shall I. But what's wanted now is to make them well. I defend them as best I can, that's all."
>
> "Against whom?"
>
> Rieux turned to the window. A shadow-line on the horizon told of the presence of the sea. He was conscious only of his

exhaustion, and at the same time was struggling against a sudden, irrational impulse to unburden himself a little more to his companion; an eccentric, perhaps, but who, he guessed, was one of his own kind.

"I haven't a notion, Tarrou; I assure you I haven't a notion. When I entered this profession, I did it 'abstractedly,' so to speak; because I had a desire for it, because it meant a career like another, one that young men often aspire to. Perhaps, too, because it was particularly difficult for a workman's son, like myself. And then I had to see people die. Do you know that there are some who refuse to die? Have you ever heard a woman scream 'Never!' with her last gasp? Well, I have. And then I saw that I could never get hardened to it. I was young then, and I was outraged by the whole scheme of things, or so I thought. Subsequently I grew more modest. Only, I've never managed to get used to seeing people die. That's all I know. Yet after all—"

Rieux fell silent and sat down. He felt his mouth dry.

"After all—?" Tarrou prompted softly.

"After all," the doctor repeated, then hesitated again, fixing his eyes on Tarrou, "it's something that a man of your sort can understand most likely, but, since the order of the world is shaped by death, mightn't it be better for God if we refuse to believe in Him and struggle with all our might against death, without raising our eyes toward the heaven where He sits in silence?"

Tarrou nodded.

"Yes. But your victories will never be lasting; that's all." Rieux's face darkened.

"Yes, I know that. But it's no reason for giving up the struggle."

"No reason, I agree. Only, I now can picture what this plague must mean for you."

"Yes. A never ending defeat."

Tarrou stared at the doctor for a moment, then turned and tramped heavily toward the door. Rieux followed him and was almost at his side when Tarrou, who was staring at the floor, suddenly said:

"Who taught you all this, Doctor?"

The reply came promptly:

"Suffering."

"Indifference" to transcendence here is a humanistic protest "in fighting against creation as he found it," a defense of the dying against death. It is a stoicism because Rieux is no longer "outraged by the whole scheme of things," even though he continues to know that "the order of the world is shaped by death." The best aesthetic touch here is the moment when Tarrou and Rieux come to understand one another, each finding the meaning of the *Plague* to be "a never ending defeat." But this is wasted when, at the conclusion of the passage I have quoted, Rieux utters the banality that "suffering" has taught him his pragmatic wisdom. Repeated rereadings will dim the passage further. "A shadow-line on the horizon told of the presence of the sea." Conrad would have known how to integrate that into his complex Impressionism, but in Camus it constitutes another mechanical manifestation of symbolism, reminding us that Oran opened itself to the Plague by turning its back upon the sea.

Camus was an admirable if confused moralist and the legitimate heir of a long tradition of rational lucidity. He did not write a *Candide* or even a *Zadig*; I cannot recall one humorous moment anywhere in his fiction. *The Stranger* and *The Plague*, like his other fictions, are grand period pieces, crucial reflectors of the morale and concerns of France and the Western world in the 1940s, both before and after the Liberation from the Nazis. Powerful representations of an era have their own use and justification and offer values not in themselves aesthetic.

Further Reading

Alter, Robert. *The Art of Biblical Narrative*. New York: Basic Books, 1981.

Alter, Robert and Frank Kermode, ed. *The Literary Guide to the Bible*. Cambridge, Mass.: Belknap Press of Harvard University Press, 1987.

Barry, Peter ed. *Issues in Contemporary Literary Theory*. Houndmills: Macmillan, 1987.

Bloom, Harold. *Where Shall Wisdom Be Found?* New York: Riverhead, 2004.

———. *The Book of J*. New York: Grove, 1990.

Culler, Jonathan D. *Literary Theory: A Very Short Introduction*. Oxford: Oxford University Press, 1997.

Durant, Will. *Story of Philosophy: The Lives and Opinions of the World's Greatest Philosophers*. New York: Pocket, 1991.

Emerson, Ralph Waldo. *The Essential Writings of Ralph Waldo Emerson*. New York: Random House, 2000.

Ford, Andrew. *The Origins of Criticism: Literary Culture and Poetic Theory in Classical Greece*. Princeton: Princeton University Press, 2002.

Frye, Northrop. *The Anatomy of Criticism: Four Essays*. Princeton: Princeton University Press: 2000.

Gottlieb, Anthony. *The Dream of Reason: A History of Philosophy from the Greeks to the Renaissance*. New York: W.W. Norton & Company, 2001.

Greene, William Chase. *The Choices of Criticism*. Cambridge, Mass.: M.I.T. Press, 1965.

Hartman, Geoffrey. *Minor Prophecies: The Literary Essay in the Culture Wars*. Cambridge, Mass.: Harvard University Press, 1991.

Hume, David. *Principal Writings on Religion Including Dialogues Concerning Natural Religion; and, The Natural History of Religion*. New York: Oxford University Press, 1998.

Kuklick, Bruce. *A History of Philosophy in America*. New York: Oxford University Press, 2002.

Pater, Walter. *Essays on Literature and Art*. New York: Knopf, 1993.

Russell, Bertrand. *A History of Western Philosophy*. New York: Touchstone, 1976.

Saintsbury, George. *A History of Criticism and Literary Taste in Europe from the Earliest Texts to the Present Day*. Edinburgh: Blackwood, 1949.

Scneewind, J.B., ed. *Moral Philosophy from Montaigne to Kant*. Cambridge: Cambridge University Press, 2002

Tarnas, Richard. *Passion of the Western Mind: Understanding the Ideas that have Shaped Our World View*. New York: Harmony, 1991.

Trilling, Lionel, ed. *Literary Criticism: An Introductory Reader*. New York: Holt, Rinehart, and Winston, 1970.

Wild, Laura Hulda. *A Literary Guide to the Bible : A Study of the Types of Literature Present in the Old and New Testaments*. Philadelphia: R. West, 1978.

Wimsatt, Jr., William K, and Cleanth Brooks. *Literary Criticism: A Short History*. New York: Knopf, 1957.

Index

About the Author

HAROLD BLOOM is Sterling Professor of the Humanities at Yale University. He is the author of over 20 books, including *Shelley's Mythmaking* (1959), *The Visionary Company* (1961), *Blake's Apocalypse* (1963), *Yeats* (1970), *A Map of Misreading* (1975), *Kabbalah and Criticism* (1975), *Agon: Toward a Theory of Revisionism* (1982), *The American Religion* (1992), *The Western Canon* (1994), and *Omens of Millennium: The Gnosis of Angels, Dreams, and Resurrection* (1996). *The Anxiety of Influence* (1973) sets forth Professor Bloom's provocative theory of the literary relationships between the great writers and their predecessors. His most recent books include *Shakespeare: The Invention of the Human* (1998), a 1998 National Book Award finalist, *How to Read and Why* (2000), *Genius: A Mosaic of One Hundred Exemplary Creative Minds* (2002), *Hamlet: Poem Unlimited* (2003), and *Where Shall Wisdom be Found* (2004). In 1999, Professor Bloom received the prestigious American Academy of Arts and Letters Gold Medal for Criticism, and in 2002 he received the Catalonia International Prize.